COMPREHENSIBILITY IN LANGUAGE ASSESSMENT

British Council Monographs on Modern Language Testing

Series Editors: Karen Dunn, British Council; Tineke Brunfaut, Lancaster University
Founding Co-editors: Vivien Berry and Barry O'Sullivan, both at the British Council

This series – published in cooperation with the British Council – provides short books in the area of language testing. These titles are written by well-known language testing scholars from across the world including members of the British Council's Assessment Research Group (ARG). The books offer both a theoretical and a practical perspective to language testing and assessment – proposing, where required, models of development, which are reflected in actual test tasks. They are unique in that they are authored by individuals with considerable academic, teaching and assessment experience, thus offering the reader a unique insight into the link between theory and practice in the area. In many cases, the books illustrate their approach with reference to actual test items, from the British Council's Aptis test service.

Published:

Assessing the language of young learners
Angela Hasselgreen and Gwendydd Caudwell

Knowledge-based Vocabulary Lists
Norbert Schmitt, Karen Dunn, Barry O'Sullivan, Laurence Anthony and Benjamin Kremmel

Rethinking the second language listening test: From theory to practice
John Field

Scoring second language spoken and written performance: Issues, options and directions
Ute Knoch, Judith Fairbairn and Yan Jin

Validity: Theoretical development and integrated arguments
Micheline Chalhoub-Deville and Barry O'Sullivan

Forthcoming:

Assessing reading
Tineke Brunfaut and Jamie Dunlea

Assessing second language writing: Current and future perspectives
Anthony Green

Assessing speaking: Current and future perspectives
Fumiyo Nakatsuhara, Vivien Berry, Chihiro Inoue and Nahal Khabbazbashi

COMPREHENSIBILITY IN LANGUAGE ASSESSMENT

A Broader Perspective

Parvaneh Tavakoli and Sheryl Cooke

SHEFFIELD UK BRISTOL CT

Published by Equinox Publishing Ltd.

UK: Office 415, The Workstation, 15 Paternoster Row, Sheffield, South Yorkshire, S1 2BX
USA: ISD, 70 Enterprise Drive, Bristol, CT 06010

www.equinoxpub.com

First published 2024

British Library Cataloguing-in-Publication Data
A catalogue record for this book is available from the British Library.

ISBN-13 978 1 80050 432 5 (hardback)
978 1 80050 433 2 (paperback)
978 1 80050 434 9 (ePDF)
978 1 80050 455 4 (ePub)

Library of Congress Cataloging-in-Publication Data
Names: Tavakoli, Parvaneh, author. | Cooke, Sheryl, author.
Title: Comprehensibility in language assessment : a broader perspective / Parvaneh Tavakoli and Sheryl Cooke.
Description: Sheffield, South Yorkshire ; Bristol, CT : Equinox Publishing Ltd, 2024. | Series: British Council monographs on modern language testing ; volume 6 | Includes bibliographical references and index. | Summary: "In this book, the authors argue that conceptualising comprehensibility as a multidimensional construct and adopting a broader perspective to understanding and analysing it for communication purposes would benefit the fields of second language assessment and second language acquisition"-- Provided by publisher.
Identifiers: LCCN 2023023625 (print) | LCCN 2023023626 (ebook) | ISBN 9781800504325 (hardback) | ISBN 9781800504332 (paperback) | ISBN 9781800504349 (pdf) | ISBN 9781800504554 (epub)
Subjects: LCSH: Language and languages--Ability testing. | Comprehension--Testing. | Second language acquisition.
Classification: LCC P53.4 .T38 2024 (print) | LCC P53.4 (ebook) | DDC 418.0076--dc23/eng/20231106
LC record available at https://lccn.loc.gov/2023023625
LC ebook record available at https://lccn.loc.gov/2023023626

Typeset by S.J.I. Services, New Delhi, India

CONTENTS

LIST OF FIGURES

LIST OF TABLES

Credits

ACKNOWLEDGEMENTS

Writing this book has been an enjoyable experience and an enlightening journey which would have not been possible without the help and support of a number of individuals and teams. First, we are grateful to the Assessment Research and Development Group at the British Council and to Dr Jamie Dunlea and Professor Barry O'Sullivan in particular for providing us with the opportunity to make a valuable contribution to the Monographs on Modern Language Testing series. We would sincerely like to thank the series editors, Dr Karen Dunn and Professor Tineke Brunfaut for their constructive feedback and continuous support throughout the process. Last but not least, we are grateful to the two anonymous reviewers for their extremely valuable and insightful feedback.

ABOUT THE AUTHORS

Parvaneh Tavakoli is Professor of Applied Linguistics at the University of Reading, UK. Parvaneh's main research interest lies in the interface of second language acquisition and language assessment. Over the past two decades, Parvaneh has led several international research projects investigating the construct of spoken language and its assessment. Her research, which is widely cited in the field, has been published in the form of articles in prestigious peer-reviewed journals (e.g. The Modern Language Journal, SSLA and Language Learning), policy reports (e.g. Report to Welsh Government), and monographs by key publishers (e.g. Cambridge University Press and TESOL Press).

Sheryl Cooke is an Assessment Researcher with the British Council Assessment Research Group. Sheryl has 20 years' experience in various areas of language assessment and her qualifications include an MA Language Testing (Lancaster University) and an MA Linguistics (SOAS). She is currently a PhD candidate at the University of Jyväskylä (Finland), focusing on the assessment of spoken English and the potential implications for English as a Lingua Franca. Her research interests include assessment of speaking, the use of new technologies in language testing and the ethics of language assessment in the global context.

CHAPTER 1

INTRODUCTION

This book presents an overview of features that have been identified as contributing to spoken comprehensibility. From a linguistic point of view, we start from the bottom up and Chapter 2 focuses on pronunciation, exploring the phoneme, word and utterance level components of meaning. The focus of the third chapter shifts to spoken texts and the features associated with longer turns of monologic speech. The key aspects of pragmatic knowledge that affect comprehensibility are discussed in Chapter 4; a summary of research in this area is presented and contextual and cultural differences that might have an impact on comprehensibility are explored. Chapter 5 presents a discussion of the effects of fluency on listeners and their judgements of comprehensibility. While each of these chapters focuses on comprehensibility indicators at those levels of linguistic enquiry, the aim is also to illustrate how these components function as part of a broad, intricate system of meaning creation and should not be evaluated independently.

Chapter 6 takes a higher-level perspective of the opportunities and threats automated assessment might present to the construct of comprehensibility. Chapter 7 takes the discussion into the classroom and looks at how a broader understanding of comprehensibility can support teachers and learners. The final chapter draws together the approach discussed in the monograph and summarises key implications for language assessment. A visual representation of the framework we present throughout is included in the concluding chapter.

Meaning in Spoken Language

What does it mean to *understand* someone? What does it mean to be *understood*?

> An examiner in a face-to-face test of spoken English presents the test-taker with a topic for an extended monologue. The task is to speak for two minutes on the topic of 'a successful person you know'. The test-taker talks about her favourite celebrity and

> spends most of the time allotted describing the star's appearance in detail. After the extended monologue, the examiner follows up with further questions designed to elicit more spontaneous, interactive language. He asks, "Does success depend more on hard work or on good luck?" His particular variety of English means that he pronounces 'luck' as most speakers of English pronounce 'look'. The test-taker, whose first language is morphologically uncomplex, seems not to pick up on the form of the word, interpreting the question as "Does success depend more on hard work or good looks?" and begins to talk about success and beauty, a perspective that fits with the broader topic area, too. The examiner interrupts and repeats, "hard work or good luck" still using his variety of English pronunciation and, when the test-taker responds again by talking about beauty, he interrupts and repeats the words, "not good looking, good luck!" agitatedly three times without any modification of his own pronunciation, perhaps assuming that the morphology of the word (good luck rather than good lucking (ungrammatical)) will provide the information necessary to achieve mutual comprehension. When this does not succeed, the examiner draws on a gloss for the phrase by saying, "you know, good luck like winning a raffle draw" but as the test-taker is seemingly unfamiliar with this culturally specific concept, she still does not understand the examiner's intended meaning and, finally, when the test-taker, now flustered and anxious, still responds by talking about appearance, he gives up and moves to a different question.

The example of a breakdown in communication above illustrates just some of the factors that cause misunderstanding or contribute to a lack of comprehensibility. There is clearly an issue around pronunciation of a particular word – a reasonably straightforward linguistic factor – that could have been resolved by an empathetic communicator who understood the need to make himself understood through whatever means necessary, such as modification of pronunciation, providing a gloss, rephrasing. Yet there is more than a simple phoneme production factor at play: the examiner seems to expect the test-taker to accommodate his particular regional accent (sociolinguistic factor), the test-taker fails to pick up on the morphology of the word (lexico-grammatical factor), the examiner makes the assumption that responsibility for successful communication lies entirely with the test-taker (sociolinguistic and pragmatic factors), and the broader discourse structure and conventions make the test-taker's misinterpretation completely plausible (discourse and pragmatic factors) given the topic of focus in the extended monologue.

Comprehensibility is considered central to successful communication (Munro and Derwing, 1995a, 2006) but despite the crucial role comprehensibility plays in communication and the contribution it makes in the assessment of spoken language ability, its realisation in language tests has been approached very differently: from often vague and intuitive holistic ratings of how 'intelligible' the test-taker is or how much 'effort' is required from the examiner to understand to a focus on purely technical aspects of language with little consideration of communicative effect. This book seeks to engage with the construct of communicative comprehensibility in the context of language assessment. It aims to provoke a reconsideration of spoken comprehensibility within language teaching and assessment as a far broader construct at two inter-related levels. First, comprehensibility is not just a set of linguistic components at acoustic, word and utterance level; rather, it includes elements at discourse and pragmatic level. Second, comprehensibility goes beyond the utterances of the speaker to include listener characteristics. Finally, comprehensibility is inextricably linked to the communication event it facilitates and is not an abstract construct that exists in linguistic components alone and independent of the speech context. We highlight the challenges associated with a purely atomic approach to comprehensibility (i.e. comprehensibility in general being linked to a range of distinct linguistics features without taking purpose and context of the speech event into consideration) and argue that the current approach as realised in language assessment does not fully take into consideration the range of contributing linguistic and non-linguistic factors, multimodality, plurilingualism and translanguaging – all crucial components in creating shared understanding in today's communicative landscape. From this position of a broader perspective on comprehensibility, we consider a sample of language tests and standards of reference, and discuss pedagogy and technology in light of this approach. It is hoped that this volume will contribute to a renewed understanding of comprehensibility that will go some way to informing the design, development and use of tests of spoken language.

At the core of this book is the concept of *comprehensibility*. While there are various technical definitions of the term and it overlaps with other related concepts, our fundamental premise is that comprehensibility is the successful communication of a message between one person and (an) other(s); this is a somewhat broader definition than currently used in language teaching and assessment. While the perspective we take can be applied to other forms of communication and language skills in the traditional sense, in this book, the focus is on the comprehensibility of spoken language because the aural dimension of the speaking skill has led to a forefronting of linguistic indicators such as pronunciation and fluency in terms of their overall impact on comprehensibility and this allows us to interrogate how these features could be included in this broader perspective. While the intention is that the approach in this book applies to all languages, English predominates, as it does in much international academic discourse. This is due to the relative wealth of research into comprehensibility in English, the more explicit and detailed rating scales and test specifications – most likely due to the commercial nature of English language testing and the associated investment in research and development, as well as support for test validation in the face of competing products – and access to published research.

Key Terms and Definitions

We start with an overview of concepts and terminology that form the basis of our discussion throughout this book: from general terms used in applied linguistics more broadly to a description of current understanding of key concepts related to comprehensibility within language learning. We introduce alternative viewpoints on comprehensibility from other disciplines and end this brief section with a clear description of the broader conceptualisation of comprehensibility we are advocating in this book. This is the foundation for the subsequent discussion around comprehensibility in language testing.

Table 1.1 provides a reference list of key terms for the reader to return to if necessary.

Co-construction of meaning: The roles played by both speaker and listener in achieving understanding of a speech event (whether synchronous or asynchronous).

Construct: The underlying ability that is being evaluated.

Discourse: Spoken language that functions as a whole beyond the level of the sentence; in this book, discourse will be used interchangeably with the term spoken text (as distinct from written text).

Features: Technical linguistic characteristics of speech, e.g. the ability to produce long utterances without hesitation or correctly articulate individual sounds of the target language.

ELF: English as a Lingua Franca – English used as a common language between a variety of speakers from different language backgrounds.

Inner / Outer / Expanding Circles: Traditional categorisation of different English varieties and speakers; Inner Circle – US, UK, Canada, Australia, New Zealand and Ireland; Outer Circle – mostly ex-British colonies where English functions as a predominant language, e.g. Singapore, India, Jamaica, South Africa; Expanding Circle – countries where English is not generally used as a means of communication but is learned at school or university.

L1/L2: First language or second language (of the speaker); see NS & NNS below.

Lingua Franca: Any language used as a common language between speakers of a variety of languages (including possibly the LF); e.g. English, Spanish, French, Hausa, Mandarin.

Macro features or approach: Starting with the largest contributors to establishing meaning (e.g. communicative context), and working down the hierarchy towards the micro, linguistics or acoustic features of speech; also referred to as 'top-down'.

Micro features or approach: Starting with the smallest units of language (e.g. phonemes) and considering how they contribute to establishing meaning; also referred to as 'bottom-up'.

Multimodality: "The use of more than one semiotic mode in meaning-making, communication, and representation generally, or in a specific situation. Such modes include all forms of verbal, non-verbal, and contextual communication." Oxford Reference online dictionary (Dec, 2022); this is considered to be increasingly prevalent given technology facilitated communication that draws on various modes simultaneously.

NS: Native speaker – the speaker of a language as their first, most predominant language; this is usually, but not always, their mother tongue; *NNS* – Non-native speaker. While this term is used occasionally or cited throughout this book, we prefer the term L1 speaker (NS) or L2 speaker (NNS) in recognition of the challenges and issues associated with 'nativeness'.

Plurilingualism and translanguaging: A speaker's ability to draw on different languages and knowledge of language (even partial) within their individual linguistic and cultural portfolio to get meaning across.

Rating criteria: Aspects of linguistic and/or communicative performance used by language assessors to assess samples of language produced by a test-taker.

Test validity: Various approaches to validity exist, for example, building an evidence based argument to support score interpretation for the intended test use situation. In this book, we take the more traditional definition of test validity as our foundation: whether a test measures what it purports to measure, not more or less.

Test reliability: Whether a test delivers accurate and consistent results across different instances and variables.

TLU: Target Language Use domain – the intended context where the test-taker will most likely use the language being tested, e.g. university studies

Table 1.1: Key terms used in this book

Comprehensibility is a complex concept complicated further by the interchangeable use of the terms *comprehensibility* and *intelligibility* within the literature as well as the confounding nature of other concepts such as *accent* and *accentedness*. The *intelligibility principle* (in contrast to the *nativeness principle*) presented by Levis (2005) provides a good starting point:

> [The intelligibility principle] holds that learners simply need to be understandable. The intelligibility principle recognizes that communication can be remarkably successful when foreign accents are noticeable or even strong, that there is no clear correlation between accent and understanding (Munro and Derwing, 1999), and that certain types of pronunciation errors may have a disproportionate role in impairing comprehensibility. (p. 307)

Levis (2006) describes intelligibility in a broad and narrow sense: in the narrow sense, it refers to the understanding of a speaker's every word; more broadly, it describes overall or perceived intelligibility, that is, whether a listener understood the overall meaning the speaker intended to convey, even if they missed individual words. The narrow sense corresponds to the definition of intelligibility used by many researchers today, and the broad sense links to comprehensibility as it is typically used in applied linguistics research. Thomson (2017) provides a detailed account of how these terms have been used by different scholars; the confusion that has arisen due to the various uses of these terms is reflected in his call for more consistency in use.

Applied linguists generally agree that comprehensibility, intelligibility and accentedness are interrelated yet distinct (Flege, Munro & MacKay, 1995; Major, 2007; Munro & Derwing, 1995a; Derwing & Munro, 1997). Intelligibility is defined by Munro and Derwing (1995a, 1995b) as "the extent to which a speaker's message is actually understood" (p. 76, p. 291) and comprehensibility as "listeners' perceptions of difficulty in understanding particular utterances" (1995b, p. 291), the latter building on the notion of effort introduced by Abercrombie in as early as 1949 in relation to understanding of speech and also reflecting the broad sense in the definition of Levis (2006). They offer no explicit definition for accent, however. Thomson (2017) points to accent as "being as a perceptual phenomenon on the part of a listener" (p. 3), citing Scovel (1969) who puts the existence of foreign accents squarely on the shoulders of the listener who perceives them as such. More recently, definitions of accent have achieved more clarity, although many continue to refer to deviance from L1 forms of the language, introducing a conundrum regarding which L1 variant and failing to encapsulate the notion that one

L1 speaker may perceive another L1 speaker as 'having an accent'. The first part of the description of accent as offered by Saito, Trofimovich and Isaacs (2016) is therefore much more intuitively acceptable: "listeners' perceptions of the degree to which L2 speech is influenced by his/her native language…" although the second part of their definition is less so: "…and/or colored by other non-native features" as the L1 'standard' is once again introduced.

While there is broad agreement within the field of applied linguistics that comprehensibility and intelligibility are separate but related concepts, given that the terms are less definitively used in language teaching and assessment literature and tools, for the sake of clarity, Table 1.2 outlines the definitions of the terms as they are typically used in applied linguistics.

Intelligibility: The listener's actual understanding of each word and utterance in a sample of speech. This is reliant on more bottom up features (but not entirely), often measured through transcription of speech samples or selection of the correct word/phrase from a pair or set. In this book, intelligibility overlaps with comprehensibility in that a certain degree of intelligibility is usually necessary to achieve overall understanding; the extent to which acoustic, phonemic or other micro-level linguistic feature understanding is necessary is dependent on communicative purpose and macro-level factors.
Comprehensibility: The listener's perceived ease of understanding a sample of speech. This can be seen as a result of a number of complex and interrelated factors that allow the listener to ascribe overall meaning to a sample of speech. This is frequently measured on a 9-band scale where 1 = easy to understand and 9 = extremely difficult to understand. It is this definition of comprehensibility that this book is primarily concerned with, although we argue that comprehensibility extends beyond ease of understanding for the listener; the success of the intended speech event is what renders the speech act comprehensible.The overall discussion considers the interrelatedness of the different micro- and macro-level factors in achieving mutual comprehensibility, including co-construction of meaning between speaker and listener.
Accentedness: The listener's perception of the degree to which a speech sample deviates from a particular form of the target language (usually the one that the speaker is most familiar with or regards as standard). Accent is usually measured using a Likert-type scale. Accent might impact intelligibility, listeners' perception of their understanding, or both, and is particularly relevant in our discussion of communication in a LF context.
Accent: The listener's perceived association of a speaker's pronunciation with a particular social, cultural, ethnic or socio-economic group, e.g. 'an Irish accent', 'an educated accent'.

Table 1.2: Definitions of intelligibility, comprehensibility, accent and accentedness typically used in applied linguistics

The definitions above show how the contrast between intelligibility and comprehensibility and accent/accentedness in applied linguistics is between 'actual' or literal understanding at a concrete, linguistic level (*intelligibility*) and the *listener's* perceptions in the case of the other concepts. It is almost inevitable that this subjective approach to comprehensibility leads to both listener-primacy and the abstraction of the linguistic elements involved in the communicative act, suggesting that the actual meaning of the utterance exists independently of the context, purpose and audience, and that the comprehensibility of the utterance can be assessed in this abstract form.

Other disciplines offer different perspectives. In speech therapy, comprehensibility is defined as "the extent to which a listener can understand (comprehend) a spoken utterance in a communicative context" and "understandable spoken language" (Camarata, 2019: p. 448). Speech therapists distinguish between three different levels of speech production: *accuracy*, which refers to the production of individual phonemes, *intelligibility*, which is described as "the extent to which an utterance can be understood when the intended message is known" (2019, p. 448), and *comprehensibility*, which relates to understanding in authentic communication contexts. Speech therapists use these three distinctions to treat speech disorders such as apraxia and dysarthria. Camarata (2019) identifies comprehensibility as a more functional level of speech production and recommends that interventions should be targeted at this level, with other words that while therapy targeted at accuracy might have an impact on intelligibility and comprehensibility, it is not necessarily the case and that comprehension "should be a high-priority goal for remediation" (p. 448). In clinical linguistics, intelligibility is used to refer to what applied linguistics would view as comprehensibility: "Speech intelligibility is a relative measure of the degree to which a speaker's speech signal is understood, the relativity depending at a minimum on the identities of speaker and listener, what is spoken and where it is spoken" (Weismer, 2008, p. 569), which includes non-linguistic factors such as context. The definitions from other disciplines above do not focus on listener perception of ease of understanding, but on the comprehensibility of the message in relation to context and audience.

These insights from related disciplines suggest that while linguistic features (e.g. accuracy of pronunciation) are crucial components of making meaning, they are only part of what constitutes making a speech act comprehensible. We argue for a broader perspective on comprehensibility than typically taken in teaching and language assessment, one that encompasses linguistic intelligibility but is not reduced to linguistic indicators only, and one that is not measured in terms of listener ease of understanding, but extends to the communicative success of the speech event. Our argument is for comprehensibility, in this broader sense, to be the focus of the teaching and testing of spoken language. The measurement of a speaker's ability to make their ideas comprehensible to another cannot be limited to linguistic proxies and cannot be abstracted from the communicative context and the audience only, which together play a role in achieving shared meaning and communicative success.

Rationale and Justification

The main impetus for a reconsideration of comprehensibility in language learning and assessment is recognition of the wide-ranging and complex factors involved in the creation of meaning at a time when the focus is primarily on the atomic linguistic components that contribute to making spoken communication comprehensible. While the importance of linguistic elements (sounds, words, syntax, etc.) to achieving meaning is not disputed, there is a danger that the operationalisation of comprehensibility within teaching and testing will be reduced to these elements only (i.e., to form and accuracy), abstracted from context, communicative purpose and outcome, and the participants in the speech act, both speaker and listener. Particularly as research investigates more 'computable' components of comprehensibility in order to inform not only human evaluations of communicative proficiency, but also the algorithms underlying automated assessment of speaking, we feel that it is important to take a step back and look at comprehensibility from a broader perspective.

There are historical shifts that make this reconsideration especially pertinent: how language is used by diverse groups of speakers, contemporary modes of communication, and changing theoretical perspectives on how communication is achieved. These are discussed in more detail under the headings of complexity and lingua franca below.

Complexity in Defining Comprehensibility for Assessment

The difficulty in reaching a consensus on what constitutes comprehensibility underscores the complexity of the construct. Even at an atomic level, while studies (Derwing & Munro, 1997; Zielinski, 2008; Isaacs & Trofimovich, 2012; Jin & Mak, 2013; Trofimovich & Isaacs, 2012;

Saito et al., 2015, 2017) have investigated the features associated with comprehensibility ratings, there is insufficient evidence to make any conclusive decisions about a 'comprehensibility inventory', even for English. Confounding factors such as limited and varied L1 backgrounds of speakers and/or raters across studies make a definitive overview more elusive. While perfect pronunciation has traditionally been seen as the intelligibility/comprehensibility panacea, that seems far from the case and, although phonological factors may play a significant role, fluency, lexis, grammar as well as discourse and pragmatic aspects all contribute to achieving communicative success.

Aspects outside of the purely linguistic realm such as pragmatic context, familiarity with the topic, or sociocultural factors have an impact and can determine which linguistic features carry more weight in getting the meaning across (See Chapters 2, 3 and 4). Also, although tests of comprehensibility place the onus on the speaker to get meaning across, comprehensibility is co-constructed and the listener has a part to play. This introduces not only the listener's own linguistic skills, but also attitude (e.g. towards accent), motivation and tolerance (e.g. of slow speech or ambiguity). Disentangling speaker from listener in assessing comprehensibility is hardly possible and one of the motivations for reconsidering the primacy of listener ease in assessing comprehensibility.

To further exacerbate the intricacy of interrelated components, comprehensibility is context-dependent and, therefore, dynamic (Harding & McNamara, 2017). The immediate situation in which an utterance occurs can radically change the meaning, and the evaluation of communicative success will depend on the purpose of the communicative act. Even within a short conversation, comprehensibility can change depending on the strategies and motivation of the speaker and listener to reach a point of shared understanding.

Finally, even if an extensive inventory of atomic features could be identified and agreed upon, it is impossible that a human would be able to consciously consider each one and award an overall score; in the case of machine marking, which aspects have an influence on the final rating will most likely remain unclear. The potential danger of abstracting comprehensibility and reducing successful communication skills to a set of linguistic features (or narrowing the construct) extends to test-taker 'gamification' of assessment systems, for example, university applicants who score well on tests of English but disappoint their lecturers when they are unable to engage in meaningful discussion in the academic realm.

Lingua Francas and Assessing Comprehensibility

Languages that serve as major lingua francas, either regionally or globally, present particular challenges for teaching and assessment which have typically relied on standard points of reference as goals or for evaluation of success. English, the predominant global lingua franca in many fields, is an example where the tension between L1 speaker norms and increasingly diverse varieties has been evident in both language teaching and testing for numerous years.

The L1 speaker is still referenced in language tests, or influences the test design, albeit less often or explicitly than in the past. Proponents of an L1-speaker focus in testing see the use of standard forms as a means to make the test more consistent and, therefore, more reliable, and more fair to all test-takers. The rationale behind this is that if a variety of accents were included in, for example, the listening section of a test, those more familiar with those accents might have an advantage. This ignores the reality of English language use around the world, however, and the fundamental requirement to validate a test through demonstrating the connection to the Target Language Use (TLU) domain (Chalhoub-Deville & O'Sullivan, 2020). Berns (2006, p. 723–724) identified three key assumptions behind L1-speaker norms for English (L1 speaker referred to as 'native speaker' in this excerpt). These can be adapted to apply to the use of any language as a lingua franca:

(1) everyone learning [X] does so in order to interact with native speakers;
(2) the communicative competence learners need to develop is the native speaker's; and
(3) learning [X] means dealing with the sociocultural realities of [X country], that is, [X] ways of doing, thinking and being.

In the case of lingua francas, this has changed, as explicated in the work of Seidlhofer (2009) who argued for a new perspective on English as a lingua franca (ELF) that sees the primary role of ELF as facilitating communication within communities of practice. These communities of practice could (but needn't) include speakers whose first language is English and cut across the traditional boundaries between Kachru's (1985) Inner, Outer and Expanding circles. Globalisation and the internet facilitate the interaction of geographically dispersed community members who share an interest and an ability to speak English to varying degrees. Taken from this perspective, ELF is not a standard variety of English or, indeed one particular form at all, but an instance of communication in the language that allows for shared understanding of meaning between speaker and listener.

This is a major impetus for a focus on comprehensibility. It also muddies the waters with regards to researching the linguistic features contributing to comprehensibility when speakers of different varieties of English, for example, can easily achieve mutual understanding despite differences in lexis, idiosyncracies in grammar, and differently pronounced phonemes.

Multimodality and Plurilingualism

Two other key drivers for a broader perspective on the comprehensibility construct are multimodality and plurilingualism. The communicative landscape has changed rapidly over the past several decades and continues to evolve significantly with the use of technology, demanding an ability to draw together different sources of information and modes of communication to get meaning across, and to access different modalities (images, gestures, sounds, etc) in order to comprehend meaning (Kress, 2000; Lotherington & Jenson, 2011; Early, et al., 2015). A traditional speaking test that focuses narrowly on pronunciation accuracy, range of lexis and speech rate, for example, misses the crucially important skill of leveraging tools beyond the linguistic realm to achieve communicative goals.

This extends beyond modes of communication to include different languages. This is particularly relevant in the lingua franca context, where an effective communicator will demonstrate an awareness of what non-target language resources she can draw on (e.g. cognates between her language and that of the listener) and exploit these to achieve mutual understanding. Traditional language tests (and teachers) frame this negatively as 'L1 interference' whereas the use of other languages might add significantly to communicative comprehensibility. The Common European Framework of Reference (CEFR) recognises "plurilinguals [as having] a single, interrelated, repertoire that they combine with their general competences and various strategies in order to accomplish tasks" (Companion Volume, p. 30) and, importantly for our broader conceptualisation of comprehensibility, plurilingual competence includes an ability "to call upon the knowledge of a number of languages (or dialects, or varieties) to make sense of a text" (Companion Volume, p. 30). These shifts in our understanding of meaning making and the seismic changes available in terms of what we can draw on to achieve mutual understanding demand a re-evaluation of our treatment of comprehensibility in the assessment of a person's communicative competence.

A generation ago, the world of literacy was based on paper. Now, literacy engages people in texts and discourses that traverse space and time on screens in which we can access and mix semiotic resources that include a multiplicity of languages (Lotherington & Jenson, 2011, p. 226).

Comprehensibility in Language Assessment

In this section, we explore examples of how comprehensibility in general is dealt with in language tests and proficiency scales and highlight why this is problematic and needs a much more rigorous and broad understanding of what constitutes comprehensibility.

A key component of the assessment of spoken language performance is rating scales. They contain the assessment criteria for raters to apply to language performance and they provide the users of test scores (e.g. universities, immigration agencies, HR departments, regulatory bodies) with a description (and therefore expectation) of the test-taker's ability. In essence, rating scales are the operationalisation of the underlying construct being assessed and provide useful insight into whether and how comprehensibility is being incorporated in a particular test of speaking proficiency.

The approach to assessing language proficiency in English has, largely, shifted from an almost wholly L1-speaker, intuitively-assessed, benchmark seen in rating scales such as the Australian Second Language Proficiency Ratings (ASLPR) (Ingram, 1985) and early versions of the American Council for the Teaching of Foreign Languages (ACTFL) scales towards a focus on communicative performance using 'can-do' statements in the 1990s and beyond (Fulcher, 2003, 2010). The last two decades have seen another shift towards a more research-informed focus on features of language (Fulcher, 1996; Lazaraton, 2002; Isaacs & Trofimovich, 2012). Comprehensibility is usually implicit or vague in these descriptions of performance, as will be seen in the examples discussed below.

Examples from Language Tests

Large-scale, high-stakes tests of English are used primarily to decide whether a test-taker has the ability to function in an English language tertiary educational situation or in a skilled profession such as medicine; the same tests are also used to ascertain whether someone has the communicative skills to migrate to a predominantly English-speaking country and, presumably, meaningfully participate as a resident of that country. We focus on the assessment of spoken performance only.

Two of the most well-known tests used for these purposes are the International English Language Testing System (IELTS) and the Test of English as a Foreign Language (TOEFL) internet Based Test (iBT), both of which have speaking components. IELTS uses an analytical approach to assessing the spoken performance of a test-taker during an Oral Proficiency Interview (OPI), dividing the score for speaking into four separate criteria: Fluency and Cohesion (FC), Lexical Resource (LR), Grammatical Range and Accuracy (GRA) and Pronunciation (PRON). Looking at the public version of the IELTS Speaking Band Descriptors (n.d.), which reflect the actual band descriptors very closely, proxy terms for comprehensibility are primarily evident in the PRON criterion descriptors, as can be seen by these extracts:

- is effortless to understand (band 9)
- is easy to understand throughout; L1 accent has minimal effect on intelligibility (band 8)
- can generally be understood throughout, though mispronunciation of individual words or sounds reduces clarity at times (band 6)
- mispronunciations… cause some difficulty for the listener (band 4)
- speech is often unintelligible (band 2)

Bands 1, 3, 5 and 7 are not defined in terms of features; rather, raters are instructed to use these bands if the speaker exhibits all of the lower-band features and only some of the higher-band features. As the only criterion that takes this approach, it suggests that pronunciation is difficult to define in very granular terms and/or raters might find it difficult to put into practice.

At band 8, the IELTS descriptors include reference to accent, generally seen as a separate but related concept to comprehensibility: '*L1 accent has minimal effect on intelligibility*'.

It is noticeable that throughout many IELTS descriptors and scales that refer to spoken communicative ability the term *intelligibility* frequently overlaps with the meaning of the term *comprehensibility* (see definitions in table 2). The GRA descriptors also refer to comprehensibility, although to a lesser degree, with reference to '*comprehension problems*' at bands 6 and 5 and '*misunderstanding*' at band 4. The L1-speaker is taken as a reference point in this criterion: band 9 refers to '*'slips' characteristic of native speaker speech*'; implicit in this is that comprehension is not affected. Comprehensibility is referred to obliquely in the LR descriptors in terms of effect on the message: '*precise meaning*' (band 8) and '*make meaning clear*' (band 6). In FC, comprehensibility can be seen in the references to '*coherence*' at various bands, for example, '*may lose coherence at times*' (band 6).

There are several key take-aways from this brief look at the IELTS rating rubrics. Firstly, the construct of comprehensibility is distributed across different linguistic categories, suggesting that a complex web of linguistic features underlies the ability. Secondly, the frequent reference to comprehensibility (*understanding/intelligibility/clarity*) in the PRON descriptors suggests that the test developers view pronunciation as a core contributor to the construct being measured by the test. This could have significant impact in light of studies that have found PRON to be the most difficult for examiners to operationalise compared to the other criteria (Yates et al., 2011; Galaczi et al., 2011). Other aspects of comprehensibility are evident in that the listener (in this case, a rater) is asked to make a decision about the amount of effort required to achieve understanding, indicating that comprehensibility is a) subjective and b) co-constructed by speaker and listener (although, crucially, it is only the speaker's effort to achieve communicative success that is being measured). Finally, the assessment of *amount of effort* and the use of modifiers such as *some difficulty, at times, generally, minimal effect* point to comprehensibility being scalar, a characteristic that proves tricky for raters (Isaacs et al., 2015). Taking a broader perspective on comprehensibility, it is noticeable that the context of the speech is not taken into consideration; unlike the IELTS writing rubrics, the speaking descriptors do not make reference to task achievement, appropriacy or tone.

The TOEFL iBT has two sets of publicly available rating rubrics – one for the independent speaking task and another for the integrated task (reading and listening into speaking), both of which are rated on a 4-band scale. Comprehensibility (again, often referred to in the scales as intelligibility) is dealt with similarly in both sets of rubrics and is most evident in the *Delivery* descriptors, although there is reference to aspects of comprehensibility across the other categories, too: General Description (an over-arching descriptor), Language Use and, to a lesser extent, Topic Development. As with the IELTS descriptors, this spread attests to the complexity of the comprehensibility construct. The link to pronunciation, specifically, is also evident, but unlike IELTS, there is no reference to accent. Although not a separate criterion per se, more features of pronunciation are explicitly linked to comprehensibility across all level descriptors under the Delivery criterion: '*minor difficulties with pronunciation or intonation patterns…do not affect overall intelligibility*' (score level 4); '*speech is basically intelligible*' (score level 2), suggesting that pronunciation contributes a great deal to comprehensibility. TOEFL, however, introduces a somewhat more explicit connection between both fluency and successful communication of the message (under Language Use), and organisation of ideas and clarity (under Topic Development for the Independent Task). Again, as with IELTS, the subjective nature of comprehensibility assessments is noticeable in the references to '*listener effort*' in score levels 1 – 3, as is the scalar nature of comprehensibility in the use of terms such as *not significantly affected, does not seriously interfere with communication of the message*, and *generally clear* (all score level 3).

Other tests of English show similar rating-scale characteristics. The Trinity College London Integrated Skills in English (ISE) test refers to *Effects of inaccuracies* and *Effects on the listener*, using terms such as '*intelligibility*', '*difficulty*' [in following the message], '*impede communication*' and '*careful listening*' in the detailed descriptors; there is a reference to '*non-standard phonemes*', which could be interpreted (or operationalised by raters) as accent. Unlike the other tests discussed above which are all rated by humans, the Pearson Test of English (PTE) is auto-rated (with human rating for model training and validation purposes); while the machine itself does not make use of rating rubrics, the descriptors of performance at the different levels are intended to reflect the salient features that are measured. Speaking items are scored on two scales: Pronunciation, and Oral fluency (see PTE Score Guide for Test Takers Version 19, 2023, p. 42–43). Both are assessed using a 6-band scale (0–5) and PTE is explicit in referencing the L1-speaker benchmark – 5 is labelled '*Native-like*' while 1 is '*Intrusive*' and 0 is '*Non-English*'. Despite the auto-rating of the speaking by non-sentient machines, comprehensibility appears to be included in the construct as described in the rating rubric: '*listeners may find more than ½ of the speech unintelligible*', '*difficulty understanding about 1/3 of the words*', '*unclear*', '*distortions do not affect intelligibility*', '*easily understandable*'. Throughout the two sets of descriptors, accent and nativeness of speech are referenced: '*non-native phonological simplifications*', '*intrusive foreign accent*', '*need to adjust to the accent*' and (somewhat confusingly) '*All vowels and consonants are produced in a manner that is easily understanding by <u>regular</u> speakers of the language*' (author's emphasis). Apart from possibly reflecting a particular position with regards to the importance of accent or standard English in assessing language, the L1-speaker focus most likely also reflects the need to have a clear reference point in order for machine-rating to be possible. This has had some unintended consequences, however, as seen in the test results of an educated L1 speaker of English failing to obtain the necessary score on the speaking test, most likely due to an unfamiliar accent (Australian Associated Press, 2017). The intersection between comprehensibility and automated assessment are explored more in-depth in Chapter 6.

Turning to other languages, various tests of Mandarin Chinese draw on a range of proficiency scales to evaluate the spoken performance of foreign language learners. One such scale is the Chinese Language Proficiency Scales for Speakers of Other Languages (CLPS). The advanced level descriptor reads: *Able to make oneself understood and communicate effectively with others on concrete or abstract topics and able to give a description or argumentation on a topic that one is interested in, expressing oneself clearly and coherently with appropriate details*. As with rating scales in the other languages shown above, there is reference to comprehensibility of the spoken communication as well as clarity. Despite the overt communicative focus of the descriptors, it would seem that testers of Mandarin focus on linguistic features when rating; in their analysis of four sets of documents for the teaching and assessment of foreign language learners of Mandarin in mainland China, Jin and Mak (2013) identified seven distinguishing features used in the teaching and testing of L2 Chinese speaking: 'target-like syllables, speech rate, pause time, word tokens, word types, grammatical accuracy and grammatical complexity' (Jin & Mak, 2013, p. 27). Again, we see that the ability to make oneself comprehensible is narrowed down to a number of different linguistic variables.

The Test Deutsch als Fremdsprache (TestDaF), is a test for foreign language learners of German offered at three different levels covering a range from B2 to C1 on the CEFR. While explicitly linked to the CEFR scales, the test makes use of very concise band descriptors at three levels or *TestDaF-Niveaustufen* (TDN) (TestDaF (2012) levels): TDN3, 4 and 5. Comprehensibility is realised in the speaking descriptors as '*communicate clearly*' (TDN 5), '*linguistic deficiencies do not impair communication*' (TDN 4), and '*linguistic deficiencies may, however, slow down understanding*' and '*the communicative intention is only partly realised*' (TDN 3). In contrast to make of the tests discussed above, these descriptors focus on communicative comprehensibility rather than linguistic indicators, it would seem.

Examples from Standards and Frameworks

The Common European Framework of Reference for Languages: Learning, teaching, assessment (CEFR; Council of Europe, 2001) and the Companion Volume (Companion Volume; Council of Europe, 2020) scales provide a useful reference by which educators, students and others can evaluate ability and interpret test scores not only in relation to requirements and other test-takers in a language, but across languages.

Comprehensibility is most explicitly reflected in the CEFR Companion Volume Phonological Control and Plurilingual Competence scales. As with other rating scales discussed above, *intelligibility* overlaps in meaning with *comprehensibility* – "Intelligibility: accessibility of meaning for listeners, covering also the listeners' perceived difficulty in understanding (normally referred to as comprehensibility)" (Council of Europe, 2020, p. 134). Notably, the Phonological Control scale was completely replaced in the revised CEFR, for reasons explained in the publication:

> In language teaching, the phonological control of an idealised native speaker has traditionally been seen as the target, with accent being seen as a marker of poor phonological control. The focus on accent and on accuracy instead of on intelligibility has been detrimental to the development of the teaching of pronunciation. (Council of Europe, 2020, p. 134)

The revised Phonological Control scales include reference to specific features of speech (*individual sounds, prosodic features (e.g. stress, rhythm and intonation)*) as well as to speaker intelligibility and to communicative effect. Comprehensibility is only occasionally and obliquely referred to in other scales (e.g. *give clear descriptions* under the Range criterion (Council of Europe, 2020, p. 171)). In the description of Plurilingual Competence, there is a clear focus on communicative success: "fully participate in social and educational contexts, achieving mutual understanding" and "different languages can be used purposefully for conveying messages in the same situation" (Council of Europe, 2020, p. 123); in the Plurilingual Comprehension scales, we see the phrases, "to support comprehension" (B2) and "develop comprehension" (B1) (Council of Europe, 2020, p. 126).

The American Council for the Teaching of Foreign Languages (ACTFL) takes a can-do approach, with detailed descriptions at each of the eleven levels identified. While communicative effect or outcome is included in the descriptors, it is unclear how these might be effectively operationalised, given the level of detail and vagueness. In addition, there is liberal reference to L1-speakers, for example, in this extract from the level Low Advanced: *Their speech can be understood by native speakers unaccustomed to dealing with non-natives* (ACTFL, 2012). It is seemingly implicit that comprehensibility ('*can be understood*') is measured with reference to the L1-speaker listener only.

This brief overview of how comprehensibility is reflected (or not) in language tests and standards of reference reflects several of the tensions and key issues associated with a shift towards the assessment of comprehensibility put forward in this book. The key concern around a narrow definition of comprehensibility where the construct is distilled down to linguistic indicators only and insufficient consideration is given to wider contributors to making meaning is that it will result in construct underrepresentation and render the generalisation of performance on a test to a broader communicative context invalid. McNamara points out, "[t]he empirical validation in language testing is to ensure the defensibility and fairness of interpretations based on test performance" (2006, p. 33). If a test score is used to decide whether someone can carry out particular communicative functions in a certain context or TLU domain (e.g. university or a profession), test developers need to prove that the test reflects the range of contributors to that ability. It follows that a broader view of the comprehensibility construct demands tests that are linked to the context of use and are not limited to the ability to use language in an abstract sense regardless of communicative achievement or effect.

Aims and Structure of the Book

This book aims to provoke a reconsideration of the comprehensibility construct in the assessment of communicative competence by:

- unravelling the micro- and macro- threads that contribute to the understanding of spoken communication
- considering how wider components of the communicative landscape contribute to the making of meaning and the success of a communicative endeavour
- allowing comprehensibility to be defined in terms of dynamic and changing patterns of features that are linked to context and purpose

Implicit in this approach to comprehensibility of spoken language is the recognition that a shift towards accounting for and including the broader, communicative task specific features and factors crucial to communicating successfully in a contemporary speech landscape is necessary in both language teaching and assessment. During the course of this monograph, comprehensibility is presented as a complex concept: co-constructed, context-dependent, dynamic construct that evolves through the course of interaction, it is differentiated from intelligibility as it is not a characteristic specifically displayed by a speaker or a listener. It is linked to communicative purpose and affected by pragmatic factors including contextual, sociolinguistic and sociocultural elements of communication; a multidimensional construct affecting spoken communication in a number of different ways.

The rationale for a book dedicated to exploring comprehensibility in the context of language testing builds on the position expressed in Levis' (2005) intelligibility principle: that it is comprehensibility that we, as testers and educators, should be assessing. There are implications of an insistence on placing comprehensibility at the core of a testing approach: first, atomic linguistic features should only be referenced where they have an impact on meaning or there is evidence that they are key contributors to a more general view of comprehensibility and, secondly, comprehensibility cannot be divorced from the context of the communicative task and the purpose of the test itself. The exploration of comprehensibility at this point in time is partly motivated by the adoption of technology for the rating of spoken communication skills. In the context of a relative lack of understanding of or agreement on what constitutes comprehensibility, the use of automated rating systems could have unforeseen consequences. Investigating how comprehensibility between speakers and listeners is achieved – and understanding how much we do not know – is especially important to guard against encoding an insufficiently understood construct that potentially results in negative consequences on individuals and societies in the assessment of communicative proficiency.

For the overall structure of this book, we refer the reader back to the outline provided at the start of this chapter. Starting from the bottom up, in the next chapter we review a linguistic point of view on comprehensibility, focusing on pronunciation, and exploring phoneme, word and utterance level components of meaning. The concluding chapter includes a diagramatic representation of our approach to comprehensibility; the authors feel that this is more meaningful as a summary of the overall discussion, although some readers might find it useful to refer to this intermittently.

CHAPTER 2

COMPREHENSIBILITY AT A PHONOLOGICAL LEVEL

'Whatever you say, say nothing.'
Seamus Heaney, 1975.

Pronunciation is recognised as a signifier of tribe: language background, social group, or socio-economic background; it can result in acceptance or discrimination, admission or exclusion. It is also a key contributor to communicative comprehensibility in spoken language. This chapter serves to recognise the essential contribution of phonological factors to the overall construct of comprehensibility and highlight the issues that come with erroneously or gratuitously focusing on linguistic features of pronunciation in the assessment of communicative ability. The chapter looks specifically at the link between phonological features and comprehensibility, their realisation in tests of spoken language and the challenges that occur particularly in tests of languages that function as lingua francas. We consider how different research approaches attempt to explicitly link pronunciation and the understanding of spoken language. Finally, we examine the challenges in determining and operationalising aspects of pronunciation that affect comprehensibility and argue against focusing on atomic features of pronunciation to the exclusion of other intersecting aspects of the comprehensibility construct.

In this chapter, we argue that while it is important to continue investigating the linguistic features associated with comprehensibility, the assessment and teaching of spoken communicative proficiency should not take a purely atomic approach. In other words, a speaker's spoken language ability cannot be determined only by whether a particular feature is present or absent in the speech sample, e.g. the '*th*' (/δ/ or /φ/) sounds in English. Rather, the importance of what we are terming micro-level features (like minimal pairs where single phonemes can change the meaning, e.g. *ship/sheep* in English) for comprehensibility is determined by the context and communicative purpose of the utterance; it is also influenced by sociolinguistic factors (particularly accent, in relation to pronunciation). In some situations, a particular feature will carry greater weight in terms of achieving comprehensibility; in other instances, that exact same feature will assume a peripheral role, if any – Figure 2.1 towards the end of this chapter provides a visual representation of this thinking. If a particular speech sample is being 'marked down' because the rating system (human-rated or automated rating) requires evidence of a certain linguistic feature that is not there, despite the speech being comprehensible, this leads to serious questions around the test score being representative of an ability to communicate effectively. Overall, we advocate that it is only where certain phonological features serve to resolve ambiguity that arises due to a paucity of other linguistic and context-related factors that they should be considered explicitly in assessments of spoken language, i.e. if they do not obfuscate the intended communicative outcome or effect, they should not be negatively assessed.

Key Terms

The terminology we use in this chapter and beyond is common to most discussions of pronunciation more broadly. While this chapter does not engage in technical discussion of articulatory phonetics or phonology, a brief description of key terms will help to establish a common framework for the subsequent exploration of pronunciation and comprehensibility.

The conceptualisation of 'pronunciation' used in Second Language Pronunciation Assessment (Isaacs & Trofimovich, 2016) serves as a useful touchstone here:

> (1) individual consonant and vowel sounds, commonly referred to in the literature as 'segments', and (2) features that span a larger unit than a single segment, such as word stress, rhythm and intonation, referred to synonymously in the literature as 'suprasegmentals' or 'prosody' – terms that are, therefore, used interchangeably. (p. 9)

In this chapter, we also use *suprasegmentals* and *prosody* interchangeably. However, we recognise that the term suprasegmentals includes both prosodic features ("suprasegmental properties that influence oral productions, especially when producing connected speech" (Ghanem & Kang, 2018, p. 115)) and features associated with fluency. While the term suprasegmental in this chapter refers mostly to features associated with oral production, some of the studies referenced include temporal (i.e. fluency) features in their analyses, an indication of how the different features of communicative comprehensibility are intertwined. For a more detailed discussion of current thinking on pronunciation features that encompasses both segmental and suprasegmental features, see Ghanem and Kang, 2018.

Languages in general are made up of a collection of individual phonetic segments – most commonly vowels and consonants – which are combined to form words and meaning. Segments which serve to differentiate between meaning are phonemes, or "the smallest phonological units that can create a linguistic difference in meaning" (Rogersten-Revell, 2011, p. 93). An example in English is the difference between the words *very* and *berry*, where */v/* and */b/* are distinct phonemes which affect meaning directly, i.e. minimal pairs. A distinction needs to be made between *phonemic* differences – where the meaning of the word changes due to the substitution of a different phoneme as in the example above – and *phonetic* differences, where the sound might change but the meaning does not, like the dialectal variation between */tæsk/* (General American (GA) English *'task'*) and */ta:sk/ 'task'* in Received Pronunciation (RP) British English.

Since this book aims to consider comprehensibility from a view that goes beyond just English we recognise that it is not only the articulation of individual sounds that might affect comprehensibility. For example, tone in Chinese dialects is associated with meaning at the syllable and word level and has been demonstrated as playing as an important role in determining meaning as phonemes themselves (Surendran & Levow, 2004); this is likely to extend to other Asian and African tonal languages such as Mandarin and Hausa respectively (Newman, 1996; Yip, 1996). This is not discussed here, however, due to limitations in scope.

As suggested in the Isaacs and Trofimovich (2016) definition of 'pronunciation' above, phonemes are considered segmental level features while at the suprasegmental level other features occur. The latter include word stress (e.g. *refuse* in English, where stress on the second syllable signifies the verb to mean to say 'no', and on the first, the noun meaning 'rubbish' or 'garbage'); sentence stress which serves, amongst other functions, in English, to introduce new information or contrasting information; intonation – rising and/or falling pitch spanning more than just one syllable; and pitch itself. However, even at this early stage of labelling the components of pronunciation we run into challenges. There is not, for example, agreement on what constitutes a syllable (Blevins, 1996; Goldsmith, 2011; Ladefoged & Johnson, 2014). In discussing the link between pronunciation and comprehensibility, while we do not wish to neglect the myriad of articulatory and psycholinguistic complexities that are associated with producing speech, this chapter will focus on the broader implications of assessing pronunciation in the context of communicative effect.

Approaches to Linking Phonological Features and Comprehensibility

As has been stated, the premise of this book is that communicative comprehensibility is not contingent on linguistic features only, but needs to be considered in the broader context of the speech act. This position does not suggest that intelligibility achieved through the control of sound articulation and oral production is not important; indeed, it can be the origin of much confusion in spoken communication. While the cases where these cannot be resolved through linguistic context, the context of the conversation, or paralinguistic strategies are rare, understanding what the meaning distinguishing phonological features are in a certain language is in the interests of not only assessors, but also teachers and students. Faced with the daunting task of mastering or teaching a foreign language, learners and educators alike have sought to find the most expedient way to do this (Brown, 1988) – see Chapter 7 for a discussion of pedagogy and comprehensibility. Whether learning focuses on the (elusive) native-speaker accent as a benchmark or on communicative ability, there is obvious interest in which characteristics of the speaking skill will bring the biggest return on investment of learning time. In the case of English, the need to know what features of pronunciation to prioritise in the classroom has led to a vast body of research into the link between comprehensibility and phonological features (Derwing & Munro, 2015), as well as approaches to establishing this correlation. We briefly present an overview of different approaches to linking phonological features to comprehensibility, suggesting some limitations to each. We then move on to consider some phonological features that have been found to contribute to comprehensibility in different studies and, in doing so, highlight the complexities and difficulties that preclude the production of a neat inventory of phonological features for comprehensibility, even for one language.

Correlation Focused Approach

One approach is to investigate which linguistic features correlate most strongly with high ratings of comprehensibility. As Nagle et al. (2019) point out, "...nearly all current evidence about the linguistic aspects of

L2 comprehensibility is correlational, based on associations between comprehensibility ratings and coded or rated measures of L2 speech" (p. 4).

This approach was led by the 1992 study by Anderson-Hsieh, Johnson and Koehler that focused specifically on features of pronunciation and since then, various studies have attempted to tap into the underlying linguistic features of comprehensibility. In this method, listeners rate comprehensibility (typically using a 9-point 'ease of understanding' scale) of samples of speech; listeners can be naïve (non-experts) or experienced assessors; overwhelmingly, studies tend to rely on L1 speakers of the target L2. Comprehensibility ratings are subsequently correlated with features identified in linguistic analysis of the spoken performances; analysis typically uses expert coding and categorisation or sophisticated software for more technical examination of acoustic data. The Isaacs and Trofimovich (2012) study provides an example of this approach; for a broader overview of studies, see Isaacs and Harding (2017). This approach is attractive in that it attempts to 'unpick' the complex web of phonological features that contribute to achieving meaning.

The Lingua Franca Core

One particularly influential approach to defining phonological components of comprehensibility for teachers and learners is Jenkins' Phonology of English of International Language (EIL) (2000). Jenkins investigated data gathered at a UK university, generated by L2 speakers of English. She identified 40 communication breakdowns and attributed 27 of these to phonological issues. Her proposed Lingua Franca Core (LFC) balanced evidence from miscommunication data and what Jenkins – in her experience as a teacher – found to be practically 'teachable'. With a focus on teaching practice and a shift from English L1 speaker pronunciation as the learning goal towards understanding, Jenkins' core inventory proposal was revolutionary and is considered the 'first wave' of research into ELF (Harding & McNamara, 2017) but it suffers from several limitations. Firstly, sample paucity – only 27 instances of phonologically-induced misunderstanding were used (Isaacs, 2018; Sewell, 2017). Secondly, only communication between L2 speakers of English was focused on, thereby potentially defining alternative inventories and setting different standards, continuing the manufactured division between L1 and L2 speakers of English within the global community of ELF users in the World Englishes tradition (Harding & McNamara, 2017; Jenkins, Cogo & Dewey, 2011). A related weakness of the LFC is that it seeks to codify an ephemeral, elusive 'variety' before it can be taught or tested.

The Functional Load Principle

Another approach to identifying linguistic features underlying the comprehensibility construct is the Functional Load Principle (FLP). It is characterised by more top-down, deductive, theory-led (Meyerstein, 1970) thinking where evidence is used to confirm the hypotheses about which phonological features affect comprehensibility. The FLP as it applies to phonological features uses information from minimal pairs, contrastive analysis, and articulatory phonetics to whittle down the list of discrete sounds that contribute most significantly to clarity of communication. It shares, with other approaches, the goal of identifying which phonological features teachers and learners of a language should focus on to achieve understanding.

The FLP is used across various domains and was initially applied to phonology by King (1967b), Catford (1987) and later Brown (1988). The approach uses statistics to analyse the 'burden' carried by a particular phonological feature in terms of disambiguating meaning. As such, the FLP is sometimes expressed in highly technical terms (e.g. Sundrendran & Levow, 2004) which can be difficult for non-statisticians to understand and the calculations are not transparent. The description by Suzukida and Saito (2021) helps to clarify the approach in more lay terminology:

> FL [Functional Load] is a list of segmental contrasts that are ranked based on their communicative value. These contrasts were developed from minimal pairs in frequently used words, the degree of neutralization among regional English dialects, and the segmental position within a word. (p. 4)

To clarify further, 'segmental contrasts' are differences between phonemes or individual sounds that have a direct impact on meaning (e.g. /*pin*/ vs /*pen*/ in English). For a concise description of the FLP, see Munro and Derwing (2006), who empirically tested the FLP with Cantonese L1 speakers of English. For more detailed discussions about the approach, see King (1967a) and Sewell (2017).

Times have changed since Brown's (1988) paper and eyebrows will certainly be raised about some of the key assumptions as his model was based on RP, now considered a highly affected variety of English. The approach, however, has been revisited by Munro and Derwing (2006) and, more recently, by Suzukida and Saito (2021). While these studies pertain to segmentals only, other (far more technical) studies have applied the FLP to the comparison of the 'functional yield' between word stress in German, Dutch and English and tone in Chinese (Surendran & Levow, 2004) and there is potential to exploit this approach to cover a wider range of phonological features at both the segmental and suprasegmental levels.

The Dynamic Approach

There is increasing recognition that comprehensibility is not fixed but fluid, that it is highly context-dependent rather than abstract and context-independent, and that it relies on co-construction and negotiation of meaning rather than residing with the speaker only (Leung & Lewkowitz, 2006; Canagarajah, 2007; Jenkins et al., 2011; Seidlhofer, 2011; Harding & McNamara, 2017).

In contrast to the early proposals by Elder and Davies (2006) to either a) measure ELF using Standard English (i.e. British or American standard forms) with 'accommodations' operationalised through the review of test materials for cultural bias or rater training, or b) evaluate alternative varieties as standards once they had become encoded (e.g. Hong Kong English), Harding and McNamara's (2017) discussion of ELF in language assessment emphasised the dynamic nature of communication and highlighted just how slippery the construct of comprehensibility in ELF (or indeed any LF) is. Their recommendations for an (E)LF construct in testing include two references to phonological features and accent variation, and the unfixed nature of comprehensibility can be seen in the liberal use of the word *different*:

- The ability to tolerate and comprehend different varieties of English: different accents, different syntactic forms and different discourse styles.
- The ability to use those phonological features that are crucial for intelligibility across speakers of different L1 backgrounds.
- Co-construction of meaning is also evident in the mention of the receiver of the message (*tolerate and comprehend*) and the creator of the message (*ability to use*). (Harding & McNamara, 2017, p. 577).

This unfixed, dynamic and co-constructed approach to comprehensibility is echoed in the recent research by Nagle et al. (2019) into understanding the components at play as speakers and listeners work to achieve common understanding:

> As L2 speakers produce varying levels of accuracy, complexity, and fluency over time, listeners must continuously process this variability to interpret the intended message within an emergent discourse structure, suggesting that a speaker's comprehensibility is likely a dynamic, time-sensitive construct for the listener. (p. 5)

As such, the focus is on communicative success emerging as a result of an interplay of changing factors. Nagle et al.'s (2019) study into comprehensibility of Spanish L2 speech focused on how the raters changed their comprehensibility decisions as they listened by using Idiodynamic Software (MacIntyre, 2012) that recorded rating changes as they listened, followed by stimulated recall interviews. Nagle et al. (2019) motivate their research as follows:

> If comprehensibility is a dynamic construct, then it should display some of the core properties of dynamic systems, including change over time, interconnectedness of elements, self-organization into preferred and dispreferred states, and nonlinearity or threshold effects (de Bot et al., 2007; de Bot, Lowie, Thorne, and Verspoor, 2013). (p. 21)

While the research included the use of only three samples of speech, it takes an important step towards recognising and investigating the dynamic nature of comprehensibility. Their findings also point to the importance of macro-level factors (discourse, in particular) and the negative impact of patches of miscomprehension on overall understanding.

Phonological Features Associated with Comprehensibility

In this section we report some phonological features that various research studies suggest might be key contributors to comprehensibility; with other words, findings suggest these features could have a stronger impact on achieving meaning or, in FLP terms, the features carry a heavier burden in contributing to the shared understanding between speaker and listener. Before we delve into the features themselves, a caveat: this discussion of features is not intended to be conclusive or exhaustive, or to provide a neat inventory of features, but rather to provide a sense of what research has yielded thus far; the discussion itself also illustrates why a set of phonological features contributing to comprehensibility – even in one language – remains elusive.

There are several reasons this overview can be neither definitive nor comprehensive. Firstly, the findings need to be qualified or restricted because variables such as speaker and listener L1, familiarity with accents, topic familiarity, as well as task types have all been shown to have an impact on performance and/or comprehensibility ratings (Gass & Veronis, 1984; Foster & Skehan, 1996; Tauroza & Luk, 1997; Major et al., 2002; Crowther et al., 2015; Suzukida & Saito, 2021), with other words they are not generalisable across speaker, listener or communicative task. Secondly, the research designs are so varied as to make comparison difficult: studies focus on comprehensibility, or intelligibility, or accent – or conflate two or more of these (studies reported below include one or more of these concepts). Indeed, to what degree accent and comprehensibility are being conflated by listeners is unclear and worth bearing in mind as studies suggest that there is significant overlap in these constructs when phonological features are investigated (Kang, 2010; Kang et al., 2010). Finally, some linguistic analysis draws on human intuition (e.g. 'goodness' of intonation, Derwing & Munro, 1997) while other studies employ technical tools like PRAAT (e.g. Isaacs & Trofimovich, 2012), making comparison tricky.

The following overview moves from a micro-level, granular phonological component point of view towards higher-level, 'bigger' phonological units not only to provide a logical structure to the reporting of features, but also in recognition of the trajectory of typical teaching and testing traditions and the 'prosodic hierarchy' (Nespor & Vogel, 1986). Like the complex web of various linguistic and non-linguistic aspects of communicative language, however, discrete phonological features cannot easily be teased apart and there is significant interaction between segmental and suprasegmental components, and beyond. Indeed, Zielinski argues that the segmental/suprasegmental categorisation is a "false dichotomy" (2015, p. 409) that ignores the interaction and cumulative effect of different levels of phonology on intelligibility and comprehensibility. The interrelatedness of phonological factors is evident in the discussion below.

Segmentals

Segmentals refer to the phoneme level, i.e. the oral production characteristics of vowels and consonants. and are clear contributors to overall communicative comprehensibility.

Correlation studies have identified a clear link between the production of certain segmental features and comprehensibility (overwhelmingly in

English target language studies) (Derwing & Munro, 1995a; Zielinski, 2008; Trofimovich & Isaacs, 2012; Kang & Moran, 2014) but these remain inconclusive. While much research into comprehensibility features focuses on segmentals, Suzukida and Saito (2021) point out that these are often treated as a single measurement (i.e. mispronunciation) and the type of phoneme is neglected. This results in having little insight into what types of phonemes might be more influential and correlation studies yield no agreed inventory about which segmental features carry more weight in terms of comprehensibility for a particular language. For example, consonants might contribute more to the message than vowels in some languages.

Apart from phoneme quality (i.e., close articulatory proximity to a recognised form), position within the lexical-grammatical context also seems to play a role. For example, in English, consonant clusters at the beginning and in the middle of words are also seen as key contributors to understanding, as are long and short vowel contrasts and the 'nurse' /ɜː/ vowel. Deterding's (2013) study supports this, with the exception of vowel length which listeners did not always perceive (and is not a feature in some World Englishes, Kirkpatrick, 2007). Deterding and Kirkpatrick (2006) found that segmental features caused miscommunication amongst speakers of ASEAN languages only where those errors were not common to the English variety of both speaker and listener such as the insertion of */t/* in the Myanmar speaker's articulation of *us* (realised as */uts/*).

The LFC and FLP offer more clarity and certainty around lists of phonemes necessary for learners to master in order to make themselves understood in English, whether evidence supports this or not. Jenkins' (2000) LFC proposal included primarily segmental features, with consonants making up the core part of the overall inventory. The LFC, which applies to English only, sees the whole range of English consonants being of importance for the learner, with notable exceptions being the dental fricatives */θ/* and */ð/*, although this is challenged by Luchini and Kennedy (2013) who provide an example of miscommunication as a result of */θ/* substituted with */t/* (the data set, however, is small). Jenkins (2000) singles out vowel length as a key comprehensibility distinction; this is supported by Jurado-Bravo (2018) who, however, adds vowel quality (i.e., how the individual sound is formed (lips, tongue, etc), not just the length) as a crucial contributor to intelligibility in Spanish speakers of English.

Rank Ordering of RP Phoneme Pairs Commonly Conflated by Learners			
	Vowels		Consonants
10	/e, æ/	10	/p, b/
	/æ, ʌ/		/p, f/
	/æ, ɒ/		/m, n/
	/ʌ, ɒ/		/n, l/
	/ɔː, əʊ /		/l, r/
9	/e, ɪ/	9	/f, h/
	/e, eɪ/		/t, d/
	/ɑː, aɪ/		/k, g/
	/ɜː, əʊ /		
8	/iː, ɪ/	8	/w. v/
			/s, z/
7	–	7	/b, v/
			/f, v/
			/ð, z/
			/s, ʃ/
6	/ɔː, ɜː/	6	/v, ð/
	/ɒ, əʊ /		/s, ʒ/
5	/ɑː, ʌ/	5	/θ, ð/
	/ɔː, ɒ/		/θ, s/
	/ɜː, ʌ/		/ð, d/
			/z, dʒ/
			/n, ŋ/
4	/e, eə/	4	/θ, t/
	/æ, ɑː/		
	/ɑː, ɒ/		
	/ɔː, ʊ/		
	/ɜː, e/		
3	/iː, ɪə/	3	/tʃ, dʒ/
	/ɑː, aʊ/		
	/uː, ʊ/		
2	/ɪə, eə/	2	/tʃ, ʃ/
			/ʃ, ʒ/
			/j, ʒ/
1	/ɔː, ɔɪ/	1	/f, θ/
	/uː, ʊə/		/dʒ, j/

Table 2.1: Brown's list of key contrasts in RP English used to illustrate his application of the FLP (Brown, 1988, p. 604).

Despite its adherence to an English L1 speaker benchmark variety, the FLP approach yielded an intuitively attractive list of segmental feature production in English that is crucial to meaning, and Brown's (1988) rank ordering of the contrastive pairs generated by this approach is shown in Table 1. Although based on Received Pronunciation (RP), Brown argues that this is acceptable as it is the target variety of most learners of English and that the variety bias is mitigated by the 'neutralisation' of differences between regional dialects (limited to Inner Circle prestige varieties). Brown's focus is limited to segmentals and his analysis will resonate with any teacher of English.

Several studies have recently revisited the FLP in the context of comprehensibility and intelligibility. Munro and Derwing (2006) showed that phonemes with a higher functional load had a great impact on both comprehensibility and accentedness; Suzukida and Saito's (2021) results (Japanese L1) were in line with this and concluded, further, that it is consonants with high functional load that are more strongly correlated with comprehensibility, providing the useful shorthand for this finding - *high FL > low FL; consonants > vowels* (p. 14). In a subsequent study, Suzukida and Saito (2022) found that high FL phonemes contributed to expert rater assessment between low to medium pronunciation ratings, while low FL phonemes had an impact when raters are deciding between rating pronunciation as medium or high in terms of proficiency level. In a study that brings together two approaches to identifying phonologically significant features, Sewell (2017) applied FLP to the LFC, effectively 'testing' whether Jenkins' (2000) inventory also demonstrates a high functional load. The results suggested that particular phonological features at the segmental level (especially consonants and their location in the utterance) are, indeed, of significance to ELF.

In a study that has methodological characteristics of both the LFC and the FLP, Neri et al. (2006) focused on segmentals in Dutch drawing on large corpora of spoken language and identifying the salience, frequency, persistent and the likeliness of impact on comprehensibility to arrive at an inventory of 11 'problematic' phonemes for teachers to concentrate on during teaching. Interestingly, the majority of the segmental features identified were vowels and diphthongs, rather than consonants which are thought to carry the primary segmental 'load' in meaning differentiation in English.

Findings from studies are further confounded by correlations showing marked differences between different L1 speakers, for example, segmental features were important for comprehensibility for Chinese L1 speakers of English, but much less so for speakers of Hindi or Farsi (Crowther et al., 2015). Other studies have found that segmental errors do not affect comprehensibility ratings, or that they correlate more strongly with ratings of accent than either comprehensibility or even intelligibility (reinforcing the notion that these are related, but separate, concepts) (Munro & Derwing, 1995a; Derwing & Munro, 1997; Saito et al., 2017); while the majority of studies focused on English, Saito and Akiyama (2017) also noticed only minor impact of segmentals on comprehensibility in the speech of Japanese L2 learners.

Suprasegmentals

Suprasegmentals refer to features that go beyond the level of consonants and vowels, i.e. at syllable, word and utterance level, and include word stress, sentence stress, intonation, pitch and rhythm; this term includes temporal indicators often associated with fluency, although here we are focused on the phonological aspects while fluency indicators will be directly dealt with in Chapter 4.

Evidence from research shows that suprasegmentals play a key role in achieving understanding (Field, 2005; Kang, 2010; Winters & O'Brien, 2013; Saito et al., 2015) and some researchers suggest that these features may have an even stronger impact on understanding than segmentals (Anderson-Hsieh et al., 1992; Kang et al., 2010). Suzukida and Saito's (2022) study suggests that accuracy in word stress and production of syllables (e.g. avoiding errors due to elision, substitution or insertion of individual sounds within the syllable) affect whether Japanese L1 speakers of English are rated as mid- or high-level in terms of pronunciation. Other studies also suggest that the teaching of suprasegmentals could lead to better comprehensibility ratings or pronunciation scores (Derwing et al., 1998) and even that undue pedagogical focus on segmentals rather than global pronunciation could be detrimental to achieving comprehensibility (Derwing & Rossiter, 2003, Derwing et al., 2004). Suprasegmentals have often been investigated as a unitary construct, for example, Munro and Derwing (1995a) who included 'nativeness of prosody' in their investigation, Derwing and Munro (1997) ('goodness of prosody'), and Saito et al. (2015) where 'good' prosody correlated with higher proficiency ratings. Isaacs (2018), in an overview of the study of phonological feature correlates to comprehensibility over the years, pointed out that segmentals received 'primacy' in the pre-communicative language teaching years and that suprasegmental features were relatively neglected. This has changed and researchers now recognise the effect of higher level phonological components on the production of comprehensible speech (Derwing & Munro, 1997; Wennerstrom, 1994; Hahn, 2004; Derwing & Munro, 2005; Kang, 2010).

A key non-segmental level in the phonological hierarchy of English (Demuth, 2009) is word stress. Kager (1996) refers to word stress being concerned with "the location of prominent syllables within words, as well as the rhythmic, positional, quantitative, and morphological factors that govern patterns of syllable prominence" where 'prominence' can be achieved through various acoustic means like pitch intensity and syllable duration, amplification, and vowel quality. There is great variation across languages: for example, German and English show a tendency to carry distinctive word stress that is stored and encoded in the lexicon (Cutler, 1984; Field, 2005), while Finnish has fixed stress on the first syllable of words. Most studies cited below are based on English where stressed syllables in polysyllabic words are associated with vowel realisation (i.e. 'reduced' or not). For a detailed, more technical, overview, see Kager (1996).

Various studies have identified word stress as being a key predictor of comprehensibility and/or intelligibility in English (Kang et al., 2010; Isaacs & Trofimovich, 2012; Luchini & Kennedy, 2013), and Jenkins (2000) included it in the LFC inventory. One possible reason word stress is so strongly related to ease of understanding in English (and, most likely, other stress-based languages) is because it is encoded and stored in the mental lexicon – lexical stress seems to act as a 'look-up' function that assists in retrieving vocabulary in these languages (Field, 2005). This could explain the salience of lexical stress over segmental accuracy in English, as 'whole word matching' overrides segmental errors (Cutler and Clifton, 1984). Following on from Cutler and Clifton's (1984) research, Field's (2005) study supported their finding that the *direction* of stress misplacement is also important in English: a 'leftward' shift appears to be acceptable, a 'rightward' shift less so, especially if accompanied by changes in vowel quality.

The interaction between word stress and vowel quality in English is an important one (Field, 2005; Sicola & Darcy, 2015): typically, vowels in unstressed syllables are 'reduced', that is, they undergo centralisation (usually replaced with *schwa* /ə/) and are shorter in duration and intensity while stressed syllables are realised as 'full' vowels. It is not uncommon that, for English L2 speakers, the ratio of stressed to unstressed syllables in English L2 learners is low (e.g. Nakamura, 2011). This relationship between phonemes and word stress is reflected in Isaacs and Trofimovich's (2012) study, which found that the ratio of correctly reduced vowels correlated positively with comprehensibility ratings (.74) while segmental error ratio (incorrect production of individual phonemes) showed only moderate correlation (-.54) and errors in syllable structure (elision or insertion) even less strongly correlated (only -.37): unsurprisingly, the more word stress errors occur, the fewer appropriate vowel reductions produced by the speaker. In what seems to be returning full-circle, Cutler's (2015) article argues that word stress in English is redundant, in other words, that it is the vowel quality (full or reduced) that triggers 'look-up' for the listener, rather than the word stress that leads to retrieval of lexical information. To support this, she points to the very rare instances of contrastive word stress patterns in English like INsight vs inCITE (capitals indicating word stress placement), showing that it is rare that word stress alone has an impact alone on meaning at the word level.

Word-level stress is interrelated with other temporal features such as sentence stress and rhythm. Sentence stress – also *primary stress*, *nuclear stress*, *contrastive stress* or *accent* – is where the acoustic means to achieve stress (e.g. duration and loudness) is used, in English and languages like Turkish and Arabic, to introduce new or contradictory information into an utterance. Jenkins (2000) includes nuclear stress as part of the LFC, and Hahn's study (2004) found that primary stress misplacement affected content recall by English L1 speakers of monologic speech produced by a high-proficiency Korean speaker of English. Low (2006), on the other hand, demonstrated that Singaporean English did *not* use prosodic tools to de-accent given information and that this did not affect intelligibility, calling into question the impact of sentence stress on comprehensibility. There are few comprehensibility correlational studies where primary stress is isolated, however, most likely because of the interwovenness with other temporal features, lexical stress patterns, and with the role nuclear stress plays in interactional speech which is less well researched from a phonological point of view in relation to comprehensibility and intelligibility.

Rhythm, which Crystal (1992) defines as "the perceived regularity of prominent units in speech" (p. 334), can be seen as 'how a language divides up time' ("how groups of syllables are organised into larger units such as feet and phrases" (Tajima et al., 1997, p. 2)) and is achieved through the placement of stress in the stream of speech. This confounding temporal feature (from a comprehensibility perspective) is typically measured by the duration between stressed speech elements and can be highly technical (see Tan & Low (2014) for a specialist discussion). Languages vary greatly in terms of timing and there is currently general agreement that rhythm is not a dichotomy of stress-timed languages (e.g. English and German) or syllable-timed languages (e.g. French and Chinese), as suggested by Abercrombie, 1967. Rather, languages fall along a continuum, with isochronous languages (like German) at one end and isosyllabic languages (like Spanish) at the other (see Low (2015) for a detailed discussion of previous literature, including mora-timing as proposed for Japanese). Temporal features in general have been seen to link to comprehensibility, intelligibility and perceptions of accent: Zielinski's (2008) study measured intelligibility for English L1 listeners of various East Asian L1 speakers of English, finding that listeners relied on syllable stress timing for understanding and, in particular, that the (accurate) production of strong syllables had a positive effect on comprehensibility; Tajima, Port and Dalby (1997), using technical means to manipulate temporal features in the English speech of a L1 speaker of English and a Chinese L1 speaker of English, concluded that intelligibility is affected by temporal properties. There are examples that suggest, however, that rhythm may be primarily associated with accent rather than actual comprehensibility in English; Low (2006), Tan and Low (2014) and Low (2015) show that two recognised and widely accepted varieties of English – Malaysian and Singaporean English – are closer to the syllable-timed side of the spectrum and do not de-accent given information or reduce vowels frequently. In her research, Szczepek Reed (2012) takes a Conversational Analysis approach and in one study of Mandarin (syllable-tendency timing) L1 speakers of German as a L2 (tending towards isochronous timing), identifies rhythm as a prosodic device used for interactional purposes, with the L2 speakers of German able to mirror the stress timing of their interlocutors at crucial turn-taking junctures, even where their speech tended, otherwise, towards syllable-timing. In other studies, this also occurred with Singaporean English speakers interacting with British English speakers, with Russian L1s conversing in German, and with Mandarin L1s interacting in German with L1 speakers of that language.

Tone functions differently across languages: shift in pitch across a syllable can change the meaning of a word (e.g. Mandarin), and tone on one syllable relative to the adjacent one (up-step/down-step) (e.g. Shona, a Bantu language spoken primarily in Zimbabwe) can change lexical meaning – this has an obvious impact on comprehensibility, although top-down or context components are significant mitigating aspects. Moving up the prosodic ladder, beyond the word level, according to Levis and Wichmann (2015), "Intonation is the use of pitch variations in the voice to communicate phrasing and discourse meaning in varied linguistic environments" (p. 138), where pitch is typically measured in frequency levels, denoted in F0, etc. While studies linking comprehensibility/intelligibility/accent to intonation often rely on intuitive evaluations (Munro & Derwing, 1995a – 'goodness of intonation'; Pickering, 2009), the use of technology allows more objective measurement of pitch variation (Isaacs & Trofimovich, 2012, using PRAAT). Across various languages, pitch has been shown to be associated with communicating emotion and that less proficient speakers of L2 English tend to use a narrower pitch range (see Pickering, 2009, for a more detailed discussion), although the Isaacs and Trofimovich (2012) study showed no correlation between pitch range and comprehensibility, and in Suzukida and Saito (2022) intonation was not a factor in proficiency ratings. Pickering's study (2009) recognised the interactive role pitch plays, finding that ELF interlocutors orient to pitch movement and height in order to manage sources of communicative 'trouble', using these to alert them to comprehensibility issues and whether they have been resolved. From a non-English perspective, a study of L2 Japanese learners found comprehensibility to be more strongly correlated with pitch accent than segmentals (Saito & Akiyama, 2017).

Other studies have identified a range of suprasegmental features contributing to comprehensibility. Kang et al. (2010) used regression analysis to evaluate the link between a range of 29 suprasegmental features and comprehensibility of English, identifying lexical stress as one of the predictors of comprehensibility; suprasegmental fluency (a combination of tone choices and temporal features), tones, boundary markers and pitch were other predictors. Kang (2010), on the other hand (also for English), found that word stress and pitch range were associated with accent ratings whereas speech rate (a temporal indicator, traditionally categorised under 'fluency' but with clear links to rhythm) was an indicator of comprehensibility. As above with segmental features, Ghanem and Kang's (2018) overview of the technical aspects of suprasegmental features serves as a rich reference here, with primary stress (as measured in pitch, length and intensity) being a key indicator; other phonetic indicators of proficiency are prominence and tone height (related to primary stress), tone choice (related to intonation) and pitch range (with L2 speakers displaying a narrower range than L1s).

The discussion above reflects not only the interrelatedness of phonological features as contributing factors to comprehensibility, but also the influence of suprasegmentals in the processing of spoken language, as well as on interactive communication. Suprasegmental features are important parsing devices: intonation, pausing, nucleic stress, etc., are key components in the identification of grammatical constructions, as O'Brien et al. (2014) have found for German and Nguyen et al. (2008) have shown for English as spoken by Vietnamese L1 speakers; intonation also helps define meaning and idea units or boundaries (Levis & Wichmann, 2015). The function of suprasegmental features in spoken interaction is significant, as seen in the examples above, and, as such, how speakers of lingua francas use these devices (or do not) to facilitate communicative goals requires further inquiry.

Phonological Features in Test Constructs

As we have seen in this chapter so far, there is a strong association between pronunciation features and comprehensibility. Phonological features are also frequently manifested within rating descriptors that focus on or include pronunciation indicators. In this section we consider the role of phonological features in rating scales and standards for a number of prominent language tests plus the CEFR.

There are several main issues to consider here. Firstly, the tests considered here are intended to test the general proficiency of speakers from a range of L1s in the target language. Because comprehensibility features seem to be L1-specific (as discussed earlier in this chapter), one of the key issues with designing a rating scale (or descriptors) intended to apply to all language groups is that it is destined to be generic (Isaacs et al., 2018). Indeed, Isaacs et al. point to two dichotomous trends in scale development: a task- and context-specific approach, and a more universal approach to the broader trait of speaking ability. If linguistic features of comprehensibility (as seems to be the case) are linked to language background and the purpose of the task, then it is not feasible (nor is it fair) to consider them in ratings of pronunciation unless the assessment applies to that L1 only, or to that particular context of evaluation.

Secondly, in the case of human rated-tests, pronunciation scales are notoriously difficult to operationalise (Isaacs et al, 2015; Harding 2017). For example, even where discrete phonological features can be confidently referenced in scales, issues with ensuring that human raters have sufficient linguistic expertise, have the same understanding of the features, and that the cognitive load during rating is not unduly heavy preclude extremely detailed, feature-rich scales from being implemented. Dimova (2018) also points out that the use of the term pronunciation across scales is often left open to interpretation.

As will be discussed in more detail in Chapter 6, auto-rating also grapples with the conundrum in terms of trying to 'unpick' the underlying construct that the test aims to evaluate. In some cases, specific features of pronunciation may be deliberately programmed into the auto-rater, usually based on research into the link between comprehensibility and these features In other cases where 'big data' is used to train the machine, it is less clear exactly what the 'black-box' auto-rater is taking into account; sometimes, not even the test developers are aware and rating reliability is based solely on post-hoc correlation statistics between human raters and the computer (see Chapter 6). Test-takers, teachers and the users of test scores (like universities and immigration agencies), however, would often like to interpret the meaning of a particular score and some auto-rated test developers provide descriptions of the construct being measured and some test developers have provided validation studies (e.g. TOEFL SpeechRater (Xi et al., 2008; Chen, et al., 2018) and the guides produced by the Pearson Test of English (PTE)). We draw on the latter to understand more about how phonological features, in particular, are reflected in auto-rated tests of spoken language.

Finally, a key component of comprehensibility that was raised in Chapter 1 is co-construction of meaning and the role of the listener in the success of the message. As is reflected in the scales and descriptors below, pronunciation skills are evaluated in terms of the impact on the listener (rater) and the implicit onus is on the speaker to make themselves comprehensible through control and manipulation of a range of phonological features. From a broader comprehensibility point of view, this is problematic, as is discussed below.

Overview	
IELTS	IELTS 9-band rating scale (9 = most proficient) for the Oral Proficiency Interview (OPI) delivered and rated by human examiners. Public band descriptors are referred to here, although these closely resemble the rating scales used by examiners. Phonological features are contained within the Pronunciation category of the Speaking descriptors; there is a separate Fluency scale which includes reference to hesitation, pausing and coherence, but not phonological features beyond the segmental level.
TOEFL iBT	TOEFL iBT speaking is human rated on a scale of 30 points divided into 5 sections: Below Basic, Basic, Low-Intermediate, High-Intermediate, and Advanced. The comments below refer to the public performance descriptors in which can-do type statements at different levels include one bullet point referring to both fluency and phonological features.
PTE	PTE scale descriptors (0 = non-English, 5 = Native-like) cover phonological features as part of the 'enabling' scores component of test reporting under 'Pronunciation' and 'Oral fluency'. These are viewed as linguistic 'traits' and are included in the machine assessment of all the speaking item types except the short question listening-into-speaking task.
TestDaF	In the sub-test level descriptions speaking section, the three levels (3 = lowest, 5 = highest) do not mention specific language components; rather, the phrase 'linguistic deficiencies' is used and linked to impact on meaning. The CEFR is used as a reference point.
HSK	The original HSK was developed using word (character) lists including frequency (Meyer, 2012, p. 121) and there was no speaking test. Currently, speaking proficiency is described in relation to the CEFR, i.e. in CEFR can-do statements and there is no explicit mention of pronunciation features, only communicative outcomes.
CEFR Companion Volume	As many tests rely on the CEFR levels to describe speaking proficiency, these are covered here. The CEFR Companion Volume is referred to given the significant changes to the pronunciation descriptors – the 'Phonological Control' scale (see Chapter 1). The CEFR Phonological descriptors are informed by four factors related to pronunciation: articulation of phonemes, prosodic features, accent, and intelligibility (Council of Europe, p. 134).

Table 2.2: Phonological features in rating scales and standards: Overview

Segmental features	
IELTS	Unspecified 'pronunciation features' are referred to throughout from three perspectives: range of features, control of the features, and effect of the use. It is unclear, in the public band descriptors, whether these are at segmental or suprasegmental level, but ordering of the descriptor sentences suggests that they go from discrete to holistic.
TOEFL iBT	At the lower levels, the impact of 'mispronunciation' on meaning seems to refer to discrete sounds although this is not made explicit.
PTE	Under the detailed Pronunciation trait descriptors, 'mispronunciation' of individual consonants and vowels is referred to, with frequency of inaccuracies decreasing with proficiency. Mispronunciation at the phoneme level is in reference to 'native-like', 'regular speaker' and influence of other languages. Reference to problems with 'consonant sequences' at the lower levels.
TestDaF	N/A
HSK	N/A
CEFR Companion Volume	Dealt with explicitly under the broad category under the 'Overall Phonological Control' descriptors and, in a more detailed manner, under 'Sound Articulation'. The focus is on clarity and precision of the articulation of phonemes (although no benchmark is provided). Descriptions are generic, e.g. 'sounds in the target language' and mispronunciation is tolerated in the mid-range if intelligibility is not affected, although L1 influence on phoneme production is referenced at the lower and higher levels.

Table 2.3: Phonological features in rating scales and standards: Segmentals

Suprasegmental features	
IELTS	See above.
TOEFL iBT	At the higher levels, intonation is made mention of explicitly.
PTE	Correct word stress is covered under the Pronunciation trait with reference at some levels to vowel reduction; as with segmentals, frequency of 'correct' stress increases with proficiency levels. Sentence stress is referred to as a positive indicator at the two highest levels. Lack of stress-timing and 'staccato' delivery referenced throughout the Oral fluency descriptors, as well as 'phrasing' and 'phonological simplifications' (although what these are is unclear).

TestDaF	N/A
HSK	N/A
CEFR Companion Volume	As with segmental features, suprasegmentals are covered in both the over-arching 'Overall Phonological Control' category and the more detailed 'Prosodic Features' scale descriptors. The focus is on range of suprasegmentals ('repertoire'), intelligibility and influence of L1.

Table 2.4: Phonological features in rating scales and standards: Suprasegmentals

Holistic references		Comments
IELTS	Reference to intelligibility and, at the lower levels, the impact of mispronunciation on intelligibility are made. Difficulty for the listener is also referred to.	The descriptors lack specificity.
TOEFL iBT	Reference to clarity and ease of understanding are made throughout; the term 'intelligibility' used when describing pronunciation, 'comprehensibility' is used at the highest level when describing overall coherence.	The descriptors lack specificity.
PTE	References to effect on intelligibility and clarity.	Detailed phonological feature and frequency of errors as indicators of proficiency could only be operationalised by a machine. Requirement for no errors at the highest 'native-like' band 5 is unrealistic and inauthentic.
TestDaF	Clarity is referred to at the highest level; the impact of 'linguistic deficiencies' on communication is mentioned at the lower two levels and again at the lower level in terms of how they might 'slow down understanding [for the listener]' at the lowest level.	Descriptors are exceptionally brief and lacking in specificity; there is a clear focus on communicative impact.
HSK	N/A	

CEFR Companion volume	Intelligibility and clarity are referred to, although L1 influence is also mentioned throughout.	The descriptors seem to be appropriate for European languages although whether they encapsulate all the features of non-European languages is questionable (e.g. tones). The CEFR takes the co-construction of meaning into account in the Phonological Control descriptors, e.g. "interlocutor needs to be collaborative" at A1.

Table 2.5: Phonological features in rating scales and standards: Holistic approach and comments

The overviews in Tables 2.2 – 2.5 highlight several aspects of phonological feature representation in test constructs. Firstly, while the generic nature of descriptors that apply to a range of L1 learners is to be expected, the only auto-rated example included in the overview (PTE) contains the most specific references to phonological features (although these are still largely generic). This most likely reflects the cognitive difficulties human interlocutors would have operationalising this level of detail, even if the features are shown to be significant to the construct – only computers have the processing power necessary for this task. Secondly, the more detailed descriptors reflect the hierarchy of pronunciation features in contributing to creating meaning (also reflected in language teaching) – segmentals are a focus at lower levels, while these become more 'assumed' at higher levels where attention is on suprasegmentals. Finally, in most of the scales reviewed, the responsibility for communicative success lies squarely with the speaker, even where listener effort is referenced; the exception is the CEFR Companion Volume Phonological Control descriptors which bring in collaborative willingness and other interlocutor traits that contribute to the co-construction of meaning.

The importance of rating scales in realisation of pronunciation as a key contributor to the broader comprehensibility construct is crucial. Knoch (2016) identifies three approaches to developing rating scales – expert intuition (e.g. IELTS), empirical data (as used in many of the studies described in the above section on approaches to linking features to the comprehensibility construct) and the use of theoretical models – discussing how the latter has not been drawn on for speaking scale development.

The first two, of course, are vulnerable to incorporating bias into the scales and, therefore, the construct. Knoch (2016) also emphasises the need to validate scale development, perhaps by contextualising the criteria within a validation argument structure, and stresses the importance of going beyond the more common investigations into reliability and level discrimination, suggesting that (in this case, for the skill of writing, but it can be generalised across language skills):

> [researchers] can also focus their investigations on how well the writing construct is captured in the scale and how relevant the scale is to the wider domain being measured. Researchers can also examine whether the scale has positive consequences on stakeholders. (p. 59)

The relevance of descriptors to the wider domain is of particular interest to ELF and other LFs, especially in relation to evaluation of pronunciation given its prime position at the intersection of language assessment and sociolinguistic factors underpinning accent and variation. A key question is whether the scale criteria adequately reflect what impacts understanding in the real-world context: "What the descriptors are based on and whether that input reflects the communicative reality needs investigation", as Knoch (2016, p. 18) recommends. Importantly, how the descriptors are realised by raters (or technology-driven rating systems) deserves attention, given the potential of rater-bias that is driven by attitudes towards accent rather than an assessment of comprehensibility. The decisions based on scores obtained through the application of rating scales, which are central to the realisation of the construct, can have a serious impact on the lives of people and the structure of societies.

Challenges and Considerations

The discussion so far demonstrates that while there is increasing insight into how phonological aspects affect communicative comprehensibility, we are still some way from any conclusive evidence and any inventory of phonological features is subject to a myriad of variables. Situated within a broader perspective on comprehensibility with an emphasis on communicative context, purpose and outcome, the inclusion of phonological features in the assessment of communicative ability faces several challenges, primarily around generalisability. These are discussed under three main areas below: speakers, listeners, and communicative context.

Speakers

The L1 background of the speakers has a major influence on the acquisition and production of segmentals in the target language as is evident in various models of language acquisition (Eckman, 2004; Escudero & Boersma, 2004; Best & Tyler, 2007; Flege & Bohn, 2021) which demonstrate that the closer the target language is to the L1 in terms of phonetic realisation at the phoneme level, the more easily the L2 phoneme will be learnt and produced, and the less it will impact intelligibility. This is supported in relation to comprehensibility by other research, for example, Crowther, Trofimovich, Saito, and Isaacs' (2015) study across different L2 English learners shows that substitutions at the segmental level had a much more profound effect on comprehensibility ratings for Chinese-L1 speakers compared to their Hindi- and Farsi-L1 counterparts. This has implications for rating scales or automated assessment models that include specific phonemes as indicators of communicative proficiency if they are intended to be generalised across a range of L1 speakers. Generalisation (of descriptors or a model) to a wider group of English L2 speakers is only possible if the test-taker population is adequately represented in the sampling. It seems unlikely that more than a narrow range of indicators will be identified for a wide range of speaker backgrounds (as the LFC attempted on a small scale), suggesting that until there is more conclusive evidence, mention of articulation of individual phonemes should be linked to the impact on the overall message, or clearly restricted to a particular L1 profile.

Suprasegmentals, however, appear to be more generalisable across language background and, if they have an impact on communicative comprehensibility as is indicated in numerous studies, then Levis' (2005) suggestion that they be incorporated into pronunciation instruction for different language backgrounds could extend to rating scales and the development of automated models.

The question of speaker background is one that will be revisited in Chapter 6 in our discussion on automated rating within the broader comprehensibility perspective. This relates specifically to sample size and profile, and the need to ensure that the data is representative of the target population the rating model will be used to assess.

Listeners

It is not only the speech samples drawn on in the studies that suffer from under-representation of a range of L2 speakers of the target language when investigating the comprehensibility construct. Another key question centres on who the judges are of what is easy to understand and, in most studies (including Spanish, see Nagle, 2019), the arbitrators have been L1 or near-L1 raters of the target L2. With other words, the data on which the studies are based are not reflective of real-world lingua franca communication in terms of listeners either. In particular, as ELF has grown and English language users have found themselves more likely to be in conversations that do not include a 'native speaker' (Graddol, 1999), students and teachers of English have concentrated their efforts on making themselves understood in the first instance rather than striving for a particular native-speaker accent (Derwing & Munro, 2005; Field, 2005; Levis, 2005). It is crucial, then, that the raters used for research into comprehensibility features are representative of the real-life users of the language if the test is to be valid (Cooke, 2020). This applies to pronunciation in particular, given that this is the linguistic skill that shows most variation, not only amongst users of 'big-language' Lingua Francas (French, Spanish, Chinese, Swahili and, of course, English), but also amongst speakers who are considered native-speakers of those languages. Unfortunately, research in the area of English-language comprehensibility correlates has, so far, been biased towards small groups of 'expert' L1 speakers of English. There are exceptions, mostly where an explicit comparison between L1- and L2 speakers has been a core focus of the research but findings are contradictory, with some results suggesting that there is a difference between how these groups rate comprehensibility (e.g. Kang, 2012) and others finding no difference (e.g. Derwing & Munro, 2013). Any evidence indicating a difference, however, supports the need to ensure that raters are representative of the language users themselves.

Other listener related factors that can influence the findings include familiarity of the listener with the topic, whether naïve or expert raters are used (Yan & Ginther, 2018), and the motivation of the listener to understand the speaker. Rater background and familiarity with the L1 of test-takers (Winke et al., 2013; Carey et al., 2013) could also impact comprehensibility ratings, particularly in relation to pronunciation.

Context

In this broader perspective on comprehensibility, we are advocating for language to be viewed not as an abstract entity that achieves meaning only through linguistic devices, but as inextricable from the context in which the communicative event occurs. This applies to phonological features that no doubt play an important role in achieving the overall message. However, the extent to which the accuracy or presence of certain features should be explicitly measured in the assessment of communicative comprehensibility depends on the communicative goal of the speech event, to what degree non-phonological features (including other linguistic features such as grammar and lexis, and paralinguistic factors) contribute to the making of meaning, and, in interactive, dialogic speech, how the dynamic, shifting nature of comprehensibility between speaker and listener works towards achieving the communicative goal.

Different contexts place varying loads of work on pronunciation to achieve communicative success and convey meaning. Different components – phonological features – of pronunciation will rise (and fall) in prominence and relevance depending on the particular context and purpose of communication, including what the speaker and listener wish to achieve. For example, articulation of segments is crucial when prompted to read a credit card number into an automated phone banking system; however, in most everyday conversations, mispronunciation or 'mis-hearing' of a word can easily have the message 'rescued' by providing additional linguistic or paralinguistic information – an example is the confusion in English numbers such as *50* and *15* where even L1 English speakers who share a dialect have to resort to emphatic stress of the last syllable or provide other information to disambiguate their utterance (e.g. 'one five'). Further examples of this are discussed in relation to Figure 2.1 below.

The co-construction of meaning is another push factor towards considering pronunciation within the broader communicative context and as one of many variables. Communication is an act of negotiation between speaker and listener, one that relies on a diverse and constantly changing set of input variables in order to achieve the transfer of meaning (or opinion, or attitude). It also relies on non-linguistic factors such as the motivation of the listener to understand the speaker's communicative goal, on their tolerance of ambiguity and willingness to forgo the understanding of every individual word in the interest of the wider communicative goal, and attitude and bias towards particular accents (or other speaker characteristics). Clearly this is a challenge for assessment without easy solutions; however, a shift towards testing interaction with a focus on task achievement could go some way to mitigating this.

Shifting Importance of Features of Comprehensibility

Figure 2.1 is an initial attempt to map the multiple, fuzzy intersections between macro-level factors (including higher level linguistic factors such as lexis, syntax and discourse), sociolinguistic factors, and phonological features. The *y*-axis takes into account the context of the speech, ranging from situations where the accuracy of the acoustic-signal is crucial to convey meaning because contextual clues are missing (or wholly ignored, such as with shibboleth tests) to situations where macro-level, non-linguistic factors do much of the work in getting meaning across and linguistic features carry less weight in this regard. The *x*-axis represents the demands of the wider social milieu set for the language such as politeness, persuasion, or indicating identity.

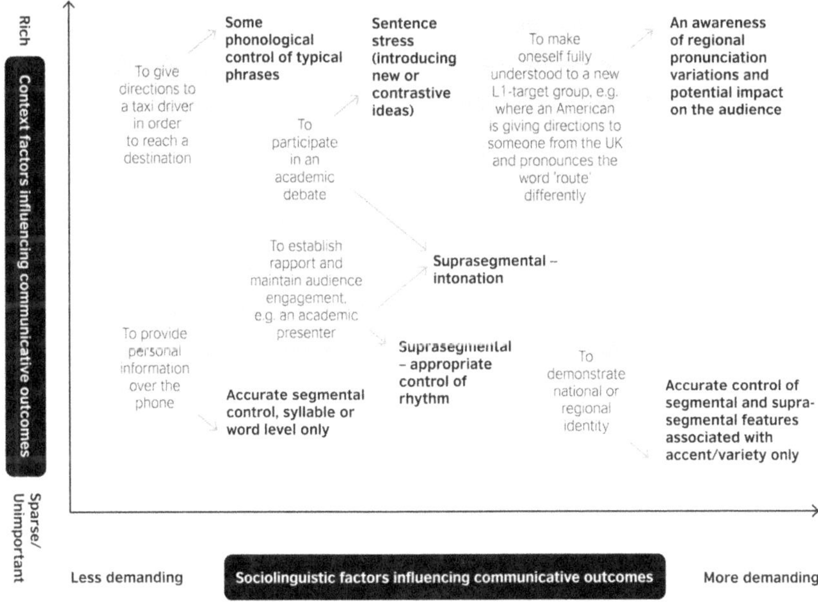

Figure 2.1. Pronunciation located in a broader, dynamic view of comprehensibility

Figure 2.1 is intended to be an example of how the identification of the pronunciation features to be measured (e.g. to be included in a rating scale or in a feature-driven automated assessment model) should be informed by both context and sociolinguistic factors. Importantly, these factors intersect as the *purpose* of the evaluation of spoken language – represented by the grey ovals in Figure 2.1 – within a certain context of use.

At the top end of the *y*-axis, context is rich and even if someone is speaking a foreign language and using hand gestures, it is likely that meaning will come across reasonably well. In the example on the top left-hand side of the grid, both the speaker (the passenger) and the listener (the taxi driver) are highly familiar with the particular scenario and a few badly pronounced words (such as *'go straight'* or *'turn right'*) could most likely still result in a positive outcome. Those speech events that have sparse contextual factors or macro-level aspects will rely more heavily on pure linguistic elements to get meaning across, such as when someone is required to state their full name on the phone, similar to the example in the bottom left-hand side of the figure. The arrows in the figure indicate which phonological features would most likely be most significant in terms of achieving comprehensibility.

Sociolinguistic factors intersect along the *x*-axis, demonstrating the relative importance of listener perception of phonological features that do not otherwise impact meaning *per se*. While there is a cumulative aspect to the features as we move diagonally along the intersection of the axes – excellent control of intonation without an ability to generally produce the individual sounds of the language would not yield a positive communicative effect in an academic debate, for example – the underlying aim of the figure is to consider which phonological features carry the greatest burden of communicative load in the different instances of communicative outcome, and guide which features could play a greater role in language assessment that is both purpose- and context-driven. An example of where literal meaning might be clear but the speaker does not achieve the purpose of the communicative event is the delivery of a presentation that fails to engage the audience because supra-segmental features such as intonation are not used; consider the monotone delivery of an exciting news item, for example.

At the top right-hand quadrant of the grid is an example of how a regional difference in pronunciation of a lexical item (US vs UK pronunciation of the word *route*) might cause a momentary lapse in comprehensibility, one which is most likely quickly resolved through the plentiful contextual clues, but could also be the target of a test of regional origin (see also the example of the interlocutor's regional pronunciation affecting the test-taker's understanding at the beginning of Chapter 1). In the bottom right-hand section of Figure 2.1, another test of origin ignores context entirely (i.e. it is unimportant because meaning is not the focus) in a shibboleth test. Ultimately, what constitutes acceptable purpose for language testing is an ethical consideration.

The extent to which features of pronunciation work in tandem with a range of other linguistic and contextual features and the degree to which co-construction of meaning between speaker and listener are illustrated by the difficulty in providing examples that are wholly reliant on pronunciation only. Even unexpected information – such as the opening of a narration or the first lines of a poem – seem to be quickly informed with predictions of what's to come in the mind of the listener. It would seem we are predisposed to build shared mental models of meaning and to make sense of the sensory input around us.

The onus is on test developers to understand the context in which pronunciation is contributing towards the evaluation of comprehensibility, to consider how this impacts comprehensibility indicators and to develop tasks relevant to the specific context where rating scales focus on or give much greater weighting to the relevant aspects of pronunciation. Essentially, this can be used to construct map pronunciation features, once the purpose of the test is established. This has obvious implications for large-scale, international tests in which a range of generic features are included in the rating scales and apply to different task types. Highly generalised, communicative context-independent scales could result in potentially serious, negative implications for test-takers.

Conclusion

In this chapter, we have investigated the connection between features of pronunciation and the construct of comprehensibility, as well as looking at how these features are reflected in language tests.

While segmental and suprasegmental features are key contributors to the comprehensibility construct, the connection between these is complex and context-dependent, and they need to be considered in light of their actual impact on the message. Although there is increasing understanding around which phonological features have an impact on comprehensibility, it is crucial that the assessment of phonological features:

- is not gratuitous, that is, they are only referenced when there is clear evidence, from research, that they impact meaning or communicative effectiveness in that context
- ensures that there is adequate representation of both the speakers and listeners involved in the real-world use of the language in the test construct, not just L1 speaker or elite varieties

- considers the purpose of the test itself so that undue weight is not put on phonological features when there are other macro-level and linguistic factors that contribute to comprehensibility.

The interplay of phonological features with other linguistic and non-linguistic factors in the speech event ecosystem is visually represented in Figure 8.1 in the last chapter of this book.The strong link between accent, phonological features and potential bias unrelated to comprehensibility warrants particular attention by testers. This convergence of sociological factors and test consequences in the assessment of pronunciation makes it imperative that test developers and users take an ethical stance in relation to this.

CHAPTER 3

COMPREHENSIBILITY AT A DISCOURSE / TEXT LEVEL

In this chapter we move further up the rungs of the linguistic ladder to focus on extended spoken texts, that is, beyond the word and sentence or utterance levels. While Chapter 4 considers speech in terms of how it achieves meaning and is understood within the broader contextual and sociocultural aspects in which it occurs, here we focus on the features associated with longer turns of monologic speech. Monologues warrant investigation not only because many Oral Proficiency Interviews (OPIs) include an extended turn on a specific topic (e.g. IELTS, Cambridge's B2 First and C1 Advanced) but also because the increasing move towards computer-based testing (human- or machine-rated) means that speaking tasks are typically restricted to the elicitation of extended speech in response to visual, aural or written prompts and input in the form of presentations and narrations, for example.

The key assumption underlying this chapter is that comprehensibility is linked to communicative purpose (see Chapter 2) and that, above the utterance level, the aim is for the listener to understand the spoken text as a whole, for example, the argument a lecturer is putting across in a presentation. In this chapter, we are interested in whole-text comprehensibility, in other words, we are not concerned with listening-for-specific-information (acoustic-signal, lexical-retrieval driven) such as train station announcements. Comprehensibility at the whole-text level can only be achieved through adequate (co-)construction of a mental model in the mind of the listener and discourse strategies and devices are crucial to this.

This volume takes a micro- to macro-level approach to the exploration of linguistic features of comprehensibility and readers might consider that moving from a focus on phonology to a discussion on discourse omits the lexical and syntactical levels of language. Obviously, these have a significant impact on whether a speaker can be understood or not: knowledge of, and ability to, control the grammatical structures of a language and the range of vocabulary at the speaker's disposal will determine the richness and precision of the message she is attempting to convey. Much research has been done in these areas, both in terms of language testing and comprehensibility itself (Varonis & Gass, 1982; Read & Nation, 2006; Saito et al., 2016; Tavakoli & Foster, 2008; Webb & Rodgers, 2009a and 2009b) and we direct readers to these detailed studies for further reading. We do not ignore these important components of comprehensibility, however: as will become evident below, both grammar and lexis are key contributors to creating an extended-text mental model in the minds of speaker and listener, thus establishing mutual understanding, or comprehensibility.

First, this chapter identifies the scope and definition of discourse as it is explored here and covers some challenges and tensions. Next, a general overview of discourse features that have been researched and theorised is presented with an example from a language test. We then consider research into the link between spoken discourse features and comprehensibility. Finally, we turn our focus to how discourse features contribute (or otherwise) to the assessment of overall understanding of speech in rating scales and the role of raters in interpreting these as factors affecting comprehensibility.

What is Discourse?

'Discourse' is a confusing term because it is used to describe wide and diverse instances of human communication, from linguistic analysis of extended speech to the broad analysis of language in use in the socio-political landscape (Harris, 1952; Widdowson, 2004; Sealey, 2020). Furthermore, within applied linguistics, the terms discourse and text are used differently by different researchers (Widdowson, 2004; Tanskanen, 2006). For the purposes of clarification, in this chapter, discourse refers to spoken language that functions as a whole beyond the level of the sentence, and discourse will be used interchangeably with the term spoken text (as distinct from written text). While spoken language does not necessarily use 'sentences' in the formal grammatical sense, and researchers typically use AS-units ("a single speaker's utterance consisting of an independent clause or subclausal unit, together with any subordinate clause(s) associated with it" (Foster et al. 2000, p. 365)) or similar for analysis, 'sentence' will be used here to refer to a unit of spoken language that generally corresponds in terms of function and form to that of a written sentence, although we explicitly recognise that spoken language is different to the written form, and that the degree of variation is linked to the wider communicative context of the speech under scrutiny.

In this sense, discourse refers to how spoken sentences or shorter utterances are connected to each other in extended speech that forms a coherent whole, such as a story or a presentation. This level of textual 'connection' has been recognised, theorised and studied for many years and the literature yields some useful descriptions and definitions, although different – and sometimes opposing – positions are taken. Halliday and Hasan (using the word 'text' rather than discourse) describe it as "any passage, spoken or written, of whatever length, that does form a unified whole" and stress how "a text is a unit of language in use" (1976, p. 1); Cook (1989) also describes discourse as "language in use, for communication" (p. 6). Yet it is more than just how sentences are connected to each other: Widdowson (2004) points out that there are also features within sentences that connect ideas into larger units of coherent meaning.

As instances of communication – as examples of language in use – discourse is necessarily context-dependent and meaning (comprehensibility) is achieved through a complex web of relationships at different levels of the situation in which the language occurs. Researchers have typically taken a tripartite approach to context in discourse, seeing it as linguistic (also referred to as 'cotext'), cognitive (e.g. building mental models of the extended text by drawing on linguistic and other sources), and social. This discussion is limited to the exploration of linguistic cotext and, to a lesser degree, the cognitive aspect, in relation to comprehensibility and testing. The study of discourse as discussed here is primarily the study of coherence and cohesion which Tanskanen describes as "how the sequences we hear or see hang together" (2006, p. 1); we also touch briefly on prosodic features associated with spoken text in terms of their influence on the discourse structure.

Although we are focusing on monologic spoken discourse, it is worthwhile considering that neither the 'monologic' nor the 'spoken' represent binary dichotomies in relation to 'dialogic' or 'written'. Monologues take different forms, from short, casual voice messages to long, formal speeches and, even as extended lectures or presentations, the mental model of meaning is formulated by the speaker with the virtual or asynchronous listener or audience in mind (Linell, 1998). Speeches and presentations display some properties of dialogic speech, for example, as the speakers generally attempt to establish a relationship with the audience, and the use of cohesive devices reflects this (Tanskanen, 2006). While there are different discourse characteristics associated with written and spoken texts (Brown & Yule, 1993), there is recognition that printed and verbal texts are not always distinct from each other in terms of linguistic discourse features and may fall along a continuum depending on level of formality or informality, or whether the text is planned or spontaneous (Ochs, 1979; Tannen, 1980; Crystal, 1995). These writers from almost three decades ago were prescient: consider the characteristics of written forms of social media in comparison to pre-recorded lectures available to students as online resources, for example, with the former showing more characteristics of spoken language and the latter of written language.

Before looking at features of cohesion and coherence, a brief acknowledgement that there are broader factors that influence the linguistic features that are elicited from a speaker, including those associated with discourse, is necessary as these are the speech samples to which rating criteria will be applied. First of all, the mode is likely to affect the response elicited, for example, whether the test is delivered by a human interlocutor face-to-face, over the phone, or through a synchronous computer-mediated platform, or through a digital device with no human interlocutor. Even where a test-taker is engaging in an extended monologic task, whether there are visual clues or back-channelling will have an impact on the strategies they use to achieve comprehensibility. Audience is a second consideration: whether the performance is for a human interlocutor, synchronous or asynchronous, or for a machine-rated evaluation. Thirdly, task-type, linked to genre, is a fundamental factor in determining the text type and could subsequently affect the rater's (or rating system's) evaluation of overall comprehensibility as manifested in text coherence.

In summary, we have delimited the scope of this chapter to monologic spoken discourse, although as the discussion above indicates, distinctions and categorisations are not always clear cut and the factors influencing the use of discourse features are myriad. In the next section, we consider how discourse and comprehensibility are connected and describe the features associated with extended, monologic discourse that help to make spoken texts meaningful as a whole.

Monologic Spoken Discourse and Comprehensibility

This deeper dive into the linguistic and structural features of monologic texts that contribute to the 'wholeness' of extended speech is not meant to be exhaustive; rather, the intention is to provide an overview of the features along with an example to illustrate the link to comprehensibility, to highlight the complexity of interactions and lay the groundwork for discussion of discourse features in the evaluation of spoken communication.

To illustrate how discourse features contribute to comprehensibility, we draw on an example taken from a test of English, a 'long turn' task typical in many tests of spoken language. Consider, first, just the utterances or propositions that a test-taker might make as part of their response (the test and task are deliberately not mentioned here) and assume they are made in this order:

1. There is a net.
2. Many people are gathered together.
3. A tall girl is second.
4. The sun is shining brightly.
5. There are only five girls wearing t-shirts and running.
6. A man is serving.
7. There is the shade of trees.
8. A crowd is watching intently.
9. No observers can be seen.
10. There is a very large venue.
11. An opponent looks nervous.

These propositions, taken individually, are comprehensible, but are as yet difficult to make sense of *as a whole*, although – already – readers' knowledge of the world (and of language tests!) is most likely being drawn upon to link these together into a mental picture. From an assessment perspective, while all the individual utterances might be comprehensible, grammatical and factual, the 'long turn' cannot be evaluated as *comprehensible overall*.

The first step in deciphering how these sentences could collectively create a comprehensible monologue is to understand the task (the context), taken from the Cambridge B2 First for Schools speaking test practice materials (Cambridge English, 2015) (Part 2 – "Long Turn") which includes two thematically linked photographs and instructions uttered by an examiner-interlocutor, *"Here are your photographs. They show people trying to win in different situations. I'd like you to compare the photographs… "* (see Appendix 1). While there is a second component to the task *("…and say what you think might be difficult for the people ")*, in the interests of brevity, we will concentrate only on the first requirement. Already, knowledge that the pictures depict a competitive activity gives a different meaning to some of the words (*net, serve, second,* and the type of *crowd* (spectators)). Knowledge that the response will be a comparison helps to solve the apparent contradiction between propositions 2, 5, 8, 9. Another step that could be taken without manipulating the actual words or grammar is for the reader-listener to re-order the utterances in their mind in a way that provides a structure that 'flows' in a more logical way, one that meets the expectations of a comparative text in the mind of the listener.

Mere organisation, however, is not enough to properly link the ideas together in a truly comprehensible way that allows the listener to understand the situation without too much cognitive 'work' and without the message losing some meaning or arriving only half-formed in the mind of the listener. Grammatical structures and words need to be changed and added so that the response might sound something like this:

> In the first photograph, many people are gathered together in a large venue where the sun is shining brightly. A man is serving across a net to an opponent who looks very nervous while the crowd watches intently. In the other photograph, there are no observers and only five girls wearing t-shirts are running in the shade of trees. A tall girl is second.

Yet this still feels disjointed and could be made more 'whole' through not only the addition of references to the task, but also better grammatical and lexical choices:

> I'm going to compare two photographs where people are competing to win. The one on the left shows many people gathered together in a large sports stadium to watch a tennis match. As the sun shines brightly, a player is serving across the net to his opponent who looks very nervous while the crowd watches intently. The other picture is quite different. Firstly, there are no spectators and only five girls wearing t-shirts can be seen running a race in which the tallest girl is coming second. Secondly, in contrast to the championship where there is bright sunlight, these girls are competing in the shade of trees. Overall, while the first seems to be a professional sports event for adults, the second is a more intimate competition for young athletes.

In this imagined response, which is intended to be more comprehensible at the broader text level, there are additional external references to the photographs and a stronger framing structure; furthermore, both grammatical and lexical changes facilitate a more detailed mental model in the mind of the listener. In other words, the listener links the concepts and actions to make the description more comprehensible. These features will be covered in more technical detail in the discussion below, with references to this example where helpful.

Extended speech such as this achieves its connectedness chiefly through cohesion and coherence. While there is broad agreement that both cohesion and coherence exist and that these are separate concepts, there are, nevertheless, tensions between functional grammar and structuralist schools of thought who see one or the other area as contributing more weight to the achievement of textual unity (Brown & Yule, 1978; Halliday & Hasan, 1976; Carrell, 1982; Tanskanen, 2006). Tanskanen (2006) provides a clear differentiation of the two:

> cohesion refers to the grammatical and lexical elements on the surface of a text which can form connections between parts of the text. Coherence, on the other hand, resides not in the text, but is rather the outcome of a dialogue between the text and its listener or reader. (p. 7).

Cohesion is linguistic in nature, generally obvious to the listener, objective and quantifiable; it resides in the words and grammar of the text itself, in the technical nuts and bolts of language. Coherence, on the other hand, eludes surface-level analysis and offers up few bite-sized, concrete tools, suggesting, instead, that there is an underlying system that establishes the extended speech as one entity. The locus of coherence is predominantly in the minds of the speaker and listener, making it subjective and ethereal. However, as Tanskanen (2006) puts it, "[i]nstead of trying to decide which is more important or more necessary for guaranteeing identification as text, […] both cohesion and coherence can be said to have a role to play in contributing to the unity in discourse" (2006, p. 18–19). Metaphorically, if extended discourse is a house, cohesion is the mortar connecting the bricks of meaning and ideas, and coherence is the unseen frame of the building without which the other elements would be an unstructured mess. Both are necessary to produce a recognisable, single unit that is comprehensible to the listener as such.

Cohesion

There are many different ways to achieve textual 'wholeness' and there are diverse approaches to the categorisation of cohesion. Several influential works provide detailed analyses of cohesion in English including Halliday and Hasan (1976), Brown and Yule (1978), Hoey, (1991),

McCarthy (1991), and Halliday and Matthiessen (2013). Readers are directed to the works referred to in this section for a detailed understanding.

Cohesion is typically separated into grammatical and lexical cohesion. Halliday and Matthiessen identify four mechanisms by which cohesion is achieved in English: conjunction, reference, ellipsis, and lexical organisation (2013, p. 603). Conjunction refers to a collection of devices (including adverbial linkers like *actually*) and grammatical constructions that express the relationships between clauses in the text including causal (*because*), additive (*and, not only... but also...*), contrastive (*but, while x..., y...*), and temporal (*while, after*) connections. Teachers and testers are most likely familiar with the clumsy (over-) use of these by less proficient learners of language. Reference covers a myriad of devices to link, situate and order components of the text, including personal pronouns (*they, his*), demonstrative (or deictic) features (*there, now*), and (in some languages) articles, like *a tennis player* followed by *the tennis player* in subsequent mentions; these devices can refer to items within the text itself, or that are text-external (e.g. *the one on the left*), and they tend to form a reference chain that helps to keep the text together. In language assessment tests where the response is in relation to rich input data such as graphs, photographs, or integrated reading or listening into speaking tasks (such as the one from which the example at the start of this chapter is taken), it would seem that the ability to reference effectively to input material is especially important.

Other grammatical linking devices in English include relative constructions (*his opponent who is looking nervous*) and ellipsis (substitution or complete omission as in *the first [photograph] shows*) – see Halliday and Matthiessen (2013, p. 605–606) for a detailed discussion). Other aspects of grammar also contribute to cohesion at the text level, such as the choice of voice, tense or aspect. In the example above, the use of progressive aspect in *a player is serving across the net* grammatically 'stretches' the event in the mind of the listener and allows her to comprehend the action as 'currently' occurring (in the context of the static photograph in the test task). These choices are usually informed by the genre or domain of the speech event (e.g. descriptive, narrative), vary a great deal across languages and contribute to the success of constructing the mental representation.

Vocabulary range and choice have an obvious effect on comprehensibility (the greater the lexicon available and the appropriacy of word selection, the more precise and nuanced the meaning that can be conveyed), and lexical cohesion also plays an important role in creating a connected mental representation of a concept or event, without which comprehensibility would not be achievable. Tanskanen (2006) highlights the importance of "the choice of lexis [as] one of the primary means available to speakers and writers for creating continuity in their messages" (p. 2). Lexical cohesion is essentially about building chains of meaning across a text; "cohesive harmony" in Hasan's terms (1984); "patterns of lexis" that represent multiple relationships within the text and beyond in Hoey's (1991) work. This is achieved in many different and complex ways as seen in the example put forward earlier in this chapter, including simple repetition (*girl... girls... girl...*), complex repetition (*competing... competition...*), use of synonyms (*competition... race...*), exploitation of the hierarchical relationships between lexical items (hypernymy) such as *match --- player*, and lexical sets (the chains or patterns of meaning) (*competing --- sports stadium --- match --- opponent --- race --- second*), to name a few.

There are several considerations around lexical cohesion in particular that have bearing on comprehensibility. Firstly, the discourse-specificity of the lexical chains and patterns means that the impact these have on meaning are likely to be prompt-specific, that is, a relationship between two lexical items might exist in one text but not in another where the genre or topic is different (Hasan, 1984), such as *serve* and *net*. Secondly, these triggers and associations need to be shared by both speaker and listener (e.g. a knowledge of sports events and, specifically, tennis matches and athletics) (Linell 1998) and this, in turn, is subject to socio-cultural and pragmatic factors. This underlies the criticism that global, one-size-fits-all tests of the 'big' languages test more than comprehensibility of language and, in fact, also expect test-takers to be able to navigate and understand first-world, privileged scenarios (such as tennis matches). Finally, lexical chains come in waves as the speech evolves and may last for the duration of the text or end after just a few utterances (Halliday & Matthiessen, 2013), as in our example above where the lexical chain referencing the visuals (*photograph... the one on the left... picture....*) gives way to referencing of the situations they represent (*match... championship... race... sports event... competition...*); this shift from one lexical chain to the other needs to be carefully managed to avoid jarring the mental representation the listener is building and ensure comprehensibility at an extended text level.

Coherence

As was mentioned earlier in this chapter, coherence resides in the minds of speakers and listeners, rather than within the text itself. To revisit the building metaphor, coherence is the realisation of the house, achieved through the building blocks of meaning and the bonding characteristics of cohesive devices, as well as through the use of structural elements that form the frame of the abode. Coherence requires a stepping back from the building blocks to see the text as a unified whole, as a bricklayer would to see the effect of their craft on the shape of the building.

Cook (1989) describes coherence as "the quality of being meaningful and unified" (1989, p. 4). Gernsbacher and Givon (1995) explain:

> Coherence is a property of what emerges during speech production and comprehension – the mentally represented text, and in particular the mental processes that partake in constructing that mental representation. A coherently produced text – spoken or written – allows the "receiver" (listener or reader) to form roughly the same text-representation as the "sender" (writer or speaker) had in mind. (p. vii)

The authors also point out that the degree of coherence is about how well these mental models in different minds match up, and point out that coherence involves collaboration and negotiation (see also Tanskanen, 2006). Even where the text is not synchronously interactive, such as a speech or pre-recorded piece of spoken discourse, the speaker is working towards creating a comprehensible 'whole' for the real or imagined listener.

The broader ordering and structuring of information and ideas in the discourse event is of crucial importance to establishing overall comprehensibility. Celcé-Murcia (2008) proposes a model for communicative competence that includes a central role for discourse competence which

> refers to the selection, sequencing, and arrangement of words, structures, and utterances to achieve a unified spoken message. This is where the top-down communicative intent and sociocultural knowledge intersect with the lexical and grammatical resources to express messages and attitudes and to create coherent texts. (p. 46)

and includes:

> coherence: expressing purpose/intent through appropriate content schemata, managing old and new information, maintaining temporal continuity and other organizational schemata through conventionally recognized means.
>
> generic structure: formal schemata that allow the user to identify an oral discourse segment as a conversation, narrative, interview, service encounter, report, lecture, sermon, etc. (p. 47)

Understanding the speaker's purpose or intent as well as identifying the genre (which would inform register) are fundamental to comprehensibility of the text as a whole – knowing that the speaker's intent in the task described above is to compare/contrast two photographs immediately renders the extended monologue more comprehensible, even without the cohesive devices.

Coherence is influenced by the richness of information (story breadth and depth), topic development, generic structure, and theme and rheme. As might be expected, density of information contributes to the unity of text and various measures have been used as criteria in evaluating the correlation between coherence and comprehensibility. These include story cohesion (measured as the number of adverbials used as cohesive devices), and story breadth (number of distinct propositions), and story depth (number of different types of propositions, e.g. situation setting, action, etc.) (Isaacs and Trofimovich, 2012). Topic development includes introducing a topic (or identifying one in a testing situation where the prompt is provided) and then expanding this topic in what Seedhouse and Harris (2011) term a 'stepwise' manner, that is, without un-signalled topic shifts. Generic structure acts as a template that guides both speaker and listener in terms of how the information and ideas should be ordered and helps drive topic identification, development and shift. This allows the listener to know what to expect next and is strongly linked to genre and function, for example, narration, description, argument. Theme and rheme (or topic and comment) is another key tool to achieve coherence, with the theme being 'fronted', followed by a comment in relation to this theme which subsequently links to the following theme, either directly or through inference.

The key principle underlying this chapter is that comprehensibility of extended spoken text is achieved through the successful construction of a shared mental representation in the minds of speaker and listener. These macro, structural aspects of coherence in monologic speech are crucial to the building of this mental model and to subsequent perceptions of comprehensibility.

Prosodic Features Contributing to Comprehensibility at the Discourse Level

Chapters 2 and 5 provide an in-depth description of phonological and fluency features in relation to comprehensibility. Prosodic features play a key facilitative role in the building of mental models because spoken (as opposed to written) discourse carries the added complication that the aural signal needs to be recognised and parsed by the listener. Features of both phonology (e.g. intonation, pitch) and fluency (e.g. pausing) play a role in breaking the stream of speech into units of meaning that the listener is able to process, and relating these semantic chunks to one another, contributing significantly to the comprehensibility of the overall message. Thompson (1994) provides a succinct summary:

> The intonation system thus offers the presenter of a monologue resources for signalling the underlying meaning relations of the monologue, by connecting together parts of the text. The system of prominence enables the speaker to indicate the functional relationship between two words which enter into a cohesive tie; for example, whether they are equivalent or in opposition to each other. Similarly, the use of contrastive high pitch can be used to signal a contrastive relation between lexical items. The system of tone choice allows the speaker to indicate the relative newsworthiness of different elements of the message. (p. 65).

There is a wealth of literature on the relationship between prosodic features and discourse structure and processing. For detailed linguistic analyses, both from the teaching and linguistic analysis perspectives, readers are directed to Chun (2002), McCarthy (1991), Wennerstrom (2001a and 2001b), and Wichmann (2000).

The discussion above aimed to provide a foundation for our analysis of research into the link between discourse features and comprehensibility in the next section, as well as the subsequent review of a selection of rating scales from the point of the discourse-comprehensibility intersection.

Research into Discourse Features and Comprehensibility

Finding evidence that links discourse features to comprehensibility is challenging. Firstly, research specifically investigating comprehensibility is scarce and those pertaining to spoken discourse features and comprehensibility are rarer still; below, we focus on those related to comprehensibility, with minimal reference to other more general discourse-proficiency studies. A second reason why links between discourse features and comprehensibility are tenacious at best is because equation between studies is seldom possible. This is due to the variation inherent in the data used, and due to the extraneous factors discussed in the first section of this chapter. The mish-mash of data types drawn on across the studies defies comparison or findings that can be generalised; on the other hand, some studies mentioned below draw on one and the same, relatively small data set, and this sparse input resource further limits our understanding of the comprehensibility construct. Finally, many of the studies simultaneously investigate a variety of linguistic features; this risks conflating discourse devices under other categories. Below, we start by briefly considering the non-phonological linguistic correlates of comprehensibility that have been, to some extent, identified by researchers. The sample of studies cited here is not meant to be an exhaustive review, nor does it aim to identify clear trends in the findings. Rather, this serves to illustrate the challenges highlighted in the previous paragraph and to provide a sense of the complex interplay between a variety of features in the (co-)construction of a shared mental model of meaning.

In the oft-cited 'comprehensibility deconstruction' study by Isaacs and Trofimovich (2012), three discourse-level indicators were measured in the extraneous narrative speech of 40 French-L1 learners of English: story cohesion which counted adverbials (*like actually, but, etc*); story breadth, which counted the number of propositions; and story depth, which counted different story-telling components or proposition categories (e.g. setting, action, etc.). Only story breadth showed a strong correlation with comprehensibility (.71). Using what appears to be the same speech data (but different raters), Saito et al. (2015) looked into the difference between linguistic features associated with either comprehensibility or accentedness, measuring the same components as the previous study, and conflating the discourse measures into the broader category of lexicogrammar which was shown to impact comprehensibility (but not accentedness), with only discourse richness (number of propositions) showing a direct correlation (.62). The researchers add that the reason for a low count of cohesive devices in the speech samples could be the short length of the responses. While not explicitly investigating discourse devices, Saito et al.'s (2016) study into pronunciation and lexis is relevant because it includes two lexical features directly associated with discourse and lexical cohesion: polysemy ("related senses in a single lexical entry" (Saito et al., 2016, p. 149 such as the word *man* which has distinct but related meanings) and hypernymy (levels of connections between general and specific terms, e.g. *colour* and *blue*). Of these, only polysemy is associated with comprehensibility scores. Again, it seems the same data set as above was used with different raters, both novice and expert.

Crowther et al. (2015) considered ten linguistic variables in their study of comprehensibility correlates – which drew on responses from Chinese, Hindi-Urdu and Farsi L1 speakers learning English – including discourse richness which refers to the content of the speech measured by listeners on a scale of 1 (lack of detail and sophistication) to 1,000 (lots of ideas and sophisticated structure). This was subsequently conflated under the lexicogrammar category but did, as a discrete measure, correlate strongly with comprehensibility ratings overall (0.95). To confound things further, the overall lexicogrammatical category was strongly associated with comprehensibility for Hindi-Urdu speakers, while the phonological features impacted comprehensibility of the Chinese L1s and there was no clear association between either of the categories and the Farsi speakers. In another study, Suzuki and Kormos (2020) included three explicit measures of discourse in their research into linguistic correlates of comprehensibility: total number of words, frequency of connectives, and latent semantic analysis (LSA). LSA is the semantic overlap of words in adjacent sentences to measure how conceptually similar they are and the researchers used CohMetrix to measure this indicator. Their study included 120 samples of extraneous speech produced by Japanese L1 speakers of English and was notable in that they did not use a picture-prompt; rather, they provided the test-takers with a statement designed to elicit an argumentative response. While there was no significant correlation between comprehensibility and the frequency of connectives or LSA, there was a correlation with the total number of words. Given that the study also found a strong correlation between speech rate and comprehensibility, this might reflect those indicators.

An additional area where there has been ongoing research into the linguistic indicators of comprehensibility is pronunciation and there are several studies that are relevant to our exploration of discourse and comprehensibility. Hahn (2004) focused on primary stress in the speech of a male Korean International Teaching Assistant (ITA) and concluded that while correct placement of primary stress allowed English L1 listeners to process speech with more ease (i.e. it signalled units of meaning, topic shift, etc.), the finding was not significant. Kang et al. (2010) also investigated how intonation and pitch help to 'chunk' speech into units of meaning or thought groups, and how paratones (the intonational equivalent of a paragraph in writing) contribute to the overall informational structure of the discourse, facilitating comprehension. They conclude that the end of an utterance is signalled by both pitch variation and length of pause; where these are missing, the speakers are considered to be less comprehensible. It should be noted that listeners were restricted to L1 speakers of English only and as Jenkins (2000) argued, the results may be different for English L2 listeners. Pausing seems to be a key indicator linked to discourse and comprehensibility. Pickering (2001) found that longer, irregularly occurring silent pauses (within, not between, units of meaning) broke up conceptual units in ITA lectures and had an impact on the perceived ease of understanding. Kang's (2010) study of ITA speech from a range of language backgrounds, rated for comprehensibility by 58 English L1 novice listeners, highlights that the L2 speakers do not follow the same pausing conventions (e.g. longer pauses at discourse junctures) as English L1 speakers; however, the findings show that pauses, stress-related variables and pitch range did not contribute to comprehensibility ratings.

There are several studies that focused quite narrowly on discourse features in relation to distinguishing proficiency levels rather than comprehensibility. These are not within the scope of this book, and the reader is directed to Fung and Carter (2007), Seedhouse and Harris (2011), Iwashita and Vasquez (2015), and Iwashita, May and Moore (2017) for further reading.

This overview of research points strongly towards the need for not only further research into discourse features and comprehensibility, but a clear and coherent research agenda to progress understanding and support the building of better tests and rating systems.

Discourse Features and Comprehensibility in Rating Scales

It is clear, from the discussion in this chapter so far, that, beyond the word and phoneme levels and especially beyond the utterance level, discourse features have a significant impact on the ease with which a listener is able to build a mental model – in other words, on comprehensibility – even if there is not a large body of empirical evidence to support how as yet. In the last section of this chapter, we turn our attention to discourse features in rating scales and we are specifically interested in whether the link between discourse features and comprehensibility is reflected in the scales.

In general, where discourse features (including aspects of coherence) are explicitly referenced in spoken performance descriptors, there are two broad approaches. The first is to dedicate a specific criterion on the scale to discourse features; the second is to subsume reference to the features under other criteria such as fluency, lexis or phonology. Our analysis below considers descriptors of four English language tests set along a continuum between these approaches.

An underlying consideration for both approaches is around task-specificity, that is, whether discourse descriptors (separate or integrated) reflect the genre of the response to which they are being applied. Chalhoub-Deville (1995) cautions against one-size-fits-all rating descriptors precisely because different task-types draw out different aspects of the construct, that is, discourse characteristics of the response are shaped by the genre demanded by the task itself.

Before we consider descriptors of particular language tests, the CEFR is a useful place to begin as it increasingly informs or acts as the foundation for scale development. At first glance, the importance of genre in describing spoken performance is clear: while there is an overall spoken production scale, sub-scales related to sustained oral monologues are explicitly linked to what the communicative task demands of the speaker. These are divided into three macro-functions (describing experience (interpersonal), giving information (transactional) and 'putting a case'(evaluative)), and two specialised genres – public announcements, and addressing audiences. In relation to production of language in academic and professional domains, the CEFR Companion Volume (2020) explicitly states:

> Judgments are made about the linguistic quality of what has been submitted in writing or in a signed video, and about the fluency and articulateness of expression in real time, especially when addressing an audience. Ability in this more formal production is not acquired naturally; it is a product of literacy learnt through education and experience. It involves learning the expectations and conventions of the genre concerned. (p. 60–61)

As previously discussed in this chapter, genre conventions include the ability to use a range of discourse features related to both coherence and cohesion. Monologic discourse characteristics are evident throughout the CEFR spoken production descriptors (Council of Europe, 2022, p. 62–66): *appropriate highlighting of significant points* (Overall, B2); *linear sequence of points* (Overall, B1); *integrating sub-themes, developing particular points and rounding off with an appropriate conclusion* (Describing Experience, C1); *construct a chain of reasoned argument* (Putting a Case, B2); *can structure a longer presentation appropriately in order to help the audience follow the sequence of ideas* (Addressing Audiences, C1). Impact on comprehensibility is not explicit, but there is reference to clarity, particularly at the higher levels; at B2 (Giving Information) *reliably* and C2 (Addressing Audiences) *confidently and articulately* appear. Cohesive devices are mentioned less frequently or are implicit, sometimes in reference to their absence*: mainly isolated phrases* (Overall, A1); *sequential connectors* (Giving Information, A2); These references to surface-level features associated with ordering speech tend to be at the lower levels, which may suggest that less overt cohesive devices are expected at the higher levels (cf. *integrating sub-themes*, Describing Experience, C1).

In the revised CEFR, cohesion and coherence are explicitly dealt with under Pragmatic Communicative Language Competences and includes "Discourse competence [which] concerns the ability to design texts, including generic aspects like *Thematic development* and *Coherence and cohesion"* (Council of Europe, 2020, p. 138). As might be expected, various aspects of coherence and cohesion are explicitly covered in these descriptors, with many being associated with the specific genres mentioned above; again, the link to comprehensibility is indirect and focuses more on communicative effect, for example, under *Thematic development*: *an effective way* (C2), *convincingly* (C1), *clearly signal* (B1); under *Coherence and cohesion*: *clear… speech…* (C2), *mark clearly the relationship between ideas* (B2), *clear, coherent discourse* (B2). The CEFR, then, clearly recognises the role that discourse features play in effective communication and the link to comprehensibility is implicit in reference to the overall communicative effect.

Moving on to scales of specific tests, we return to the Cambridge B2 First test of English (previously the FCE or Cambridge English: First) we used as a springboard for our exploration of discourse features which treats discourse as a separate criterion. The B2 First speaking module is a 'paired' test (i.e. two candidates) and includes four parts: a two-minute 'interview', a one-minute 'long turn' (as described above), a collaborative task which involves a conversation with the other candidate, and a discussion section where the interlocutor facilitates further conversation between the test-taker pair, expanding on the topic in the previous section. The rating descriptors are intended to assess whether each of the candidates meets (level 3), fall short of (level 1 or 2), or exceeds (levels 4 or 5) the standard expected at B2 on the CEFR scale. They are divided into the following criteria: Grammar and Vocabulary, Discourse Management, Pronunciation and Interactive Communication. Focusing on Discourse Management, features of both coherence and cohesion are explicitly mentioned, as can be seen in examples like *Produces extended stretches of language despite some hesitation / Contributions are relevant and there is very little repetition / Uses a range of cohesive devices (level 3)*. Apart from the conflation of fluency and discourse features, it is also noticeable that there is no explicit reference to the effect on the overall message.

The TOEFL iBT is a step further along the continuum of separate vs integrated discourse-feature scales – discourse features are primarily covered under the Topic Development (TD) descriptors but are also referred to under the General Description (GD) descriptors (both five levels, 0–4), for the independent (computer-mediated, speaking-only) and integrated (listening-into-speaking) tasks. Features of discourse are explicitly mentioned in relative detail with some reference to the effect of coherence and cohesive devices on comprehensibility (clarity and vagueness under TD on the Independent and Integrated task scales). While *intelligibility* is referred to throughout the GD scales, it is not explicitly linked to discourse features.

In the International English Language Testing System (IELTS), coherence and cohesion features are incorporated under the Fluency and Coherence (FC) criterion and, similar to the B2 First described above, reference to discourse features tends towards the linguistic only (*speaks coherently with fully appropriate cohesive features* (Band 9); *repetitious use of simple connectives* (Band 4)), with no explicit reference to the impact these might have on the comprehensibility of the speech being assessed. In addition, IELTS examiners (who are also interlocutors) apply one set of descriptors to all parts of the Oral Proficiency Interview, despite different stages of the exam eliciting responses that display different aspects of the discourse construct: short-responses with marked topic shifts in Part

1 (Seedhouse and Harris, 2011), an extended monologic task in response to a topic in Part 2, and to the aim to build a more interactive discussion in Part 3.

The Pearson Test of English (PTE) Academic version uses a number of tasks for the assessment of speaking ability. Two of these elicit extended monologic speech, one in relation to an image (description) and the other requires the retelling of a lecture (integrated listening-into-speaking task). Although PTE Academic is machine rated, a Score Guide is available to test-takers and there are descriptions of the traits scored in each task, suggesting that the automated rating model is task-specific. Although discourse features are not referred to explicitly, cohesion and coherence are indirectly described in terms of their function as concept connectors. Consider, for example, the descriptions at the highest level (5) and lowest (0) for the *Describe image* task (Pearson, 2022, p. 35):

> 5 Describes all elements of the image and their relationships, possible development and conclusion or implications
>
> 0 Mentions some disjointed elements of the presentation

In the *Re-tell lecture* task, the importance of coherence is more explicit (levels 5 (highest) and 1 (second lowest) (Pearson, 2022, p. 36):

> 5 Re-tells all points of the presentation and describes characters, aspects and actions, their relationships, the underlying development, implications and conclusions
>
> 1 Describes some basic elements of the presentation but does not make clear their interrelations or implications

Unlike the descriptors for the other tests discussed, the PTE Academic descriptors do not include specific reference to linguistic elements used to achieve coherence and cohesion but focus rather on the relationships within the content or message. There is no indication of how these connections might be realised in terms of linguistic or other discourse features. Indeed, this is one of the concerns with machine rating – that while statistical correlation between humans and machines might be high, what is actually being counted or measured by the auto-rater is unclear. A counter-argument, however, is that (as we have seen in the more general discussion around coherence and cohesion earlier in this chapter) effective communication is about establishing similar connections between ideas in the mind of the listener as in the mind of the speaker; the achievement of this is complex and resists exact definition in linguistics terms.

Whether the complexity is located in a humanly-unfathomable algorithm used by a computer or in the equally mysterious minds of human raters, how exactly coherence and cohesion contribute to overall comprehensibility between speaker and listener remains inconclusive. (Automated rating is covered in more detail in Chapter 6.)

This section has provided an overview of how discourse features are connected (or not) to comprehensibility in a sample of rating scales. Although the descriptors in the framework and these tests differ in how explicitly linguistic ('co-text') and structural features associated with spoken discourse management are referenced, it is evident that the organisation of and linking between ideas is important in the measurement of oral proficiency and, by implication, the impact on meaning at a whole-text level. Several points arise which are relevant to our broader focus on comprehensibility:

- Where descriptors include reference to specific cohesion or cohesive devices, the risk is that raters (or an auto-rating system) could over-operationalise the aspects of the scales that are most salient and easily quantifiable like mechanical or formulaic markers (firstly, secondly, there are two sides to every coin); as a consequence, test-takers who employ more sophisticated, nuanced strategies to achieve comprehensibility might be penalised for not using a range of cohesive devices; this has the added consequence of negative washback as test-takers focus on using highly formulaic language rather than meaning-rich communication;
- Given the overlap of discourse with other linguistic criteria such as fluency and lexis, speech displaying discourse features that contribute positively to comprehensibility could be penalised under a different criterion, for example, repetition of key words might attract a lower rating under lexis where the rater (or automated rating system) is expecting a wider range of vocabulary, or repetition that contributes to establishing a unified text could be seen as negative under the fluency criterion;
- The application of a set of general descriptors to different types of responses elicited by different tasks could result in test-takers not being given the opportunity to demonstrate the discourse management skills or devices being evaluated by the descriptors, for example, in instances where the turn is too short or the topic not suitable for the inclusion of topic development.

Conclusion

We return to the underlying assumption of this chapter: that comprehensibility is linked to communicative purpose, and that, in the case of extended, monologic text, the goal is for the text to be understood as a whole. We recognised the significant contribution that discourse features make to this overall comprehension and explored the components of discourse by taking two steps back from the linguistic coal-face of comprehensibility from an extended-text perspective: first, to view the connections between semantic items within and across sentence boundaries that are achieved through cohesion; then, further back to take in the larger structuring and ordering of extended, monologic speech that, together with cohesion, results in overall coherence and allows the listener to perceive – and comprehend – the text as a unified whole. We saw that the contribution of discourse features and strategies to comprehensibility at the text level is complex and not fully understood, given the relative scarcity of studies, and that further, targeted research is necessary. The discussion also demonstrated that there is overlap between the features of discourse and other linguistic features, and that the reflection of these features in rating scales can be superficial, conflated or confounded, with potentially negative consequences on the evaluation of comprehensibility as the target construct.

As with the areas of focus of other chapters in this volume, there is a sense that an atomic approach to establishing the relationship between linguistic features and comprehensibility does not adequately reflect the intersection of various factors during any particular speech event. The reader is referred to Figure 8.1 in the concluding chapter for a visualisation of how discourse features might interact with other linguistic and non-linguistic factors within the spoken communicative environment. In the case of discourse features, we may be so concentrated on inspecting and recording the inventory of building components that we fail to appreciate how it is the combination of the bricks, the mortar, the frame, the foundation and the embellishments that produce the overall result. We are looking at the trees, not the wood.

CHAPTER 4

COMPREHENSIBILITY AT A PRAGMATIC LEVEL

In this volume, we have argued that comprehensibility is a multidimensional construct affecting spoken communication in several different ways. In Chapters 2 and 3, we focused on phonological and discourse dimensions of comprehensibility and underlined a range of variables that contribute to comprehensibility of L2 speech in these dimensions. The focus of the current chapter, however, is on the pragmatic dimension of comprehensibility, that is, when a speaker's sounds and words are clear at utterance and discourse level, but their message is not easy to understand in the given social and cultural context of the communication.

We started the book by discussing an example of a communication breakdown, during a spoken interaction, when the examiner's pronunciation of the word "luck" was not understood by the test-taker. The pronunciation of the word affected the test-taker's comprehensibility leading to incorrect responses from the test-taker. Trying to resolve the problem, the examiner provided a gloss "you know, 'good luck' like winning a raffle draw" hoping the test-taker understands the word in question is "luck". This attempt also failed but this time not owing to pronunciation problems, but because the concept of "a raffle draw" was culturally unfamiliar to the test-taker, leading to comprehensibility issues in this context of communication. It is necessary to note that comprehensibility at a pragmatic dimension, similar to other dimensions discussed in previous chapters, depends on the listener as much as on the speaker. This claim is based on strong research evidence (e.g. Hustad, 2006; Shepperd et al., 2017) suggesting that comprehensibility is a characteristic that the speaker and listener jointly bring to the act of communication by producing and comprehending the intended meaning effectively and successfully. Given the interaction between the speaker and listener in this sense, it is also important to consider comprehensibility as a dynamic and interactive phenomenon that evolves during the interaction. In the following sections, we will discuss these issues in more depth.

Another important factor to highlight in this chapter is the nature of "listener" in relation to the pragmatic dimension of comprehensibility. Most of the work conducted on comprehensibility in the 1980s and 1990s (e.g. Gass & Varinos, 1984; Derwing & Munro, 1995a, 1997) considered comprehensibility (and intelligibility) as a measure of the extent to which native speakers of an L2 (primarily English) understand and interpret nonnative speakers' speech. Here, we use the terms native and nonnative speaker in the context of these studies. As discussed in Chapter 1, given the spread of ELF we consider these terms outdated and inappropriate. While there were differences between these studies in terms of the participants' L1, level of proficiency, age and professional background, comprehensibility was consistently judged by native speakers of the target language. As discussed in Chapter 1, this practice has changed at least to some extent in language testing research. Linguists and language professionals are aware that a large majority of English communication in the world today takes place between a range of L2 users of English in different settings and for a wide range of purposes. The shift in who uses English and for what purposes English is used has invited a shift in perspective to what constitutes comprehensibility and how it should be judged. Accordingly, we propose comprehensibility should be judged based on the norms of ELF (see Chapter 1 for a more detailed discussion) when tested by international English language tests. Also note that, as discussed earlier, given the abundance of research on English language tests, our discussions in this volume predominantly focus on the assessment of English. However, we assume the same concepts and principles might be applicable to other lingua francas and their corresponding tests. The discussions provided in this chapter, therefore, are based on these principles.

The chapter's structure is as follows. After discussing pragmatic comprehensibility from a communication and intercultural perspective, the chapter will discuss key aspects of pragmatic knowledge that affect comprehensibility. Summarising research in this area (e.g. Purpura, 2004; Rover, 2011, Taguchi, 2005, 2007, 2012), we will discuss some important aspects of pragmatic knowledge that contribute to comprehensibility. Before reviewing the literature in this area, however, it is necessary to note that little research has so far focused on examining the relationship between pragmatic knowledge and L2 comprehensibility. Many studies reported in this chapter have examined the relationship between pragmatic knowledge and other aspects of L2 ability (e.g. communicative success in Purpura, 2004, and proficiency in Taguchi, 2005).

However, reviewing this literature seems imperative as it will assist us understand which pragmatic aspects of language use may be related to comprehensibility.

In our discussion in this chapter, we will then focus on two major categories of variables affecting comprehensibility at a pragmatic level: Contextual factors and sociolinguistic and socio-cultural factors. Issues such as implied meaning, topic familiarity, and mode of discourse will be discussed in relation to context. We will then discuss social factors and cultural norms in pragmatic aspects of language use, including L2 varieties and culturalingual factors that affect comprehensibility. We will then turn to assessment of comprehensibility in language test rating descriptors, rating scales and raters. More importantly, we will argue that in order to have a valid and reliable assessment of comprehensibility, issues related to pragmatic aspects of it should be carefully considered in the design of rating scales and rater training materials.

Pragmatic Knowledge and Comprehensibility

As discussed in previous chapters, comprehensibility has been defined in different ways over the past decades. The variations in these definitions are often shaped in the light of the different epistemological and/or methodological assumptions and principles that informed each definition. The way language and linguistic ability was perceived and the methods used to measure this ability have without doubt determined how comprehensibility has been defined. In this chapter, we will first focus on the development of the concept of pragmatic knowledge as a background to understanding comprehensibility. We will discuss some definitions of pragmatic knowledge to demonstrate how comprehensibility at a pragmatic level has gained currency in the field of linguistics and consequently in language testing. To do so, we provide a historical background to the emergence and development of the construct of pragmatic knowledge and its relationship to comprehensibility.

Hymes (1971) can be considered as one of the earliest scholars who highlighted the significance of the concept of pragmatic knowledge by arguing "there are rules of use without which the rules of grammar would be useless" (Hymes, 1971, p. 278). Hymes' reference to pragmatic knowledge was a milestone in the field of linguistics in general, and had an influential impact on how language was perceived and defined in a range of sub-disciplines of linguistics. In language testing, Bachman's model of communicative language ability was a turning point for the field in developing a more in-depth understanding of pragmatic knowledge and finding ways to assess it. In his model, Bachman (1990) considered pragmatic competence/knowledge as a central and essential aspect of communicative language ability. Prior to Bachman, Canale and Swain (1980) and Canale (1983) had proposed a model of communicative language ability comprising four types of knowledge: linguistic, sociolinguistic, discourse, and strategic competence. Drawing on Canale and Swain's work, Bachman's (1990) model suggested that communicative language ability goes beyond language competence to include other factors such as knowledge structures and psycho-physiological mechanisms. Language competence, in his model, comprised two types of knowledge: Organisational (abilities that are central to the formal structure of language), and pragmatic (abilities that are important when using language in context) (Bachman, 1990, p. 87–88). Bachman's pragmatic knowledge consisted of illocutionary competence and sociolinguistic competence, with the former referring to ideational, manipulative, heuristic and imaginative functions of language, and the latter representing sensitivity to variations in social and regional diversities and familiarity with the conventions related to these varieties of language use in communication.

Leech (1983) re-labelled the two types of knowledge in Bachman's pragmatic competence as *pragmalinguistics*, and *sociopragmatics*. While *pragmalinguistics* refers to the linguistic tools that are used to express and comprehend the intended meaning, *sociopragmatics* reflects understanding the social conventions that affect speakers' linguistic choices and listeners' interpretation of them. We consider Bachman's conceptualisation of pragmatic knowledge important in understanding pragmatic aspects of the construct of comprehensibility. Whether one follows Bachman's classification or Leech's categories, the importance of pragmatic knowledge lies in its relationship to conveying and understanding the intended meaning in terms of both the context of language use and the social and cultural variations of language. Analysing Bachman's view on pragmatic knowledge has allowed us to see the central role pragmatic knowledge plays in comprehensibility, although his model did not use the term 'comprehensibility' when discussing the construct.

Gass and Varonis (1984) and Varonis and Gass (1982) took the very first step towards examining the role of listener backgrounds (i.e., topic familiarity) in L1 listeners' comprehensibility judgements. These two studies are relevant to our discussion in this chapter as the researchers made the first attempt to highlight the role of factors beyond pronunciation that affect comprehensibility. In a study designed to test comprehensibility as a function of familiarity, Gass and Varinos (1984) investigated the role of pronunciation and grammar in comprehensibility of L2 speakers of English when their speech samples were judged by a group of L1 speakers. In simple language, they considered comprehensibility the extent to which native speakers comprehend non-native speakers' talk. Analysing the L1 speakers' judgements, the authors suggested that proficiency in grammar and pronunciation makes a substantial contribution to comprehensibility. However, they explained that a larger scheme should be considered if a better understanding of comprehensibility was to be achieved. Gass and Varinos (1984) proposed the following scheme to explain comprehensibility in its full sense:

$$\mathbf{C = p + g + f1 + f2 + F3, \ldots + fl + s}$$

C = comprehensibility; p = pronunciation; g = grammar;
f1 = familiarity with topic; f2 = familiarity with speaker;
F3 = familiarity with speaker's native language; fl = fluency;
s = social factors

As can be seen in Figure 4.1, the scheme primarily highlights the multidimensional nature of comprehensibility. The factors affecting comprehensibility in this model range from grammar and pronunciation to different aspects of familiarity both with the speaker and the language variety. The dots indicate that there might be other factors potentially affecting comprehensibility. While this early work should be considered a key development in providing a broader understanding of comprehensibility by referring to factors beyond word and sentence level, the proposed scheme is restricted by its predominant focus on familiarity. Looking into three aspects of familiarity (i.e., familiarity with the topic, speaker, different L1 backgrounds), the results of Gass and Varonis (1984) suggested that familiarity with topic had a major influence on comprehensibility. Familiarity in the other categories was suggested to have a facilitative role in comprehension. The scheme, however, did not make a reference to contextual, social or cultural variables that affect comprehensibility. Gass and Varonis's (1984) and Varonis and Gass's (1982) work encouraged researchers to start asking questions about the construct of comprehensibility, and opened up a forum to discuss factors beyond pronunciation and grammar that affect comprehensibility.

Another milestone in the development of the concept of comprehensibility with reference to pragmatics in the 1980s was the publication of Smith and Nelson's (1985) state-of-the-art article on 'international intelligibility' of English. In this article, the authors reviewed 163 research outputs and summarised the findings in the form of some commonly agreed principles about intelligibility. Smith and Nelson's (1985) work was particularly important as their summary highlighted (a) the widespread use of English as an international language by a range of L1 and L2 speakers, (b) the role of the listener and the interactive relationship between the speaker and listener, and (c) the complex nature of what they considered 'international intelligibility', that is, understanding a speaker's speech by both L1 and L2 speakers of English. They further argued:

> Since intelligibility depends upon so many factors of different types involved in a given speech event, it is difficult to find ways of integrating approaches and parameters. That is a challenge for future research. (P. 333)

Problematising the limited understanding of the complex construct of 'international intelligibility' at the time, Smith and Nelson's (1985) seminal work played a pivotal role in shaping and expanding the perspective towards what it takes to understand a speaker. They further criticised the existing research for using the terms intelligibility, comprehensibility and interpretability interchangeably, calling for more research to distinguish these concepts. They suggested that these three terms should be used distinctively to refer to more specific meanings, with intelligibility denoting word and utterance recognition, comprehensibility demonstrating word and utterance meaning, and interpretability focusing on meaning behind words and utterances. In effect, Smith and Nelson (1985, p.334) argued that intelligibility offered a narrow and insufficient perspective since communication problems also occur "when people fail to understand the meaning of a word or an utterance (comprehensibility), or the meaning behind the word or utterance (interpretability)". While Smith and Nelson's work was highly influential in directing researchers' attention to the pragmatic aspects of communication, it did not provide a clear explanation of how the three concepts can be distinguished or whether and to what extent they may interact with one another.

Following from this call, Kachru (2008) adopted Smith and Nelson's approach and developed a triadic framework for understanding the complex nature of comprehensibility. Being informed by the sociolinguistic specification of English as an international language, Kachru (2008, following Smith, 1992, and Smith & Nelson, 1985), considered intelligibility, comprehensibility and interpretability as the three crucial factors affecting understanding a speaker's intended meaning. As discussed in Chapter 1 and below, for reasons of scope we will not focus on the concept of interpretability in this volume. In the next paragraph, however, an analysis is provided to show how we perceive the relationship between comprehensibility and interpretability in Kachru's model.

While intelligibility, according to Kachru (2008), is understanding the intended meaning at a word level and comprehensibility at a text level, interpretability refers to understanding the intended meaning at an interactional level. In other words, it is possible to be intelligible and comprehensible, but not interpretable. Arguing that "interpretability is a matter of construction that can be put upon verbal acts by the interlocutors in social interaction" (Kachru, 2008, p. 311), Kachru suggested that interpretation of one's intended meaning is instigated, shaped and developed in interaction between the speaker and interlocutor. Therefore, one conclusion to reach is that the interpretation of the intended meaning the interlocutor brings to the conversation would help determine the degree of her/his understanding of the message. Kachru's classification is particularly interesting and novel as it considers comprehensibility as a multidimensional construct in which the role of the interlocutor/listener in understanding the intended meaning is reinforced. The distinction between Kachru's comprehensibility and interpretability, however, seems rather arbitrary, as in real-life communication, understanding the intended meaning in interaction is an inseparable part of the construct of comprehensibility. Here, it is important to note that Smith and Nelson's or Kachru's models are similar to the framework we are proposing in this volume in that they emphasise the importance of communication problems that occur at "utterance level" and "beyond utterance level" (Smith & Nelson, 1985, p. 334) with a potentially damaging impact on comprehensibility. What makes our framework different from those is that we consider comprehensibility as an overarching construct to include communication at word, utterance, discourse and pragmatic levels, with a communication problem occurring at any of the levels affecting comprehensibility. In other words, while our approach considers comprehensibility as a single construct of different facets, Smith and Nelson's and Kachru's models assume there are three different, and perhaps distinct, constructs (intelligibility, comprehensibility and interpretability) affecting listeners' understanding. In what follows in this chapter, we argue that to be comprehensible, it is necessary that the meaning is understood in the context of interaction.

In the work that followed in the 1990s, Derwing and Munro's work is particularly important as it highlighted the role of listeners' understanding of L2 speech, a framework which was then adopted by a large number of researchers in the field. For Derwing and Munro (1997, p. 2), comprehensibility referred to "native speakers' perception of intelligibility", and it was operationalised through L1 English speakers' judgments of intelligibility, on a rating scale of how difficult/easy it was to understand the L2 speaker's utterances. Based on our analysis of this definition, the word 'utterance' suggests Derwing and Munro's (1997) definition was primarily interested in comprehensibility at utterance level. This distinguishes their approach to many others who had just focused on understanding speech samples at word level. In this volume, however, we are proposing a broader perspective to understanding comprehensibility, a construct that goes beyond "utterance level" to include comprehensibility in terms of discourse and context. We will come back to this in the following sections of this chapter.

The last perspective we discuss here is Taguchi's (2005, 2007) view on the relationship between pragmatic comprehension and L2 proficiency. For Taguchi (2005), pragmatic knowledge is "the ability to comprehend and produce meaning in context" (p. 543). She argues that pragmatic competence involves knowledge at two levels of production and comprehension (i.e., pragmatic performance and pragmatic comprehension respectively), implying that both the speaker and the listener need pragmatic knowledge to take part in successful communication and interaction. Taguchi (2005) also argues that pragmatic comprehension involves "the ability to understand implied speaker intention by using linguistic knowledge, contextual clues, and the assumption of relevance" (p. 544). In her conceptualisation of the relationship between pragmatic knowledge and pragmatic comprehension, Taguchi highlights the significance of comprehensibility in the sense that we acknowledge it in this chapter, that is comprehensibility as understanding the intended meaning in the context of language use. Our proposed scheme, however, goes beyond Taguchi's definition to include sociolinguistic and sociocultural variables as well. We will discuss these variables in further detail in the section on sociolinguistic factors below.

A few important conclusions emerge from this brief historical overview of the definitions and conceptualisations of comprehensibility and its relationship to pragmatic knowledge. First of all, the concept of understanding the intended meaning in relation to context has been central to the construct of comprehensibility for a long time. Whether different researchers refer to the concept using the term 'pragmatic comprehensibility' or not, the concept is known by various researchers as an important aspect of successful communication. Second, while there have been valuable and innovative attempts at analysing this aspect of comprehensibility over the past decades, research in this area has remained limited and inconclusive. The lack of agreement on what constitutes the pragmatic aspect of comprehensibility is expected to have a knock-on effect on the assessment of comprehensibility in language testing. In our proposed scheme in this volume, we consider pragmatic knowledge a factor contributing to comprehensibility that affects communication both from a speaker and listener perspective.

Comprehensibility from a Pragmatic Knowledge Perspective

From a pragmatic perspective, there are different variables that contribute to the concept of comprehensibility, including linguistic, sociolinguistic, attitudinal, and intercultural factors. In what follows, we will discuss some of the variables that are particularly important in the assessment of comprehensibility in language testing. To structure the discussion, we have grouped these variables under two categories. The first category includes variables rooted in the coding and decoding of the linguistic components of the talk, for example, providing and interpreting contextual cues, implicatures, and references. Such variables are often called contextual aspects of pragmatic knowledge. The second category includes variables that go beyond the immediate context of communication to integrate issues related to social, sociolinguistic and sociocultural aspects of comprehensibility. Issues such as attitudes, social values, language varieties, and intercultural understanding are some of the variables in this category that influence understanding the intended meaning. We label this category sociolinguistic and sociocultural aspects of comprehensibility. In the sections that follow, we discuss each of the categories to examine how they can influence comprehensibility.

Contextual Aspects of Comprehensibility

There is little disagreement among linguists and communication experts about the impact of context on understanding a message. In this sense, context includes a range of variables from linguistic factors such as use of discourse markers to non-linguistic features of interaction such as environmental noise. Understanding the intended meaning is facilitated when there are adequate contextual cues, when the message is relevant to the discourse situation, when a speaker is discussing a topic that is familiar to the listener, or when clear references are provided to allow the listener to understand and interpret the intended meaning. Several contextual variables have been shown to have a direct impact on comprehensibility including familiarity and predictability of the message, familiarity with the topic and speech events/speech acts, and relevance. Relevance, in this sense, is defined as the need to make the output relevant to the ongoing talk in terms of both content and context. (See Cribb, 2012, for a full discussion.). Some of these variables are more important than others for assessment of comprehensibility in language testing. We focus on a few variables for which strong research evidence exists.

Familiarity. There is ample research evidence to suggest familiarity with the topic, genre, speech acts, interlocutor, and setting helps promote comprehensibility. As discussed above, Gass and Varinos (1984) showed that the different aspects of familiarity (i.e., familiarity with the topic, speaker, different L1 backgrounds, a specific L1 background) affect comprehensibility, familiarity with the topic having the greatest influence. In a more recent study, Schmidgall (2013) argues that in addition to topic familiarity, an interest in the topic would positively impact the listener's comprehensibility. We will discuss the important role of familiarity with L2 varieties under the section on sociolinguistic and sociocultural factors below.

Contextual cues. While order and organisation of information appears to be crucial for comprehensibility, research in testing pragmatic ability has shown that the overall effect of miscues is more substantial on comprehensibility than ordering of the information (Green, 1998). This finding suggests that test-takers' failure to incorporate appropriate cues such as logical corrections and references in their talk has a damaging impact on their listeners' understanding of the intended meaning. Use of discourse markers appropriately, for example, is another way of providing a solid structure and strong signposting for the interaction leading to a rich context for comprehensibility. Research in this area (e.g. Liao, 2009; Müller, 2005) has shown that not using discourse markers adequately and appropriately has a damaging impact on coherence and comprehensibility of L2 users' output.

Mode of discourse. The mode of discourse, referring to whether the talk is monologic, dialogic or group interaction, has an impact on comprehensibility. Mode, in this sense, does not just refer to the number of speakers taking part in the interaction, but more importantly it includes the degree of collaboration and amount of negotiation possible during the speech event. Therefore, the effects of mode on comprehensibility should be studied in relation to these contributing factors. In general, interaction with a higher degree of collaboration and an opportunity to negotiate meaning in a dialogue in principle helps promote comprehensibility as these opportunities enable the listener and speaker to work on problematic areas of communication and resolve them. Lack of collaboration and negotiation of meaning opportunities, for example in a monologic task, would inevitably make the listener's task more challenging when communication problems arise. Cribb (2012) argued that under such circumstances "there is a greater burden on the speaker to construct and package the utterances into a 'tighter' discourse to enable the listener to build a coherent interpretation" (Cribb, 2012, p. 71). In this sense, comprehensibility in a monologic and non-interactive mode is a more difficult goal to achieve.

The dialogic mode of interaction, on the other hand, typically involves short turns, overlaps and interrupted speech. While these are inherent characteristics of everyday conversations, they make understanding the speaker difficult for two reasons. First, longer pieces of discourse are usually considered easier to comprehend, as short exchanges and brief turns may not provide adequate contextual cues. Second, the short and interrupted nature of dialogues may lead to miscues associated with a lack of coherence, affecting listeners' ease of understanding (Cribb, 2012). These aspects of mode seem to contribute to the ease of understanding at a pragmatic level, and as such they deserve a careful consideration and more research.

Sociolinguistic and Sociocultural Aspects of Comprehensibility

There is emerging L2 research evidence to suggest that comprehensibility is influenced by a range of variables linked to social aspects of communication (Hansen Edwards, Zampini, & Cunningham, 2018, 2019; Kennedy & Trofimovich, 2019). Social factors that potentially affect comprehensibility are numerous and include a wide spectrum of social, sociolinguistic and sociocultural elements ranging from age and gender to attitudes, richness of social experiences, variations in language use, and educational and professional backgrounds. Despite the significance of research in this aspect of comprehensibility, it is surprising that this area is still under researched. In this section, we aim to provide a discussion of some important variables in this area. Given the length of this chapter, however, we will not be able to discuss all these variables. We will first discuss sociolinguistic variables before moving to sociocultural variables that affect comprehensibility.

Role of L1: One the factors that contribute to the ease or difficulty of understanding a speaker is her/his L1. It is generally hypothesised that L2 listeners may behave differently from L1 listeners when rating a speaker's comprehensibility. The existing research evidence also suggests that there are advantages for ease of understanding when the listener and speaker share the same language, and therefore difficulty is likely to arise when they don't share the same L1 background. Foote and Trofimovich's (2018) study, for example, showed clear L1 effects on ratings of L2 comprehensibility, in that speakers from the same language often found it easier to understand someone from their own language background. Interestingly, L1 background did not seem to have a major contribution to variability in comprehensibility ratings when groups of raters from different L1 backgrounds assess the same speech samples. These authors also reported that the various L1 combinations in the listener–speaker relationships resulted in "overlapping yet non-identical linguistic variables contributing to comprehensibility ratings", suggesting a range of linguistic elements (e.g. pronunciation, fluency, grammar) might be at play to affect the rating of different groups.

Familiarity with the L2 varieties. In the previous section, we discussed familiarity as a contextual factor affecting comprehensibility. From a social and sociolinguistic perspective, however, familiarity with the varieties of the L2 is perhaps the most important factor affecting comprehensibility and judgements of it. In the case of ELF, familiarity with the different varieties of English seems to be a crucial factor in comprehending speakers from these different varieties (see Chapters 1 and 2 for discussion of these at the word and sentence level). Presence of several nationally and locally well-established varieties of English in the world today (e.g. Singapore, Hong Kong, and Cockney) and emergence of new and local varieties (e.g. Jafaican, see Kerswill, 2014) makes the task of comprehending these speakers more challenging to a range of different English language users. For this reason, variables such as exposure to these varieties, extended experience of living in the target language community, and opportunities to immerse in educational and cultural contexts (e.g. immersion programmes and study abroad contexts) are variables that crucially determine the extent of the listener's comprehensibility.

A number of recent studies extend support to these claims. Saito et al. (2019), for example, examined the effects of a range of personal characteristics of L2 users (e.g. age, proficiency, familiarity and metacognition) on their judgements of comprehensibility when listening to Japanese accented English. By categorising the listeners to lenient and strict raters, the researchers compared comprehensibility ratings of the two groups. The results suggested that lenient listeners paid more attention to comprehensibility while strict listeners cared more about phonological accuracy. In addition, the examination of the listeners' language profile through a background questionnaire suggested that metacognition (awareness of the crucial role of comprehensibility), language experience (e.g. using English for professional purposes) and language distance (the distance between the raters' L1 and L2) also affected their comprehensibility ratings. In another study, Shintani, Saito and Koizumi (2019) examined the effects of raters' multilingualism on their judgement of L2 accentedness and comprehensibility. The findings suggested that multilingual raters with a better command of English over their other languages during their early childhood tended to be stricter than others in their judgement of L2 comprehensibility and accentedness. The findings also suggested that having a balanced exposure to two languages at home from early childhood can positively impact accentedness and comprehensibility judgements.

Attitudes to L2 varieties. Several studies have so far shown that listeners' attitudes to language varieties can affect comprehensibility. Before discussing this body of research, it is important to maintain that research has already shown that there are attitudes towards different varieties of English. In most studies, a consistent preference has been found for those varieties from the Inner Circle Englishes (e.g. American or British English) in contrast to local and emerging varieties (e.g. Indian English or Hong Kong English) (Ahn & Kang, 2017; Bernaisch and Koch, 2015; Bolton and Kwok, 1990). Such studies have predominantly focused on the relationship of attitudes towards accent and intelligibility (understanding meaning at word and sentence level), where only few have examined the relationship between attitudes toward varieties and comprehensibility at a pragmatic level. In line with previous research examining comprehensibility, Hansen Edwards, Zampini, and Cunningham (2018, 2019) found that perceptions of accentedness were correlated with comprehensibility ratings. They also reported that American English was perceived to be the most comprehensible and the least accented, whereas Chinese and Hong Kong varieties were rated as the most accented and least comprehensible. Interestingly, they found little relationship between these perceptions and the ability to actually understand the variety and/or speaker.

Some listeners were even found to attribute lower levels of sophistication, intelligence and creditability to L2 speakers of lower comprehensibility, suggesting comprehensibility can be perceived as a cognitive variable to some listeners (see Hansen Edward et al., 2018, for a full discussion).

Kennedy and Trofimovich (2019) highlighted the importance of social influences on ratings of comprehensibility. Reporting on studies investigating listeners' socially-oriented bias, the authors argued that having positive or negative attitudes towards the speakers may affect ratings of comprehensibility. In a study investigating university lecturers' ratings of comprehensibility, Sheppard et al. (2017) provided evidence that those reporting negative attitudes toward the English proficiency of international students gave lower ratings of comprehensibility to students' L2 English speech than those reporting positive attitudes, despite the fact that both groups provided equally accurate ratings of intelligibility in transcribing the speakers' speech.

Professional background. Shepperd et al. (2017) showed that comprehensibility was influenced by the listeners' professional background. In this study, university lecturers (teaching subject content) were compared with English for Academic Purposes (EAP) instructors (teaching language) in terms of their rating of comprehensibility. The results showed that although the two groups had similar scores when rating students' intelligibility and comprehensibility, EAP instructors were more accurate for less intelligible speakers. Positive attitudes towards international students' language abilities was suggested as a factor influencing rating of comprehensibility.

Isaacs and Thompson (2013) also examined the effects of rater experience on judgments of L2 comprehensibility, accentedness, and fluency by collecting data from 40 Canadian L1 English speakers in two groups of experienced (20 experienced English as a Second Language [ESL] teachers) and novice (20 graduate students from non-linguistic programmes) raters. Although the researchers did not find any statistically significant differences between the mean ratings of comprehensibility (or fluency and accentedness) between experienced and novice raters, the qualitative data highlighted some important differences between the two groups. For example, experienced raters were more likely to highlight pronunciation errors and more prepared to be adept at understanding L2 speech.

Gender and Age. In a study of high-school bilingual speakers in a bilingual educational context in Paraguay, Spezzini (2004) indicated that gender seemed to be a variable distinguishing speakers in terms of comprehensibility ratings. In this study, female students received a higher rating for both their verbal ability and comprehensibility ratings than their male classmates. The author interpreted the finding in terms of female students "outperforming boys in verbal ability" in general with a knock-on effect on their comprehensibility (Spezzini, 2004, p. 421). The results of the study also showed that students with higher levels of English use for social purposes received higher comprehensibility ratings, implying a relationship between social use and comprehensibility. Taylor Reid, Trofimovich and O'Brien (2019) investigated the effects of social bias, manipulated through age of listeners on comprehensibility by examining English L1 users' ratings of comprehensibility when judging French L2 users of English in Canada. Results suggested that younger listeners tended to upgrade the speakers' comprehensibility in their ratings, while the older listeners downgraded speakers on all measures of comprehensibility. The authors used the findings as evidence for the dynamic nature of comprehensibility.

Differences in cultural norms of communication practices that promote or impede communication comprise another set of variables that affect comprehensibility. Culture, in this sense, refers to the shared knowledge between the speaker and listener of a common language and cultural conventions of how the language is used in different situations in everyday life. Listeners' familiarity with the cultural norms of communication (e.g. turn taking and backchannelling) and their awareness of the sociocultural and intercultural differences in communication are central to communicating the message effectively and comprehensibly. While there are a wide range of such factors, for reasons of scope we will only discuss some important sociocultural factors that affect comprehensibility.

L1 variations. Research in comprehensibility has shown that L1 can be a source of variation in comprehensibility. Crowther, Trofimovich, Isaacs and Saito (2015), for example, examined comprehensibility of four groups of speakers (Mandarin Chinese, Hindi/Urdu, Farsi, and Romance) performing two different speaking tasks in English. The raters were L1 speakers of English and experienced experts in applied linguistics who were familiar with the language varieties under investigation. In addition to task-related differences in the speakers' comprehensibility, their study showed L1-specific influences when investigating the relationship between comprehensibility and L2 performance. For example, a strong association was reported between comprehensibility ratings and segmental errors in the pronunciation of the Chinese speaking group; a strong association was observed between comprehensibility ratings and patterns of intonation in the Hindi/Urdu speaking group; and a strong relationship was seen between comprehensibility and lexico-grammar in the Farsi speaking group. All this evidence suggests that L1 background can have an impact on comprehensibility; this would inevitably make the assessment of comprehensibility more complicated in international language testing contexts.

Cultural norms of conversations (e.g. backchannels and overlaps). Although good listeners are generally known to be able to produce backchannels when engaged in communication, providing backchannels is, to a great extent, culturally defined with some cultures requiring more backchannels, for example, than others. Given this variety of use among speakers, those listeners unaccustomed to different cultural norms could be affected when exposed to these varieties. White (1989), in a study examining the frequency of backchannels across cultures, reported that Japanese listeners produced more backchannels, both in terms of frequency and type, when engaged in intercultural talks than American listeners. Berry (1994), examining a smaller group of eight participants, reports a similar finding when comparing American and Spanish speakers, claiming that although there are several occasions for overlap in conversations of both groups, Spanish speakers have more frequent backchannels and longer overlap periods. More research is needed to examine such effects more systematically.

Culturalingual variables. Taylor Reid et al. (2019) argue that listeners' cultural differences and intercultural understanding influence comprehensibility ratings. Drawing on data collected from French and English speakers in Canada, they report that listeners who grew up as young multilingual speakers in Montreal after Bill 101 came to effect "may have felt more open to varied language use, regardless of interlocutor proficiency, even when exposed to negative comments" (Taylor Reid et al., 2019, p. 278). Bill 101, or the Charter of the French Language, came into effect in 1997 in Quebec Province in Canada to define French as the official language of the government, promoting Quebec as a multilingual society. Taylor Reid et al. (2019) have argued that listeners' perspectives on society and different linguistic groups affect listener comprehensibility, an important variable that has not been accounted for in research on L2 comprehensibility.

Pragmatic Aspects of Comprehensibility in Rater and Rating Scales

In previous sections of this chapter, we provided an analysis of the pragmatic aspects of comprehensibility and discussed a range of variables that contribute to it. The discussion above is a brief representation of the listener-based variables that potentially affect raters' L2 comprehensibility judgements. The brief discussion also highlights the dynamic nature of comprehensibility affected by both the speaker and the listener implying that different listeners may suggest different ratings of the same speech sample. This is where the task of encouraging different raters to agree on the same score/rating becomes complex and challenging particularly given the range of variables that potentially affect their ratings. In this section, we highlight the importance of such variables from a language testing perspective in relation to rating scales, raters and rater training. In language testing, when comprehensibility is assessed, testers are in fact examining the speaker's ability to communicate her/his message successfully and effectively. Typically, samples of the candidate's speech are examined by trained raters on a set of pre-established and validated rating scales. Comprehensibility of the speaker's intended message is, in effect, examined through listeners' (i.e., raters') ability to extract the speaker's meaning and interpret intentions when judging the speaker's performance against a set of rating scales and rating descriptors. This suggests that a systematic and evidence-based discussion of the assessment of comprehensibility should include an analysis of rating scales and raters. Rating scales normally present a description of proficiency and a definition of the construct at pre-determined levels of proficiency often ranging from zero to 'nativelike'/advanced mastery. Raters, usually L1 speakers of the language or proficient L2 users of it, often have sufficient experience in language teaching or testing and receive some training on how to use the rating scales. In what follows, we first discuss representations of comprehensibility in two internationally recognised tests, TOEFL iBT and IELTS. In doing this, we will analyse the extent to which comprehensibility is represented from a pragmatic perspective. We then provide a summary of research on rating scales, raters and rater training in this area.

Rating scales. TOEFL iBT speaking scales, available online, range from 0 to 4, where 0 represents a speaker who does not respond to the question or whose response is not related to the topic, whereas 4 reflects a proficient speaker who fulfils all the demands of the task for each of the constructs under investigation. The speech samples collected through

TOEFL tasks are assessed in terms of four sub-constructs of general description, delivery, language use, and topic development.

In TOEFL iBT speaking rating descriptors, Delivery seems to be the category that considers aspects of the construct of comprehensibility proposed in this volume. Delivery focuses on pace, flow and temporal aspects of speech, and predominantly examines issues central to intelligibility including pronunciation and intonation. There are occasional references to clarity of meaning, although it is not known whether this clarity is linked with phonological, discoursal or pragmatic aspects of the delivery. While one may expect to see a reference to the assessment of comprehensibility in its full form, the focus of Delivery seems to be concerned with comprehensibility at a word and utterance level. Surprisingly, the description of Delivery at lower levels (e.g. Level 3) makes a vague reference to issues of comprehensibility at a meaning level by highlighting the importance of meaning in 'meaning may be obscured in places'. Such a reference to meaning is missing in the rating description of the higher levels implying that only low-proficiency speakers may struggle with comprehensibility at a meaning level.

The IELTS speaking rating scales are assessed at nine levels of proficiency ranging from 1 where no communication is possible to 9 where an effective and successful communication is achieved (0 is assigned to non-attendance). The four sub-constructs of speaking in IELTS are Fluency and coherence, Lexical resource, Grammatical range and accuracy, and Pronunciation (see Appendix 2 for further details). The analysis of the rating descriptors suggests that the concept of comprehensibility mainly spans over the two sub-constructs of Fluency and coherence and Pronunciation, with the former reflecting some aspects of comprehensibility at a discourse level (e.g. use of connectives and discourse markers) and the latter representing comprehensibility at a word and utterance level (e.g. mispronunciation of words and sounds). The sub-construct of Fluency and coherence also focuses on fluency aspects of performance including flow of speech, hesitations and repetitions. The rating descriptors, however, do not refer to comprehensibility at a meaning level. A reference to meaning is more visible in Lexical Resource criterion (at Bands 4 and 8) at a word level where communicating 'basic meaning' and 'precise meaning' are stipulated. Grammatical Range and Accuracy criterion highlights 'misunderstanding' and 'comprehension problems' at Bands 4, 5 and 6 referring to conveying meaning accurately at utterance level. None of the two former criteria make a reference to ease or difficulty of understanding meaning at a pragmatic level. Our analysis implies that comprehensibility at word and utterance level is clearly represented in the IELTS rating descriptors, whereas comprehensibility at a meaning (pragmatic) level does not have a strong presence. TOEFL iBT values comprehensibility of meaning more explicitly although only for lower levels of proficiency. It should be noted that the two tests are fundamentally different in terms of mode of communication, with TOEFL relying on monologic tasks while IELTS uses interactive speaking tasks, although the interactive nature of speaking is restricted by the testing conditions. Such differences are expected to have implications for how comprehensibility is assessed in these tests.

For reasons of scope, we will not be able to analyse comprehensibility scales in a wider range of international language tests (e.g. Aptis or PTE). However, what seems common is that comprehensibility is not usually given a distinct set of scales. In fact, it is mostly combined with a range of other sub-constructs of speaking including fluency, coherence and delivery. Another common characteristic of these tests is that they consider comprehensibility as a continuum and adopt a scalar assessment (Crowther et al. 2015; Kang et al., 2019). The length of the scales varies from 4 to 9 points, and polar adjectives such as easy/hard to understand or totally comprehensible/incomprehensible are used to rate the extent of comprehensibility.

Issues related to raters. Research in language testing (Winke, Gass & Myford, 2013; Kang et al., 2019; etc.) has provided ample evidence that judgements of comprehensibility are influenced by a range of factors related to raters. The influence of such factors on raters' judgements introduces an unsystematic variation to the assessment of language ability. Therefore, it is possible to argue that proficiency ratings of comprehensibility are susceptible to error. Even if it is not considered an error, such variation is problematic as it results from a range of different factors including rater linguistic and professional background, their social values, attitudes, and amount of experience and training.

Taguchi (2011), for example, examined rater variations in assessing pragmatic aspects of performance of 48 Japanese English as a Foreign language (EFL) students performing two different speech acts. Four L1 speakers of English, from different cultural backgrounds (one African American, one Asian American, and two Australians), were recruited to rate the performances in terms of appropriateness of the language in relation to the speech acts. The results highlighted a core of similarities but also portrayed many differences in terms of pragmatic norms and social values the raters considered when evaluating comprehensibility.

Winke et al. (2013), among others, have provided evidence that rater's level of comprehensibility is affected by their familiarity with the candidates' L1. The results of their study indicated that raters who spoke Spanish as a second language were "significantly more lenient with L1 Spanish test takers, as were L2 Chinese raters with L1 Chinese test takers" (Winke, et al., 2013, p. 231).

Another interesting study examining the dynamic role of raters in the assessment of comprehensibility is Nagel, Trofimovich and Bergenon (2019) who focused on raters' process of rating rather than its product. Examining 24 Spanish-speaking raters assessing L2 speech samples, the authors looked into different stages of rating by checking the raters' rating as the speech unfolded. Stimulated recall interviews were then used to determine the relationship between their thoughts and ratings. The results showed that raters can be divided in to three groups of dynamic, semi-dynamic and non-dynamic raters depending on the frequency of changing their rating during the process. Surprisingly, the majority of raters belonged to the non-dynamic group implying that the raters were less likely to change their overall rating as they listened to the speech sample throughout. An important finding of the study is that it offers evidence in support of a "substantial individual variation in how listeners approached the rating task and in the speech features that elicited a response" (p. 669).

Kang, Rubin and Kemrad (2019) examined variability of comprehensibility ratings among novice raters of various backgrounds. They asked 82 untrained raters from a range of background variables (L1 or L2 speakers status, educational background, EFL teaching experience, amount of exposure to L2 speakers' speech, and formal training in language and linguistics) to judge 112 speech samples of test-takers taking the TOEFL iBT speaking test. The results showed that approximately 20% of untrained raters' score variance was due to raters' background and attitudinal factors. The most important finding of this study was that providing training to the raters significantly reduced variability resulting from rater background and attitudinal variables.

A summary of the research reported above indicates that a range of variables under investigation affected raters' variability in rating comprehensibility. Despite the strong research evidence in the field of language testing that warns language assessment organisations against issues affecting raters' rating of comprehensibility, we can still observe several factors causing variations among raters' ratings that are not accounted for in the assessment of comprehensibility. The most important factors seem to be the L1 speaker status, amount of exposure to L2 speech, and raters' background and attitudes. This is to say L1 speaker raters are more lenient, and raters with more contact with L2 varieties of the language being tested often provide higher rankings of comprehensibility, especially regarding pragmatic aspects of communication.

Conclusion

In this chapter, we have argued that comprehensibility is affected by pragmatic factors including contextual, sociolinguistic and sociocultural elements of communication. The discussions provided in this chapter highlight the dynamic and multidimensional nature of comprehensibility, and show how different variables interact with one another to help promote (or prohibit) understanding the intended meaning. The contribution of pragmatic factors to comprehensibility and its interaction with other linguistic and discourse features, and paralinguistic aspects of communication is presented in Figures 8.1. To support our proposed perspective, we have reviewed the existing research that investigates the extent to which pragmatic aspects of communication can affect comprehensibility. Despite its significance, we note that research in this area is scarce and therefore little is known about the relationship between comprehensibility and pragmatic knowledge. The existing literature is particularly limited in that there are few experiments to examine the effects of pragmatic knowledge on comprehensibility while controlling for listener variables. These limitations indicate the need for more research in this area.

The chapter further highlights the need for a careful analysis of the construct of comprehensibility at pragmatic level for language testing purposes. Our analysis of the rating scales from two current tests of English suggested that this aspect of comprehensibility is not currently carefully considered, and the potential impact of pragmatic factors of speech on listeners' ease of understanding remains unknown in the assessment of speaking ability. Research in language studies has shown that the development of pragmatic knowledge correlates with development of proficiency (see Taguchi 2005, p. 544), implying that higher level learners are better at understanding the message (e.g. the implied meaning, indirect requests, or a message with little contextual cues). However, the rating scales we have analysed do not stipulate in what ways pragmatic aspects of speech may affect ease of understanding of a speaker's message.

Our discussions have also suggested that assessing the impact of pragmatics on comprehensibility throws new challenges at language testing organisations including the development of scales, descriptors and rater training materials that can account for a reliable, valid and fair assessment of this aspect of comprehensibility. The impact of listener-related variables on L2 comprehensibility, for example, imply that different listeners may provide different comprehensibility ratings for the same speaker. In line with previous research (Carey et al., 2011; Winke et al., 2013) we consider rater background factors (e.g. L1, experience, familiarity) as "a potential rater effect" (Winke et al., 2013: p. 231), and argue that rater training programmes should include materials to make raters aware of the dynamic nature of comprehensibility and the significant role these, as listeners, plays in this dynamic system. The range of pragmatic issues affecting listeners' comprehensibility imposes another challenge for language testing as it invites the development of comprehensibility descriptors and rater training materials to help raters present a professional judgement of speech samples' comprehensibility based on their intuitive judgements of comprehensibility. One way to deal with such a challenge is to control for the influence of listener backgrounds when developing comprehensibility descriptors and/or recruiting raters. An important implication of our discussions is to appreciate the dynamic nature of comprehensibility, particularly its co-constructed and dynamic nature, and to encompass the role of listeners as an indispensable part of the process.

CHAPTER 5

COMPREHENSIBILITY AND FLUENCY

Comprehensibility has been considered central to successful communication throughout this volume, since it highlights the listener's perceptions of the level of difficulty she/he experiences in understanding the speaker. We have argued thus far that difficulty in understanding a speaker's intended meaning occurs not only at a phonological level but at discourse and pragmatic levels. For similar reasons, fluency is fundamental to successful communication as it reflects fluid, smooth, effortless, and rapid production of the message in real time. Fluency, in essence, reflects the degree of automaticity in a speaker's speech and demonstrates the speaker's ability to use the language quickly and coherently without disrupting the flow and smoothness of speech. In simple terms, we can postulate that slow, effortful and interrupted speech or speech that is uncommonly disrupted by repetitions and repairs is difficult to comprehend. Lack of fluidity, smoothness, normal speed and frequent disruption of speech in a L2 speaker's spoken performance may reflect the information processing or linguistic challenges she/he is experiencing during the speech production process or when interacting her/his intended meaning. Such challenges in producing fluent speech, to be discussed in the following sections, appear to have a direct impact on comprehensibility.

Like comprehensibility, fluency is a complex and multidimensional construct defined in terms of a number of distinct but interrelated dimensions. Much research has recently focused on investigating the nature and construct of fluency, and noticeable developments are made that provide a more in-depth understanding of how different aspects of fluency affect comprehensibility. In order to examine and understand this relationship, we will first define and analyse fluency and discuss its measurement in the field. Drawing on such definitions and discussions, the chapter will then focus on the existing research on the relationship between fluency and comprehensibility.

Defining Fluency

The term fluency, as it is used in English, refers to two different but interrelated concepts. In the general sense of the term, fluency refers to a speaker's overall language ability/proficiency, whether in L1 or L2, denoting someone's natural ability to use language efficiently. In this sense, a fluent speaker is someone who is able to use the language efficiently and skillfully where the definition may go beyond speaking to include other language skills (e.g. she/he is a fluent writer). In the more specific, and linguistically relevant sense of the term, fluency refers to the efficient and skillful speaking ability and represents speedy, smooth and uninterrupted flow of language. These two perspectives have been historically known as 'broad' and 'narrow' senses of fluency (Lennon, 1990). More recently, Tavakoli and Hunter (2018) have argued that the concept of fluency can best be considered at four levels of 'very broad', 'broad', 'narrow' and 'very narrow' where the 'very broad' reflects overall L2 proficiency or mastery of language and the 'very narrow' represents speaker's fluency in detailed, objective and measurable indices such as amount of pause or rate of speech. In our discussions in this chapter, we are interested in fluency in its narrow sense and may frequently refer to research findings in relation to the very narrow perspective proposed by Tavakoli and Hunter (2018).

Much of research examining L2 fluency is primarily informed by a psycholinguistic perspective to second language acquisition (Segalowitz, 2010; Skehan, 2009), based on which fluency can be defined as 'rapid, smooth, accurate, lucid, and efficient translation of thought or communicative intention into language' (Lennon, 2000: 26). Such definitions primarily draw on the linguistic and cognitive processes underlying speech production and comprehension in order to explain the construct of fluency. For example, they assume fluency is achieved when "the psycholinguistic processes of speech planning and speech production are functioning easily and efficiently" (Lennon, 1990: 391), and therefore disfluency in a speaker's speech may indicate issues with speech planning and processing (e.g. struggling to put the concepts and thoughts together, needing more time to access the right lexical items, being challenged not knowing a grammatical structure, etc.). Fluency is also understood as a sign of increasing implicit acquisition of linguistic forms, what is usually referred to as 'procedural knowledge' (Schmidt, 1992). This concept denotes that when linguistic knowledge becomes procedural, primarily as a result of practice and repetition, speech production processes are facilitated leading to more fluent spoken performance.

Such perspectives, in effect, argue that fluency develops from slow and effortful language planning, processing and production to fluid, uninterrupted and rapid production of speech when language knowledge is proceduralised and speech production is automatised. Tavakoli and Wright (2020, p.3) consider this perspective to defining fluency as the "cognitive dimension of fluency", and argue that although the cognitive dimension has been fundamental to researching fluency in L2 studies, there is a second and equally important perspective to understanding and researching fluency which has largely remained under-researched. Tavakoli and Wright (2020, p.3) call this second perspective "fluency in interaction", and define it as

> the ability to ensure the speaker aims to be comprehensible to the listener; the ability to manage interactions well; and the ability to keep a conversation going appropriately given the context, purpose and audience (p.3).

They argue that focusing on both perspectives when examining fluency is indispensable as it echoes current models of fluency as a dynamic multifaceted phenomenon, in which cognitive factors interrelate with social experiences of interaction (Segalowitz, 2010, 2016).

Tavakoli and Wright's (2020) proposed perspective on fluency is pertinent to our discussion of comprehensibility in this book for a number of reasons. First of all, the 'fluency in interaction' perspective considers the listener as an active component of the meaning making process, underlining the impact of a speaker's fluency on the listener. This perspective is closely linked to our argument here in which we consider comprehensibility to be a joint endeavour between the speaker and listener. Second, considering fluency from both a cognitive and interactionist perspective would provide us with a framework that allows for an analytic understanding of the relationship between fluency and comprehensibility. Finally, in the field of language testing, such interactional perspectives to understanding spoken language performance are already ingrained in language benchmarks (e.g. the CEFR) and rating descriptors (e.g. IELTS speaking descriptors). For example, the CEFR recognises proficient speakers for their ability to "interact with a degree of fluency and spontaneity that makes regular interaction with speakers of the target language quite possible without imposing strain on either party" (Council of Europe, 2018, p.144). While such a dynamic perspective to comprehensibility (i.e., successful communication relies on not only the speaker but also the listener), is recognised as a principle in language testing documents (e.g. the CEFR), there is little clarity about how such listener factors can be examined and operationalised in language testing, or included in the development of language benchmarks and rating descriptors. What seems clear is that analysing fluency from a cognitive and interactionist perspective ties in more appropriately with the language testing context central to the purpose of this book. It would also enable us to develop a more in-depth understanding of the relationship between the two constructs and how they can be represented in the assessment of L2 speaking ability. In what follows, we will discuss the construct of fluency in more detail.

Analysing the Multidimensional Construct of Fluency

Current research in L2 fluency unanimously agrees that fluency is a complex and multidimensional construct (e.g. Foster, 2020; Segalowitz, 2010; Skehan, 2014; Tavakoli & Wright, 2020) in which the different dimensions interact with one another to explain the speaker's fluency. The most widely cited framework for understanding fluency as a multidimensional construct is that of Segalowitz (2010). After years of examining L2 fluency with different groups of L2 speakers in different contexts, Segalowitz (2010) proposed that the construct of L2 fluency can best be defined in terms of three distinct but interrelated dimensions of cognitive fluency, utterance fluency, and perceived fluency. Cognitive fluency, in Segalowitz's (2010) framework, refers to the speaker's "ability to efficiently mobilize and integrate the underlying cognitive processes responsible for producing utterances" (Segalowitz, 2010, p. 48); utterance fluency signifies the measurable aspects of fluency such as speed and pausing patterns; and perceived fluency demonstrates the listener's inferences about the speaker's cognitive fluency. Perceived fluency, in this sense, represents whether the listener considers the speech fluent and what characteristics of the speaker's fluency are more salient to them.

In Segalowitz's framework, the three dimensions of fluency are interrelated, interacting with one another in a dynamic manner. Cognitive fluency requires ease of planning and processing and rapid access to, and retrieval of, linguistic knowledge during the speech production process. Issues with cognitive fluency are usually evident when the speaker is challenged by any aspects of processing (e.g. understanding the linguistic information in individual sounds) and packaging information (e.g. understanding the difference between active and passive use of verb forms), understanding the concepts, and constructing the message (e.g.

access and retrieval of linguistic items). Challenges with cognitive fluency, an abstract concept, can be observed in different tangible aspects of the speaker's speech (i.e., utterance fluency), for example, in the form of a slowed down speed, repetitions or frequent pauses. These concrete and measurable features of speech can indeed, in Segalowitz's words (2010, p.48), reflect "the operation of the underlying speech processes". We will discuss these different measurable representations of fluency in more detail in the following section.

Perceived fluency relates to both cognitive and utterance fluency. It is closely linked to cognitive fluency as it demonstrates the inferences listeners make about the speaker's cognitive fluency. For example, when judging a speaker's fluency, the listeners often consider factors such as whether the speaker is producing language with a degree of difficulty, whether the performance suggests the speaker is challenged identifying the correct lexical items, or whether the speaker finds it difficult to convey their intended meaning in a timely manner. Perceived fluency, as mentioned earlier, is also related to utterance fluency. In making their judgements about a speaker's degree of fluency, listeners in principle use concrete and observable evidence in the speaker's speech (e.g. pauses, repetitions, and hesitations) to indicate the challenges the speaker may have faced. In other words, perceived fluency results from the listener drawing on the concrete aspects of fluency (utterance fluency) to derive judgements about the challenges the speaker is facing (cognitive fluency).

A simple example to show this interrelationship could be when a listener judges the speaker as disfluent (i.e., perceived fluency) because the speaker has paused several times in the middle of their speech (utterance fluency) to search for lexical items or grammatical structures (cognitive fluency).

Several studies have to date examined the relationship between perceived and utterance fluency, and have provided solid evidence about which utterance fluency measures best predict perceived fluency. One of the earliest studies, Kormos and Denes (2004), found that speech rate, mean length of run, and the number of stressed words produced per minute were the best predictors of perceived fluency. Derwing et al. (2004) also reported that speech rate and frequency of silent pauses in the speaker's speech can predict the listeners' perceptions of fluency. Examining the link between utterance and perceived fluency, Bosker, Pinget, Quene, Sanders, and de Jong (2013) investigated rater sensitivity to speakers' pausing behaviour. The results suggested that pause and speed were reliable predictors of untrained raters' perceived fluency. They also reported that in the English language a pause of 0.025 of a second was the threshold for considering a silent pause as a sign of disfluency. Another study relevant to our discussion here is Préfontaine, Kormos, and Johnson (2016) who examined perceptions of fluency in French as a second language. Examining speech samples of 40 adult learners of French of varying levels of proficiency studying at university, the authors reported that mean length of run and articulation rate were the most influential factors in raters' judgments, while the frequency of pause played a less important role. Interestingly, they found that, unlike previous research in this area, length of pause was positively related to perceived fluency. Given this finding was in contrast with most previous studies, the authors interpreted this in the light of cross-linguistic variations specific to French. Conducting a meta-analysis of research examining the relationship between perceived and utterance fluency, Suzuki, Kormos and Uchihara (2021) reported that while perceived fluency was strongly associated with speed and pause frequency and moderately with pause duration, only a weak relationship was observed between repair fluency and perceived fluency. In summary, the findings of research in this area suggest that slow speed of performance, frequent pausing – especially if not followed by a sufficiently long stretch of talk, frequent self-repetitions, and empty fillers are the factors most closely associated with perceptions of a disfluent speaker. It is worth noting that speech that is too fast, although not a typical characteristic of most L2 speakers' speech, is also considered as dysfluent with a damaging impact on comprehensibility. Other important findings in this area include the existence of a threshold for what listeners consider to be a pause, and evidence of cross-linguistic differences in what listeners expect in different languages.

We have now presented a summary of research on the relationship between utterance and perceived fluency as it is central to our discussion of the relationship between comprehensibility and fluency to which we will return in the Comprehensibility and Fluency Section below. Before that, however, we will need to discuss whether and to what extent it is possible to measure utterance fluency reliably and objectively. This topic is necessary as most research on the relationship between comprehensibility and fluency uses these objective measures of fluency as part of their analysis.

Measuring Fluency Objectively

Since the 1980s, L2 researchers have been using a wide range of objective measures to assess fluency for teaching, assessment and research purposes. Examples of such measures include 'number of words produced per minute', 'total amount of pause per performance', and 'frequency of stressed words in an uninterrupted stretch of talk'. Over the past two decades, however, approaches to measuring fluency have received much more research attention and have consequently been examined more carefully and systematically. The development of technology has also made a major contribution to the accuracy of measuring temporal aspects of utterance fluency. As a result of these developments, it is possible to claim that the measurement of fluency has become more systematic and evidence-based since the 1980s.

Providing a historical overview of these measures, Tavakoli and Wright (2020) argue that many of these measures were initially borrowed from other neighbouring disciplines, such as clinical language sciences (e.g. speech-language pathology) and working with patients suspected to have suffered from a brain damage (e.g. diagnosing aphasia). In these disciplines, similar to L2 studies, features such as speech rate and length of utterance have been commonly used to represent patients' fluency based on which clinical decisions were to be made. Since then, L2 studies have made substantial progress in developing approaches to measuring fluency in ways that are more suitable to L2 studies, and L2 speakers. In the following section, we provide a summary of the most important developments in the field of measuring L2 fluency over the past decades. By doing this we aim to provide a measurement framework that can be used when analysing the relationship between comprehensibility and fluency.

As discussed above, different L2 studies in the field have used a range of fluency measures to evaluate L2 learners', test takers' and research participants' fluency. The wide range of measures used and the less-than-systematic approach to operationalising them raised questions about which of these measures best represented the construct of fluency. In order to respond to such questions, Skehan (2003), and Tavakoli and Skehan (2005), proposed a new framework in which fluency was characterised in terms of speed, breakdown and repair measures (see Appendix 3 for a full list of utterance fluency measures and how they are calculated). These three aspects of utterance fluency were later linked to different stages of the speech production process (de Bot, 1992; Levelt, 1989), enabling researchers to make tangible connections between observable features of speech and the speech production process (see Tavakoli & Wright, 2020, for a full discussion).

Speed fluency, in this framework, refers to the concept of how speedy someone's spoken performance is, or the speed with which her/his speech is delivered. In this sense, speed can be reflected in the number of syllables produced per minute, number of syllables produced in a stretch of talk between two pauses, or proportion of speech to total amount of performance time. Later on, Skehan (2014) and Tavakoli, Nakatsuhara, and Hunter (2017, 2020) argued that for an accurate measurement of fluency, it was necessary to distinguish between pure and composite speed measures. This suggests utterance fluency can also be measured through composite fluency, in which two aspects of fluency are combined to demonstrate the degree of fluency in one's speech (e.g. speed and pausing may combine to show speech rate). These researchers have argued that speed should be measured independently of pausing (articulation rate, i.e., total number of syllables per performance time excluding pauses) and in combination with pauses (speech rate, i.e., total number of syllables per performance time including pauses). These two aspects of speed provide very useful information about fluency especially when individual differences in speaking style in terms of speed and pausing are considered (de Jong et al., 2015).

An important progression in measuring speed has been made possible through the development of digital technology. Software such as GoldWave, Audacity, and PRAAT have made it possible for researchers to analyse speech and measure its temporal aspect with high precision and reliability. Another development in the field is the new research-based understanding of the units of measurement. For example, given the differences between morphological structures of different languages, it is now known that using syllables (rather than words) is a more appropriate unit of measuring speed. Similarly, research has indicated that the base linguistic units of analysis should be chosen carefully, that is, AS-Unit (analysis of speech unit by Foster et al., 2000) is more relevant to analysing speech than previously used units such as T-Unit (Hunt, 1965) which are considered appropriate for written language.

Breakdown fluency, in Skehan's (2003) framework, refers to the silences (pauses) that break down the flow of communication. Pause, although a natural part of communication, can be considered as a sign of disfluency if it occurs too frequently, in inappropriate positions or for long durations. In L2 fluency studies, pause can now be examined in terms of its length, frequency, location and character. That is to say, it is important to examine how long the pause is, how frequently it is happening, where it is occurring in an utterance (mid-clause or end-clause positions), and whether it is filled or unfilled. While previously researchers considered longer pauses as signs of disfluency (e.g. one second in Foster & Skehan, 1996, or 0.4 second in Freed, 2000), the latest findings of research in L2 fluency studies (De Jong et al., 2011; De Jong & Bosker, 2013) indicate that for L1 speakers of English a pause of longer than 0.25 of a second seems noticeable. This threshold may be different in other languages.

Frequency of pausing is another important characteristic of breakdown fluency to be carefully considered when assessing L2 speakers' fluency. The existing research evidence (Bosker et al., 2013) suggests that pause frequency is a more crucial indicator of breakdown fluency than pause length. Particularly relevant to our discussion of comprehensibility is that pause frequency appears to have a more substantial impact on perceived fluency, implying that it is the frequency of pause rather than its length that affects listeners (e.g. Préfontaine, 2013; Préfontaine & Kormos, 2016). In terms of pause location, there is ample research evidence to suggest pauses occurring in mid-clause positions, compared to those produced at clause or unit boundaries, are considered as a characteristic of L2 speakers and therefore signify disfluency (Kahng, 2014; Segalowitz, 2010; Tavakoli, 2011). Some researchers (Tavakoli & Wright, 2020) have suggested that location of pauses would have an important influence on the listeners' perceptions of fluency.

The final characteristic of pause to consider when assessing breakdown fluency is the character of pause, for example, whether the pause remains silent/unfilled or if it if filled with empty fillers such as 'er', and 'uhm'. L2 researchers (Clark & Fox Tree, 2002; Schmidt & Beers Fägersten, 2010) maintain that these two different forms of pause may reflect different processes. For example, while both silence and filled pauses may demonstrate language processing demands, filled pauses can highlight emphasis, discourse organisation and communication strategies (Dewaele, 1996; Schmidt & Beers Fägersten, 2010). Cross-linguistic studies (e.g. Tian, Maruyama, & Ginzburg, 2017) have also suggested that some languages vary over use of silent and filled pauses (e.g. silent pauses are commonly used for memory-retrieval in English and Chinese but to ensure appropriateness in Japanese), and there are conventions about which specific meanings different empty fillers convey in different varieties of a given language (e.g. British English, but not American English, uses "um" to signal a more severe problem than "uh").

Repair fluency represents the effort a speaker makes to repair their speech during and immediately after the production of an utterance. Repair measures, also called dysfluency measures, are usually calculated by examining the frequency of repetitions, replacements, reformulations, and self-corrections per unit of time. This aspect of utterance fluency has remained relatively under-researched, and as such its measurement has not changed a lot over the past decades.

To sum up the discussions in this section, it is possible to argue that, theoretically, the new approach to measuring fluency (speed, breakdown and repair) has helped develop a better understanding of not only how fluency is objectively measured but how these measures can be used to shed light on the L2 speech production process. For example, it is now known that speed of performance may reflect the underlying cognitive and language processing challenges (e.g. searching for ideas or linguistic units may slow down the speaker); pausing may indicate the speaker's working memory and information processing capacity (e.g. pausing to plan for what to be said next) or their communication strategies (e.g. using filled pauses to keep the listener engaged); and repair measures can highlight the underlying monitoring processes (e.g. self-correcting an error).

Despite all these developments and contributions, several important questions and challenges remain in relation to the measurement of fluency. For example, there is strong research evidence (Duran-Karaoz & Tavakoli, 2020; Peltonen, 2018; Suzuki, 2021) to suggest that L1 and L2 fluency behaviours are inter-related. That is to say, an L2 speaker's speed, pausing patterns and use of repair measures can to some extent be predicted based on their L1 speaking style and fluency behaviour. This finding implies that any measurement of fluency will inevitably include an individual-learner related variance that has to be accounted for. However, by taking account of the speaker's L1 fluency behaviour it will be possible to factor in the contribution of this individual variation in fluency that is unrelated to L2 proficiency.

As discussed above, there is also emerging evidence to indicate there are different conventions and expectations (e.g. conventions for length of pause or use of fillers) of fluency behaviour in different languages. Listeners, therefore, can be expected to transfer these conventions from one language to another when judging a speaker's fluency without realising the cross-linguistic variations. Finally, it is necessary to point out that the technical terms in this area are not always used consistently across studies. For example, while pauses are widely known as a measure of breakdown fluency (Skehan, 2003; Tavakoli & Skehan, 2005), in some studies 'hesitation' is used to denote pauses and silences (Trofimovich et al., 2017). Such inconsistencies may obscure comparison between studies.

Comprehensibility and Fluency (Utterance, Cognitive and Perceived Fluency)

In this section, we examine the relationship between comprehensibility and different aspects of fluency. Before drawing on a summary of research conducted in this area, however, it is necessary to discuss the connection between the two constructs. Comprehensibility refers to the level of ease (or difficulty) a listener experiences when interacting with a speaker. This level of ease depends on a range of factors, discussed in Chapters 1–5, including whether the speaker speaks fluently (i.e., natural, uninterrupted and fluid speech, etc.). Perceived fluency, on the other hand, examines the language features that encourage or inhibit flow, fluidity and effortlessness of speech. The two constructs are similar in that they both tap into listeners' perceptions and/or intuitions about the speaker's speech. However, they are different in that comprehensibility focuses on the difficulty/ease with which speech is understood, whereas perceived fluency demonstrates the language features that affect listeners' perceptions of flow, fluidity and effortlessness. Different aspects of utterance fluency, for example speed of performance or frequent interruptions, that affect perceived fluency would inevitably affect listeners' comprehensibility, and as such fluency is considered an important predictor of comprehensibility. It is therefore reasonable to expect that the two constructs correlate with one another and a degree of overlap is observed between the two. Reporting a high correlation of .95 between fluency and comprehensibility, Suzuki and Kormos (2020) provide support to the claim that listeners attend to overlapping features of speech when forming judgments of each of the two constructs.

The two constructs, however, are different as one requires attention to the ease of understanding (affected by a range of different linguistic factors), and the other is specifically interested in fluidity and smoothness of speech. There are two important differences to highlight about the relationship between perceived fluency and comprehensibility. First, in evaluating perceived fluency, listeners are expected to focus on specific aspects of speech (e.g. flow, speed, and repair) without taking into account the other linguistic features of speech including phonological, grammatical or lexical elements. In contrast, when evaluating comprehensibility listeners often draw on a range of linguistic features of speech (e.g. lexical, grammatical, discoursal and pragmatic) to determine how easy/difficult it is to understand the speaker's intended meaning. This reflects the broader concept of comprehensibility compared to the narrower sense of perceived fluency. Second, variations are observed, both within and between the constructs of comprehensibility and perceived fluency, in the operationalisation of the listener variables. For example, while specific questions about aspects of utterance fluency (e.g. pauses and repetitions) are asked when listeners are invited to evaluate perceived fluency, judgements of comprehensibility are often reflected in more generic concepts of ease of understanding (e.g. IELTS "the speaker can generally be understood throughout" – see Appendix 2). It is important that these similarities and differences are considered when examining the relationship between the two for language testing and research purposes.

Based on this initial discussion, a relationship between comprehensibility and utterance fluency is also anticipated. To understand the relationship between the two in more depth, we now turn to previous research that has closely examined this relationship. There is ample L2 research evidence to suggest comprehensibility is affected by the speakers' utterance fluency. The research evidence dates back to the 1980s with Gass and Varonis (1984) proposing a scheme for analysing comprehensibility in which several factors were considered (see Chapter 4 for a detailed discussion). In their framework, Gass and Varonis included fluency (i.e., what we now consider utterance fluency) as one of the key variables that affect the construct of comprehensibility. Since then, other L2 studies have provided strong and consistent research evidence that fluency is one of the main contributing factors to influence comprehensibility (Kang et al., 2010; Munro & Derwing, 1998; Saito et al., 2016).

In an early study, Derwing et al. (2004) examined whether judgements of fluency, comprehensibility and accentedness were related to measures of utterance fluency (mean length of run, pauses, and speech rate). In previous studies, these authors had shown that although comprehensibility and accentedness were related they were partially independent features of L2 speech. Recruiting 28 untrained raters to judge samples of speech produced by beginner English L2 learners of L1 Mandarin, Derwing et al. (2004) reported that fluency and comprehensibility ratings were highly correlated (e.g. correlation coefficients of up to r = .873). Their results also suggested that fluency was more strongly related to comprehensibility than to accentedness, a finding that has since been replicated in several other studies (e.g. Crowther, Trofimovich, Saito, & Isaacs, 2015; Saito, Trofimovich, & Issac, 2017; Trofimovich, Kennedy, & Blanchet, 2017).

O'Brien (2014), in a study of German L2 learners judging other L2 learner peers, also L1 speakers of German, examined the listeners' ratings of accentedness, comprehensibility and fluency. The results of her study indicated that for comprehensibility, the L2 listeners were able to understand their fellow learners' speech "in spite of their being accented and disfluent" (O'Brien, 2014: 739). When rating L1 speakers' comprehensibility, the L2 learners' ratings indicated that speech rate, filled pauses, corrections, repetitions, and factors related to morphological and lexical errors were the key characteristics of speech associated with comprehensibility. When rating fellow learners' comprehensibility, the listeners relied on a range of aspects including morphological, lexical, and stress assignment errors, suggesting comprehensibility judgements were sometimes associated with factors beyond pronunciation and accent.

Overall, and regardless of the status of the speakers (whether they were L2 or L1 speakers), the listeners in O'Brien's (2014) study consistently rated speech samples containing fewer corrections, repetitions and filled pauses as more comprehensible, highlighting the intricate relationship between repair fluency and comprehensibility. This result is worth noting as it seems processing speech samples containing disfluencies (e.g. repetitions, corrections and filled pauses) is perceived as more demanding for the listeners and therefore affecting their ratings of comprehensibility. O'Brien (2014, p.742) concludes that "it was factors related to phonetic realizations, speed and fluency of speech, stress assignment, and lexis and syntax that predicted which speech samples produced by L2 learners were easiest to understand". O'Brien's findings highlight the inter-connectedness of the concepts of comprehensibility and fluency demonstrating that different aspects of utterance fluency (speed, breakdown and repair) interact with the level of ease/difficulty the listeners experience when trying to comprehend a speaker.

Saito, Trofimovich, and Issac (2017) examined the linguistic influences on comprehensibility among 40 native French speakers of English performing narrative tasks extemporaneously. The participants' performances were rated by 20 L1 speakers of English for comprehensibility, accentedness, and 11 linguistic variables in different domains of language including phonology, grammar, and discourse structure. The results suggested that the raters' judgements of comprehensibility were associated with several linguistic variables spanning different linguistic dimensions (e.g. vowel/consonant errors, word stress, fluency, lexis, grammar) when judging comprehensibility. Of interest to the focus of our discussion is the finding that comprehensibility was closely linked with measures of speed and breakdown fluency. Saito et al. (2017) reported high correlations between mean length of run and frequency of unfilled pauses with raters' judgements of comprehensibility implying that a slow rate of speech and frequent silent pauses can negatively affect perceptions of comprehensibility. The authors explain this relationship in the light of the challenges a listener experiences when understanding the speaker by arguing that "comprehensibility is associated with all aspects of speech that contribute to listener effort in extracting the overall meaning of an utterance" (Saito et al., 2017, p. 457).

Aiming to develop a set of rating scales for comprehensibility to be used by language teachers when judging their students, Isaacs, Trofimovich, and Foote (2018, 2020) postulated comprehensibility as a multidimensional construct comprising several aspects, including pronunciation, fluency, vocabulary and grammar. In their description of the comprehensibility analytical scales for fluency, they focused on two aspects of fluency as crucial features that affect comprehensibility: speed and breakdown fluency measures. The authors suggest these two aspects of fluency, that is, whether the speaker's speech is delivered at a normal speed and whether pauses are used reasonably and at appropriate junctures determine the amount of effort needed to understand the speaker. Given O'Brien's (2014) findings summarised above, it is surprising that Isaacs et al. (2018) did not include in their study repair measures as a feature of fluency that may potentially affect comprehensibility.

In two inter-related studies, Tromfimovich and colleagues (Kennedy, Blanchet, & Trofimovich, 2014, & Trofimovich, Kennedy, & Blanchet, 2017) examined the development of comprehensibility in an instructional setting. While we will be discussing the pedagogical findings of these two studies in more depth in Chapter 6, here it seems necessary to discuss their findings in relation to the connection between fluency and comprehensibility. The two studies measured fluency in terms of mean length of run and speech hesitations. In these studies, speech hesitations refer to all instances of pauses (both filled and unfilled) and pauses inside a rhythmic group. They found that the learners developed different aspects of comprehensibility and fluency during the course of interaction.

Pertinent to our discussion in this chapter is their finding with respect to the internal relationship between different aspects of fluency and comprehensibility. They found that both comprehensibility and fluency were associated with "longer, unbroken stretches of speech" and "with fewer hesitations" (Trofimovich et al., 2017, p. 44), implying that comprehensibility and fluency may be internally connected or overlapping constructs. They argue that regardless of whether this quality of speech should be called comprehensibility or fluency, it is usually reflected in fewer intonation errors, longer runs, pitch range, and fewer pauses.

Another relevant study is Spezzini (2004) who examined patterns of use and levels of comprehensibility among 12th graders Spanish speaking learners of English in Paraguay. Similar to previous studies, Spezzini (2004) reported that the L1 speaking raters' perceptions of comprehensibility were influenced by the speakers' overall fluency and prosodic features of their speech. The final study to report here is Suzuki and Kormos (2020) who examined the linguistic dimensions of comprehensibility and perceived fluency when investigating 40 Japanese L1 English L2 speakers performing an argumentative task. The results of their study indicated that raters' comprehensibility and fluency judgements were strongly associated, confirming "the conceptual similarity between comprehensibility and higher-order fluency" (p. 159). Following Lennon, they have defined higher-order fluency as "the degree to which listener attention is held" (Lennon, 2000, p. 34), and argue that more comprehensible speech enables listeners to maintain their attention more easily while extracting, suggesting that highly comprehensible speech tends to be simultaneously perceived as highly fluent speech (Suzuki & Kormos, 2020). Their study further provides strong evidence that comprehensibility is related to articulation rate, implying that ease of understanding depends, to a great extent, on how smoothly information is presented in speech. Their results also clearly suggested that breakdown fluency also had an impact on comprehensibility, with mid-clause pauses impeding understanding.

Saito (2020) examined the relationship between collocational use of language and comprehensibility. Collocational use of language is relevant to fluency as research in second language acquisition (SLA) has provided evidence to propose collocational use of language makes speech more fluent (Tavakoli & Uchihara, 2020; Wood, 2010; Wray, 2000, 2002). Explaining the study's rationale, Saito (2020) argues that while in the area of L2 comprehensibility, much attention is paid to examining the phonological aspects of L2 speech, the lexical profile of comprehensible L2 speech has generally remained under-researched. Collecting data from 85 Japanese learners of English as a second language, Saito asked ten raters to assess learners' speech for comprehensibility and lexical appropriateness. The samples were then assessed for a range of lexical measures aimed at collocational use of language. The results demonstrated that learners' comprehensibility was determined by use of low-frequency collocations such as infrequent, abstract and complex words. In a similar study, Tavakoli and Uchihara (2020) found evidence of the relationship between the use of multi-word units and a range of fluency measures. The findings of these two studies taken together suggests that fluency and comprehensibility are inherently connected to collocational use of language. More research is certainly needed to shed light on the relationship between lexicogrammatical aspects of L2 speech and comprehensibility.

The summary we have provided above demonstrates that different aspects of utterance fluency seem to be connected to comprehensibility. Studies reported above indicate that speed of speech, amount and frequency of pauses (both filled and unfilled), and frequency of corrections, repetitions and hesitations are key aspects of fluency that affect listeners' perceptions of comprehensibility. The robust research evidence provided above encourages us to conclude that fluency and comprehensibility are inherently interrelated and may overlap to some extent. What links the two concepts together in this sense is that the observable aspects of speech (i.e., utterance fluency) play an important role in informing listeners' judgements of comprehensibility. Listeners consider longer stretches of speech, speech that is not frequently or inappropriately interrupted by pauses, and speech that is not disrupted by frequent corrections, reformulations and hesitations, as comprehensible. The existing research evidence also indicates that perhaps certain measures of utterance fluency appear to demonstrate stronger relationships with comprehensibility than others. For example, mean length of run, speech rate and distribution of pauses have been shown in numerous studies to influence ratings of comprehensibility, whereas fewer studies have shown repair fluency to affect comprehensibility. It can be hypothesised that although repair interrupts the flow of speech leading to a negative impact on perceived fluency, it does not necessarily have a damaging impact on the ease with which the speaker's message is understood since successfully conducted repair (e.g. repair that has corrected an error) can have a positive impact on comprehensibility. Repair in SLA has commonly been examined through the frequency of interruptions (e.g. repetitions, hesitations, reformulations and self-corrections) where all different types of repair are often bundled in one group. It is possible to anticipate that some kinds of repair (e.g. reformulations) are of benefit to understanding the speaker's message, whereas others (e.g. frequent false starts) are not. Without further research in which repair measures are carefully operationalised and in which they are individually investigated, it will be difficult to confirm which types of repair contribute to promoting or inhibiting comprehensibility. Overall, more research is needed to illuminate the intricate relationship between the two constructs.

Conclusion

We started this chapter by reiterating the fact that comprehensibility and fluency are constructs that are shaped and developed as a joint endeavour between the speaker and listener in the context of communication. It is therefore necessary to emphasise that what sounds comprehensible and/or fluent to one listener may not be perceived equally comprehensible and/or fluent by another; and what is acceptable as comprehensible and fluent in one context may not be considered the same in another. The dynamic nature of fluency and comprehensibility, however, deserves more attention in language testing as currently the listener contribution to the ratings of fluency and comprehensibility is not carefully taken into consideration. What remains constant in this relationship, however, is that ratings of comprehensibility and fluency are shown to be highly correlated, implying that a listener's degree of comprehensibility can, at least to some extent, depends on the speaker's fluency. In addition, it is necessary to point out that all aspects of speed, breakdown and repair fluency can affect listeners' perceptions of comprehensibility. Our discussion above also demonstrated that perceived fluency and comprehensibility are often affected by the temporal measures of speech such as speed of performance and pausing behaviour. The inter-relationship between the two constructs also highlights the challenges the listeners face in processing samples of speech and may reflect the challenges the speakers face when speaking.

Our discussions above also suggested that the relationship between fluency and comprehensibility may depend on other factors such as speakers' speaking style, L1 fluency behaviour and cross-linguistic factors. This conclusion also reminds us of the dynamic and co-constructed nature of comprehensibility and the fact that higher degrees of comprehensibility can be achieved when the listener has some knowledge of factors such as the speaker's L1 and speaking style. Finally, our discussion in this chapter suggests that while comprehensibility is linked with a broader range of linguistic categories of speech (see Figure 8.1), fluency and pronunciation seem to play a crucial role in ratings of comprehensibility. For a full discussion of such factors, see discussions in Chapters 1–4.

CHAPTER 6

TECHNOLOGY AND COMPREHENSIBILITY

At the conclusion of Kazuo Ishiguro's book Klara and the Sun (2020), a character in the novel talks to Klara, a computerised, robotic "Artificial Friend" (AF):

> Okay. Here it is. Klara, the fact is, there's growing and widespread concern about AFs right now. People are saying how you've become too clever. They're afraid because they can't follow what's going on inside any more. They can see what you do. They accept that your decisions, your recommendations, are sound and dependable, almost always correct. But they don't like not knowing how you arrive at them... [They] don't understand how AFs think. Fine, then let's go take a look under the hood. Let's reverse-engineer. What you don't like are sealed black boxes. Okay, let's open them. Once we see inside, not only do things get a lot less scary, we'll learn.

The impact of technology on our lives and society is being felt ever more profoundly. In particular, the influence of some form of artificial intelligence (AI) on individual choices – whether about purchases or presidents – has brought with it both a sense of opportunity and a sense of trepidation. Opportunity because it enables us to do so much more, so much more efficiently, and possibly more reliably; trepidation because we don't entirely understand it and we don't know what we don't know. The Ishiguro quote encapsulates the desire to remove distinctly human characteristics – such as bias, or the impact of fatigue or capacity to get a task done – from processes and decisions while retaining (human) control over the outcome. This tension is particularly acute in decisions that directly impact people's lives in a major way, such as social security eligibility, identification of potential perpetrators of a crime – and language test results that directly affect an individual's ability to progress to higher education, work in a particular job, or immigrate to a particular country. As such, this chapter presents a perspective on how the assessment of spoken comprehensibility can be impacted by technology, as well as providing key considerations to enable responsible use of technology in language assessment while mitigating the potential threats inherent in 'handing over' life-changing decision-making to algorithms.

In previous chapters we explored the complex construct of comprehensibility, focusing on linguistic proxies in Chapters 2 and 3 and venturing into the socio-pragmatic in Chapter 4. Definitive conclusions about which features contribute to comprehensibility and how these should be measured remain elusive and it is tempting to embrace technical solutions for the assessment of this complex and dynamic construct. Indeed, technological advances are having a significant impact on language assessment in general and in this chapter we examine the key ways in which these could impact our understanding of, and the insights it is possible to gain into, comprehensibility as a construct as we have presented it in this book. While this chapter recognises the potential of technology to positively influence language assessment, we consider the possible threats that it presents to the evaluation of spoken communication skills in particular and look to how we might mitigate these through open and transparent – as far as is possible – evaluation of the systems that are used.

Technology in language assessment spans a range of areas such as the mode of delivery (e.g. on computer rather than on paper), automated (i.e. machine) rating of performance, automated generation of test items, remote proctoring of computer-based tests (using either human invigilators or Artificial Intelligence [AI], or a combination), and digital test security and encrypted certification. We are primarily interested in the first two areas which are likely to have the most direct impact on the assessment of comprehensibility in speaking.

This chapter is not a technical discussion of machine capabilities or computer science as applied to spoken language use and testing. Nor does it seek to discuss the potential for technology to support language learners to achieve comprehensibility, which is beyond the scope of this book. The intention is not to be reductionist, but rather to provide educators and testing-practitioners with an easy to understand introduction to the processes at work when computers meet language assessment. We also hope this introduction can empower and encourage practitioners to critically evaluate the adoption and use of technology-enabled testing so that their responses to the changes can be informed and balanced. To this end, we present a list of considerations at the end of the chapter that can be adapted for the evaluation of technology in language assessment. The chapter includes three main sections. The first section provides an overview of some broad considerations in relation to the use of technology in language assessment, the second considers the impact of using technology to deliver speaking tests and the third focuses on the rating of speaking performance by machines. These have different, but overlapping, consequences and considerations in relation to the assessment of comprehensibility which will be discussed throughout the chapter.

Technology and Language Testing

It is not for the first time that language testing has drawn on technology to facilitate efficiencies and improvements; the use of cassette recorders and telephones, for example, is well-known to speaking test examiners. Technology brings with it many advantages for language assessment and learning. Test-takers see various benefits, including reduction in the time it takes to receive test scores, more flexibility in scheduling tests, and accessibility: for those affected by remote geography or socio-political unrest, access to a test through a local device can open up work and educational opportunities or even a lifeline to international mobility that would otherwise not be possible. For testing organisations, computer delivered tests mean scalability – more tests can be delivered more rapidly to a greater number of test-takers – and economy, given the costs of human raters and, especially, the expense of travel by interlocutors to deliver face-to-face speaking tests. The positive impact on test security is attractive to score users (such as universities or immigration departments), since the recording and storage of biometric data, in addition to the ability to invigilate tests from afar, could allow for stronger test security and more robust digitally verifiable certification, although remote invigilation also comes with potential threats to security.

There are challenges and factors that require careful consideration before wholeheartedly adopting technology in language testing. Chief of these is the widening digital divide which the COVID-19 pandemic brought into stark relief because, while technology offers increased accessibility, it is largely only to those who already have access to hardware, software, an affordable internet connection, and the ability to use these tools. In the case of international tests, an additional hurdle can be the ability to pay online. The reduction in travel to in-person testing almost certainly has a positive environmental impact but this could be off-set by the computing power required to facilitate machine learning and encryption for test-security purposes, particularly where non-renewable energy supplies electricity.

One caveat that needs to be highlighted in any discussion of technological process in general is that it is fast-moving and, increasingly, language test developers make continuous iterations and improvements to their technology-enabled systems. As readers engage with this chapter, it is worth considering that some core issues may already have been addressed; nevertheless, there are broader challenges and considerations that we need to constantly remind ourselves about when adopting technology in both testing and assessment. The last section in this chapter provides a list of questions that all language assessment stakeholders should be asking when designing, developing, using, or evaluating technology-enabled tests.

What we have discussed so far relates to the general use of technology in language assessment. From a comprehensibility perspective, we focus on two broad threats posed by technology. First, there is the potential that the ability we are measuring is changed through the use of computers to deliver and complete the tests (rather than pen-and-paper testing). The second broad threat is around automated assessment systems, where machines are used to rate spoken proficiency; while this brings with it potential benefits for the evaluation of comprehensibility, there are challenges associated with data sampling and the threat of encoding bias within automated systems. These form the main discussion areas in this chapter.

It is important to observe that the use of technology in language assessment is not an all-or-nothing dichotomy, and in acknowledgement of this O'Sullivan (2020) has outlined a spectrum of human/machine interaction in the rating of language performance. This applies to other areas mentioned above, with the degree of human collaboration varying in the application of remote proctoring systems, automated item generation and delivery of the speaking test itself. The existence of hybrid systems where there is a combination of human and machine rating, with humans focusing on different skills or rating responses that are out of tolerance range at the automated rating stage, is testimony to not only the gaps in machine capabilities but also to the unique human ability to co-construct meaning by drawing on an array of as yet not fully explicable factors. Simply put, machines are good at measuring technical traits such as grammatical complexity whereas humans provide more nuanced evaluations of communicative effect, for example.

Mode of Delivery

In this book, we consider 'delivery mode' as being the use of technological devices to deliver one or more components of a test of speaking. In other words, tapping into the ability and arriving at an assessment of a test-taker's speaking proficiency with the aid of a technical device. While the phrase 'technology-enabled language testing' brings to mind the use of computers and AI, technology has long been assisting language testers to do their job (Qian, 2009; Chapelle & Voss, 2016). An example is the PhonePass test of the 1990s (Bernstein, 1999) which was delivered over the phone and has metamorphosised into Pearson's Versant tests of Arabic, Dutch, English, French and Spanish (Pearson, 2021). Computers (e.g. TOEFL iBT (ETS, 2021)) and tape recorders (e.g. where IELTS is second marked (IELTS, 2021)) have been used for asynchronous rating for many years. Increasingly, technology is helping to deliver tests online across a range of devices. While the language testing industry was already on the tech-enabled delivery trajectory, the COVID-19 pandemic hastened the shift towards this mode as in-person Oral Proficiency Interviews (OPIs) became more difficult to administer.

The impact of mode of delivery on the assessment of comprehensibility cannot be discussed without first considering the different approaches to obtaining speech samples for evaluation, in other words, how a test-taker's speaking performance is elicited by means of the tasks on a test (Clark, 1979; O'Loughlin, 2001). These are inextricably linked to views and theories about the speaking construct itself and are best illustrated diagrammatically (Figure 6.1., expanded on below). First, however, we need to consider the general consensus on the critical link between construct definition (the ability being measured) and the inferences that are made about a test-taker's ability based on the score; Bachman and Palmer (1996) and Luoma (2004) frame this in terms of the TLU situation and how it is connected to the score. The TLU domain is the intended real-life language-use situation that test-takers will need to engage in, an ability that the test aims to assess. The TLU domain shapes the construct definition and the test and task specifications, and can be used to understand how well the test taps into the communicative skills that are required in the intended real-life situations. For example, if the test purports to assess the ability to present an academic report, the test tasks need to be shown to tap into the linguistic, cognitive and content aspects of this ability.

The ultimate and ideal test of the ability is the real-life task itself. However, no test can replicate this without encountering major practical challenges such as timing or administration; tests are 'snapshots' of a broader, underlying ability. There are different approaches to how this ability is tapped into, ranging from direct tests which seek to replicate at least some real-life TLU communicative tasks to wholly indirect tests which measure the speaking ability by proxy, where an indicator (e.g. speech rate) is considered to be representative of overall proficiency. The relative restrictions on interactive communication posed by the use of computers to deliver tests (either as a result of technological capability or in the interests of reducing costs and work associated with employing human interlocutors to deliver the tests online) make the indirect approach particularly attractive. Indicators such as vocabulary range or speech rate are easily elicited through technological means and this makes the indirect approach particularly attractive.

Figure 6.1. situates the different approaches to testing speaking along a continuum and includes examples of well-recognised international tests of English, including technology-mediated tests; this will serve as context for our discussion on the challenges posed to comprehensibility by the use of technology in test delivery. As can be seen, on the one side of the spectrum lie indirect tests. In this type of assessment, speech samples are not elicited and no attempt to reflect the TLU-domain is made; an extreme example (not involving technology) is Lado's (1961) proposal to measure pronunciation using a paper-based test – test-takers had to identify 'odd one out' sounds in a group of written words. A tech-driven example of an indirect task that reports sub-scores on 'comprehension' and 'conversation' is an item which requires the test-taker to identify, from a set of decontextualised audio-recorded words, those that are *not* part of the target language, that is, the set includes invented words (see Appendix 4 (Duolingo, n.d.), although there are increasingly components of the Duolingo English Test that are semi-direct, and this question type appears to have been discontinued in the latest iteration of the test (Duolingo, 2023)). The rationale is that indicators of general language ability (e.g. lexical range) can be extrapolated to more general skills such as conversational ability.

On the right-hand side of the continuum lie direct tests which attempt to replicate the TLU-domain as closely as test conditions and practicality will allow. Direct tests of speaking typically include an OPI, traditionally delivered face-to-face by an interviewer who may or may not also rate the performance; more recently, this person-to-person, synchronous task has been delivered online like the IELTS Video Call Speaking test (VCS) which employs a real-time computer interface (similar to Zoom) to facilitate an online interview involving both examiner and test-taker. Rating scales tend to include reference to communicative achievement (e.g. clarity of message) as well as linguistic indicators (e.g. range of phonological devices). Proponents of OPIs see them as eliciting more 'authentic' or 'natural' language, although whether they do is disputed (Fulcher, 2003). Offering an OPI for over 80 languages, the ACTFL OPI is an example of a direct test (ACTFL, n.d).

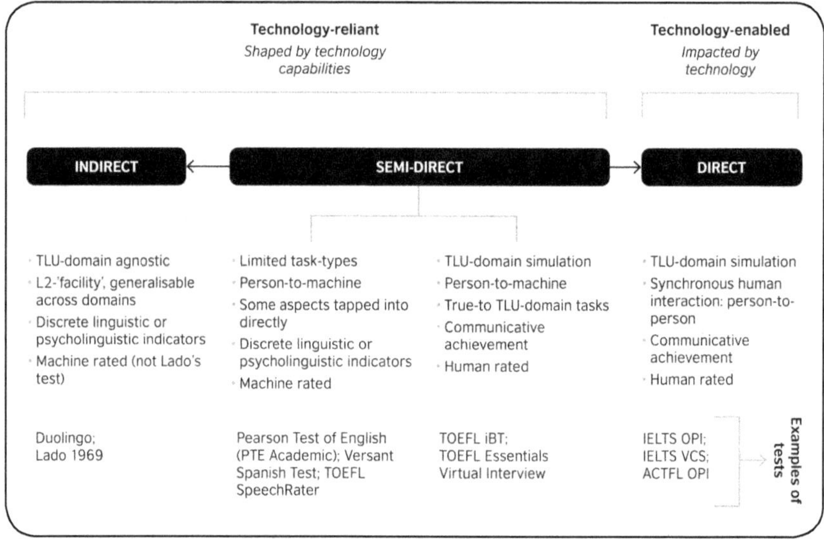

Figure 6.1. Approaches to testing speaking proficiency

Between these two test extremes on the continuum lie indirect tests which generally aim to simulate aspects of the TLU-domain in person-to-machine tasks. These tests attempt to marry the demands of validity and practicality, with validity being addressed through the reflection of some communicative tasks within the TLU-domain and some skills being tapped into directly (e.g. pronunciation of individual sounds). TOEFL Essentials is an example of a test where tasks straddle both sides of the semi-direct test types, with the 'virtual interview' including a 'prerecorded interviewer' verbally delivering the question. These computer-based, interlocutor-free tests mean that they are more easily scalable, accessible, and cost-effective.

Semi-direct tasks (rather than full tests) can be divided into two types: those limited by delivery and machine rating capabilities, and those where technology is used as a means to obtain the speech sample which is asynchronously rated by a human. In the former, as with indirect testing, measurement is of discrete indicators of a more generalisable 'facility-in-L2' that is context-independent (Bernstein et al., 2010; Van Moere, 2012). An example of an indirect task is Part B on the Versant test of Spanish which requires test-takers to repeat, verbatim, sentences they hear. The underlying rationale is that more proficient speakers are accustomed to producing 'chunks' of language in the target L2 and are able to repeat longer, more complex utterances. The underlying psycholinguistic approach is apparent in the validation document: "generally, the ability to repeat material is constrained by the size of the linguistic unit that a person can process in an automatic or nearly automatic fashion" (Versant, 2018, p. 4–5). Validation of these tests is often psychometric, such as correlating scores with other tests or comparisons between L1 and L2 speakers, or psycholinguistic, for example, gathering evidence of the cognitive processes (such as automaticity) test-takers engage in, but does not necessarily include validation of the construct itself. It should be noted that the Versant Spanish Test includes short-answer and open-ended questions which are human rated; this might suggest that, because most tasks are highly restricted, additional construct coverage is necessary to arrive at an evaluation of communicative capability.

PTE Academic (Pearson, 2022) is used to decide whether a test-taker has the skills to function in an English higher education context. Task 5 on Part 1 of the Speaking and Writing test requires the test-taker to verbally summarise key points from a 90 second academic lecture they listen to, reflecting the integrated nature of communicative skills as well as potential requirements of the TLU-domain. PTE Academic is placed towards the left of the spectrum because while a limited range of TLU-tasks is reflected, the use of automated rating pre-supposes a facility-in-L2 approach, or indirect measurement of communicative skills. While semi-direct tests often include assessment of communicative achievement (whether rated by machine, as with PTE Academic, or humans, as in the case of TOEFL iBT), there is an absence of 'authentic' interaction in the tests.

Potential Impact of Delivery Mode on Assessing Comprehensibility

Given that current international tests of English are increasingly reliant on technology for delivery, due consideration needs to be given to how this potentially changes the ability being measured. Often, the introduction of computer delivered speaking tests constrains the possibility to elicit interactive language, for example, and while strides have been made in Spoken Dialogue Systems (SDS) (Litman et al., 2018; Chukharev-Hudilainen & Ockey, 2021) that aim to mirror this element of human communication, these are still somewhat clunky and limited in application beyond being prototypes, although research suggests increasing development in this area. It should be remembered, though, that even where OPIs are 'simply' shifted online, the mode of delivery can have an effect on the linguistic and communicative features that are elicited, and, as such, could change the construct that is being assessed. This may well be the future of communication more generally, of course, and delivery will undoubtably shape the comprehensibility construct.

Two main challenges arise as a result of the use of technology in test delivery, those of construct under-representation (or narrowing of the construct) and construct irrelevance. First, considering construct under-representation, computer delivered tests may reduce the range of speaking skills that are elicited, for example, socio-pragmatic interactive skills crucial to achieving comprehensibility may be lost when the test-taker is required to engage in monologic tasks only, without a real-time interlocutor, and read aloud tasks are unlikely to reflect the cognitive processes involved in building a mental model. While proponents of indirect tests consider that these can be measured by proxy, the reliance on psychometric properties as validity evidence does not adequately address construct coverage and, while a range of indirect task types might achieve some extent of construct representation, it does not reflect the complex and dynamic relationship of these different traits in getting the message across successfully.

The second potential consequence of technology led delivery modes is the introduction of factors that are irrelevant to the comprehensibility construct. An obvious consideration is that a fully comprehensible test-taker who lacks computer skills or is unfamiliar with, for example, online interaction, will be disadvantaged not because of language ability, but because the use of technology interferes with the ability to complete the task successfully. Where computer literacy demands on the test-taker are crucial to completing the linguistic task, they become part of what is being measured; the test-taker is not just proving their language skills, but also their ability to navigate an on-screen system. While this can be mitigated by test familiarisation materials and the inclusion of clear instructions and a practice item on test tasks, it needs to be a serious consideration when evaluating the construct validity of a test. Even for those who are fully computer literate, the inevitable delays and missed turn-taking cues in simultaneous online communication means that the ability to manage this added variable is being tested in addition to the ability to make oneself comprehensible in a face-to-face interaction, for example.

These threats warrant serious consideration and should be included in test validity arguments and evaluations. The changing communication landscape needs to be recognised, however; while computer delivered tests may be different to more traditional OPIs, for example, they are likely to reflect current modes of communication and could form an integral component in the testing of the overall comprehensibility construct as it exists in real-life communication. It is, after all, becoming very important to be able to convey a message through technological means and some language users might feel more comfortable leaving a voice message than communicating face-to-face.

Finally, the purely technical impact of using technology to deliver speaking tests needs to be considered. This refers specifically to the quality of the equipment being used and the environment in which the recording is being made. A sub-standard audio recording (faulty microphone, low-quality sound-files or background noise) can impact the rating of comprehensibility whether rated by human or machine.

The use of computers to deliver speaking tests opens up many possibilities for the assessment of comprehensibility, particularly in light of new modes of communication in general. Practicality does need to be balanced with validity, however, and, during a time of crisis such as COVID-19, when it is tempting to allow the need to take examinations and obtain test scores to override concerns about the potential impact of the new modes of delivery, we need to act cautiously: a test score that does not reflect the test-taker's communicative ability or measures other skills is a compromised score and carries with it consequences. Responsible test developers will include these considerations in their validation studies (see Nakatsuhara et al., 2017, for an example), weigh the consequences for individuals and wider society over quick commercial gains, and communicate clearly with all stakeholders about what the test measures.

Automated Assessment

One of the areas anticipated to have enormous impact on language assessment is the auto-rating of productive skills. In this chapter, automated assessment is considered to be when a machine (a computer programme or software developed using 'code' (human or computer generated, or a hybrid)) is used to assign a score or other evaluation (e.g. pass/fail, CEFR level) to a sample of speech. This is not a technical explanation but, rather, a brief overview of the potential impact of auto-rating on the assessment of comprehensibility. For more detailed technical descriptions, see Xi, 2010; Xi, 2012; Xi et al., 2012; Van Moere and Downey, 2016; Isaacs, 2018; Litman et al., 2018; and Zechner and Evanini, 2020; Saito, et al., 2022.

As we are taking a comprehensibility perspective on the auto-rating of speaking, the key question underlying this section is: if a test-taker produces comprehensible speech, are there factors that might result in an auto-rated score that evaluates that speaker as not comprehensible or less comprehensible? This section identifies such potential factors. First, we provide a basic, non-technical overview of the components and processes involved in Figure 6.2.

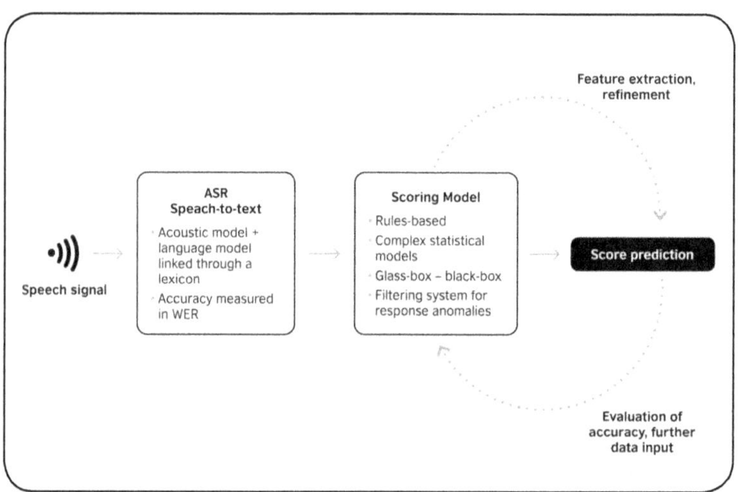

Figure 6.2. Basic overview of the process for auto-rating of spoken performance

The main components of automated assessment of speech are the speech signal itself, the automatic speech recognition (ASR) system, the scoring model (which includes a filtering model), and the score assigned to the spoken performance as a result. Figure 6.2. provides a visual representation for reference. First, the recorded speech sample needs to be converted into text in the form of transcriptions; this is done using three main sources of input: an acoustic model (the sounds of the target language); a language model (based on lexical and syntactic probabilities of certain language items occurring in a sequence in that language); and a lexicon that links the two models through entries that include items from the language model and one or more pronunciation entries for those items (e.g. if there are recognised accent variations for specific words) (Litman et al., 2018). The ASR system needs to be 'taught' using large corpora of speech and language samples. Most people will have had some experience of an ASR system, such as when using the verbal search function on a mobile phone.

The second main component is the scoring model. There are various approaches to this. One is a rules-based (or 'features-based') approach where the machine is instructed what to measure (e.g. speech rate), or to compare test-taker pronunciation of a read-aloud task to that of a 'model' (usually native) speaker; this can be considered a 'supervised' machine learning model where the rules and features are known. Other – and increasingly common – approaches move further along the continuum towards 'unsupervised' machine learning where large amounts of data, including speech samples and human ratings of those samples, are fed into a programme that then works to identify patterns (e.g. certain temporal, linguistic or other features) associated with the range of scores awarded by human raters. The end goal is to predict what score a human rater would award a speech sample based on these features, evolving into a system that is able to assign a score (a 'prediction' of a human score [Van Moere & Downey, 2016]) that is comparable, in terms of rating reliability, with that of human raters. The filtering model aims to weed out problem samples, such as memorised responses or responses in another language, for scrutiny by humans. Iterations involving further data input and refinement follow before the machine can achieve a high degree of accuracy. Scoring models are highly complex, drawing on advanced statistical tools to reach the score prediction output. The variables used by the machine to arrive at an approximation of a human rating can be known ('glass box') but, increasingly, what the machine is using to produce a score is less transparent ('black box'). This raises validation concerns: while the statistical coefficients might indicate near-agreement with human raters and we might be confident in the score awarded, we can no longer be certain about what ability the machine is measuring

– the 'black box' obfuscates understanding of the construct (see Figure 6.3.). Of course, it also opens up the possibility that AI will provide us with a much richer understanding of the components of comprehensibility than would be possible through human research alone.

This basic overview of automated assessment aims to provide background to the next section which focuses on the potential implications for the measurement of comprehensibility. While there are systems capable of measuring distinct linguistic and temporal components contributing to overall comprehensibility, a model (or combination of models) to measure comprehensibility remains elusive, primarily because the construct of comprehensibility remains a Gordian knot still in the process of being untangled (if indeed untangling is the approach that should be taken).

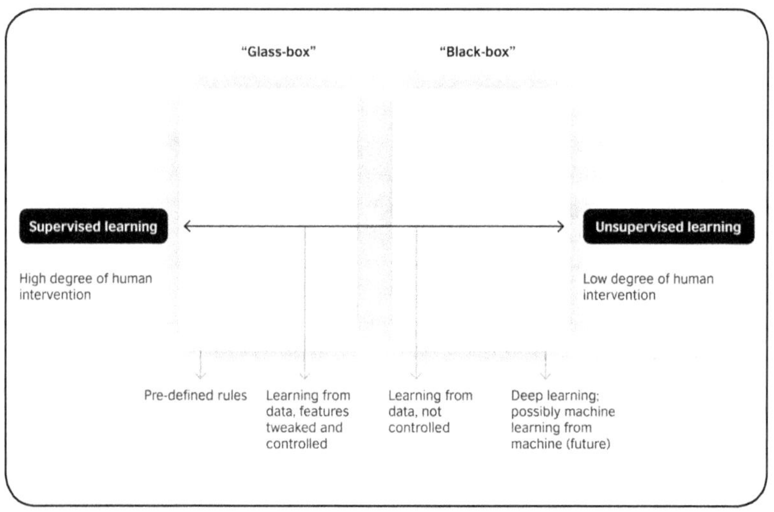

Figure 6.3. Basic overview of auto-rating training possibilities

Potential Impact of Automated Assessment on Assessing Comprehensibility

There are several points in an automated assessment process, in general, at which the validity of comprehensibility measurements could be affected. The first starts at the test design phase where task types are potentially shaped or restricted by machine capability. This concerns the sample of language elicited – predictable or unpredictable, controlled or spontaneous – because machines are most reliable when assessing highly predictable, non-spontaneous speech (Zechner et al., 2009). As Zechner & Evanini (2020) point out:

> [...] most automated scoring studies on spontaneous speech still employ only a limited set of features due to the technical challenges involved in accurately processing spontaneous speech produced by language learners, thereby resulting in partial construct coverage (e.g. van Dalen, Ragni, & Gales, 2015, p. 6).

This means in order to increase the reliability of the automated assessment, test designers will have to design tasks that elicit language samples of a predictable and controlled nature. There are implications for the rating of comprehensibility as a result. First, if a test-taker produces a response that falls out of the model 'recognised' by the machine, the results will be negative, even where the response is fully comprehensible; an example is semi-controlled speech in responses to a question like *how long have you been studying English?* where a number of years is expected and not a response such as *I never studied English because it is my first language*. Not only could this disadvantage stronger, more creative speakers, but it could also favour test-takers who employ test-wise strategies and focus on rote learning; this, in turn, could have negative washback effects and encourage a focus on form rather than learning how to make oneself comprehensible to other speakers. It also opens up the test to 'gaming' of predicted responses, such as where superficial features contributing to the test score are exploited by the test-taker to 'play' the machine rating system. For example, a test-wise candidate could memorise long tracts of spoken text and rely on speech rate and range of lexis to artificially inflate their score because this is what the machine rates rather than the more complex and dynamic construct of comprehensibility; this could result in a test-taker being assessed as highly proficient even if they are not able to function at a basic level in the L2. Second, and potentially more worrying, is that the limitations of technology could affect the range of possible task types as discussed under the potential implications of modes of delivery above, restricting the communicative skills elicited and resulting in a situation where technology determines (and narrows) the construct. To draw on Zechner and Evanini again, tests "should not depend on the scoring approach used... but should be dictated by the needs of the language use domain through a domain analysis" (2020, p. 10).

Another stage early on in the automated assessment cycle where assessment of communicative comprehensibility could be compromised is the ASR system which adds a potential dimension of error not present in the rating of writing. While the ASR also needs rules and to be 'trained' and suffers from the same potential issues that the scoring model does (see below), a particular concern at this point in the process is the reliability of the speech into text transcription. Reported in terms of Word Error Rate (WER), ASR systems may not recognise all pronunciation variations (even where fully intelligible or highly comprehensible – L2 speakers are reported as particularly problematic [Litman et al., 2018], possibly due to insufficient training using learner language) – or could be impeded by audio quality or background noise resulting in high WER; people may have had this experience with the ASR systems they use in everyday life. Thus, the text data that moves on to the next phase of the auto-rating cycle is already problematic and, however good the scoring model, it is being applied to flawed data. From a comprehensibility point of view, test-takers who are fully comprehensible in the real world could achieve low scores as a result.

A third intersection between the cycle from process to validity from a comprehensibility evaluation perspective is located at the point of the training of the scoring model. The two primary considerations here are sample representation and the potential encoding of bias. As discussed above, auto-rating systems typically 'learn' from data; they are therefore most reliable when this learning is applied to a test-taker population similar to the data set. In other words, the speech samples provided should be representative of the intended test-takers and the full range of variations in the speech of the target test population. Automated scoring test developers should ensure an adequate range of levels, voice pitch ranges (e.g. female and male), age groups (as language use can be affected by age), and language backgrounds in the data sets. Underrepresentation can lead to the machine scoring the 'majority' group with more accuracy where those not represented (e.g. certain L2s) receive inaccurate scores. This poses a particular conundrum for large-scale tests of 'international' communication: machines are data-hungry, requiring huge sets of audio and rating samples to achieve rating parity – the more data, the more accurate – and attempting to represent, for example, the global English user test population is a formidable task. Furthermore, this cannot be easily mitigated by the control of linguistic features associated with comprehensibility. As we have seen in this book, these are not only elusive, but they tend to be L2-specific and vary in their importance depending on the context.

Within the scoring model learning system, the other source of potential invalidity is the encoding of bias. While this can be as a result of sample representation issues as described above, raters and ratings can also introduce flaws that have serious repercussions for test-takers. This relates to a key dimension of comprehensibility that has been discussed elsewhere in this book: the role of the listener in the making of meaning. While monologic speech events may not draw on synchronous interaction to achieve comprehensibility, the (imagined) listener needs to, at least, be included at an early stage of model development. Firstly, who the raters are and whether they represent the most likely listener within the TLU-domain needs to be considered; often, L1 speaker raters are preferred over L2 speaker raters yet (for English) this might not reflect the people the test-taker will need to interact with in, for example, a university setting where L2-speaker classmates and lecturers outweigh L1-speaker interactants, even in English speaking countries (Universities UK International, 2018). In other words, not only does the test-taker population need be considered as part of the data sampling process, but so does the population of the intended TLU-domain. Secondly, one of the benefits that is often lauded by proponents of machine rating is that it is free of bias inherent in humans (Xi, 2012). While the machine itself is not sentient, the rating data used to train the system can carry with it rater prejudice against, for example, certain accents or age groups. As was discussed in earlier chapters, intelligibility, comprehensibility and accent are 'interrelated but separate' constructs (Munro & Derwing, 1995a) and to what degree even the most experienced, consciously objective of raters can be bias-free in this regard is doubtful (Winke et al., 2013). The counter-argument is that machine bias is no different to human rater bias. However, hard-wiring this into a system that is *believed to be* completely objective can have serious repercussions such as obstructing immigration where an L1-variety accent produced poor results on an automated test (Australian Associated Press, 2017). While the important role of the listener in achieving comprehensibility may not be sufficiently reflected in these models, at least the extent to which the listener can be represented needs to be included, and this should be a key aspect of the research agenda going forward.

Finally, increasingly sophisticated machine-learning – and 'deep learning' – potentially contributes another threat to the assessment of comprehensibility, that of construct obfuscation. As mentioned above, while statistical metrics might be reassuring, the 'black-box' factor in advanced machine-models means that we cannot be sure what is being measured and, across a plethora of AI applications, there is a call for XAI – explainable AI – where what is being measured is transparent and understood (see Saito, Macmillan, et al., 2022, for an example of the use of posteriograms to render an automated system more 'explainable', suggesting that further research could result in more XAI).

Strengths and Mitigations of Technology in Assessing Comprehensibility

The use of technology in language testing throws up several challenges and opportunities for the assessment of comprehensibility in the broader perspective we have presented in this book which should compel language testing stakeholders to ask key questions. First, we explore the challenges specific to our view of comprehensibility with reference to Figure 6.1 above.

We have argued that comprehensibility is achieved through the interweaving of various linguistic and non-linguistic components and that the importance of each of these components as contributors to comprehensibility is context-dependent and dynamic. The initial step in automated assessment of spoken language, the turning of speech into text through the ASR system, delivers the first challenge to the complexity of the comprehensibility construct. In a sense, this is a comprehensibility test in and of itself, or rather an *intelligibility* test, whereby acoustic signals are the main source of input. Depending on the sophistication of the system, rendering text from speech could unduly rely on articulation of individual sounds at this first stage of automated rating, effectively weighting pronunciation as the most important factor in achieving comprehensibility. At the next stage, the scoring model demands questions about speaker and listener representation in the training and validation data sets, as discussed earlier in this chapter. However, in the context of the broader perspective of comprehensibility we are taking here, more specific considerations are highlighted. Firstly, what type of speech (genre, monologic or dialogic, communicative task) has the model been trained on and is the model being used to assess the same type of communication event? As we have argued, some communicative events draw more on certain comprehensibility contributors than others; this suggests that task specific scoring models may better reflect the relative weighting of the different components of comprehensibility than generic models. Second, what criteria have been used to rate the training data? Feature specific or exclusively linguistic rating may result in important factors such as pragmatics being programmed out of the model, whereas human scoring that takes the achievement of a communicative goal as its measure could provide a powerful data set that allows us to leverage AI to unravel the myriad components that lead to comprehensibility.

The impact of technology on the mode of delivery also presents challenges as well as promising opportunities when comprehensibility is viewed from this broader perspective. While initial developments in using computers to test language seemed to result in construct underrepresentation due to the removal of an interlocutor, e.g. eliciting monologic speech only, rapid developments in technology and AI suggest that these advancements could elicit much richer language samples. Through the use of ChatGPT and similar systems that mimic spoken interaction and force particular communicative events, tests could deliberately include tasks that require the use of features and skills associated with comprehensibility that traditional tests have not been able to tap into, or that only the most skillful interlocutors are able to (inconsistently) elicit. Combined with a scoring model that factors in the broader elements of the comprehensibility construct, technology could have a positive impact on language assessment and, by extension, language learning.

Finally, we are cautiously optimistic that ethical, responsible development of technology-enabled language assessment could open up the possibility of enriching both the language test event and scoring to better reflect the complex nature of making oneself comprehensible in a way that humans alone cannot accomplish. Technology increasingly allows for multimodality to be reflected in communicative tasks where the test-taker can be required to draw on a range of different text types and audio/visual input, and automated assessment would most likely have greater capability than humans to measure how effectively the input material had been used (or overused). Indeed, there would be no cognitive load issues for the machine and, if the scoring model is developed with a broad, rich comprehensibility construct at its core, a wider range of factors could be assessed. Technology may offer a way to more fully and more accurately reflect the complex and dynamic interactions presented in Figure 8.1 than human only capability allows.

As this chapter has suggested so far, it is crucial that technological-enabled language testing is adopted in a critically considered way. The direction of travel for language tests is almost certainly towards technology and the inclusion of automated rating is likely in some form or another. While caution needs to be exercised, technology brings with it many benefits. Apart from the accessibility and reach that computer/device delivered tests may bring, as suggested above, algorithms that are developed using deep learning may, in fact, reflect the complexity of the comprehensibility construct. This book has delved into the myriad of potential features associated with comprehensibility in spoken language; yet, despite ongoing research, there is no definitive inventory of linguistic components of the comprehensibility construct that can be generalised across all contexts. As we have argued, it is how the features work together with contextual variables that achieves mutually understood meaning. It should come as no surprise that the mathematical model upon which a comprehensibility rating is based defies human cognition; after all, we have been unable to explain how the minds of human raters reach their decisions about whether someone is making themselves understood.

Rather than demand the impossible from an algorithm in terms of fully XAI, we should be focusing on asking the right questions and taking a responsible, ethical stance in relation to auto-rating. Raji, et al. (2020) provide a meaningful perspective:

> AI has the potential to benefit the whole of society, however there is currently an inequitable risk distribution such that those who already face patterns of structural vulnerability or bias disproportionately bear the costs and harms of many of these systems. Fairness, justice and ethics require that those bearing these risks are given due attention and that organizations that build and deploy artificial intelligence systems internalize and proactively address these social risks as well, being seriously held to account for system compliance to declared ethical principles. (p. 42)

An analogy is useful here. Consider pharmaceutical companies developing drugs through the use of complicated chemistry which the users of the medication may not be able to understand. These firms are required to explain the purpose, use, dosage, interactions, and side effects of the medication in a way so that that the user is able to understand whether the drug is the right one for them. In much the same way, test designers and developers should provide a user guide for their tests, particularly where complicated auto-rating is concerned.

The general sense that there is a need to 'explain' AI and take an ethical stance in relation to the use of machine learning while also recognising that the complexity cannot be understood by the human brain has been articulated in the call for "model cards" (Mitchel, et al., 2019). The model card is broadly analogous to the information leaflet of medication discussed above, or to nutrition labels found on food items. O'Sullivan, (2020) has argued for this concept to be applied to language tests. In tables 6.1 and 6.2, we suggest a few questions language assessment stakeholders – whether test takers, teachers, score users or testing professionals themselves – should ask about technology-enabled tests in relation to the broader view of comprehensibility we have argued for in this book. These are not exhaustive lists, but they do serve as useful starting points.

• *What ability or skills is the device based test eliciting? How does this reduce or over-extend the construct of comprehensibility as presented in the broader perspective? Does the technologically based delivery mode result in the elicitation of an abstracted sample of language devoid of communicative context factors?*   • *Do the tasks reflect, at least to some degree, communicative tasks the test takers will be required to do in real-life in the TLU domain? Does the technology allow for a richer, multimodal interaction that more effectively elicits the range of skills required to achieve communicative comprehensibility?*   • *If the test is an indirect test of ability (it does not elicit spoken performance samples), is it a measure of knowledge rather than ability or is sufficient evidence provided that the features being measured are proxies for the spoken communicative ability?*   • *If the test focuses on eliciting a narrow range of spoken linguistic features, are the other range of linguistic and non-linguistic features and factors elicited through other tests or components of the wider test battery?*   • *Do test takers have the necessary technology skills to complete the test and focus on the communicative demands rather than manipulation of the technological application? What can be done to familiarise test takers with the test format so that they are able to focus on achieving the communicative goal?*   • *What is the potential washback of the delivery mode on the development of skills to facilitate spoken comprehensibility? Does it encourage learners to develop the full range of real communicative skills necessary to achieve comprehensibility in real world communication?*

Table 6.1: Questions about the potential impact of technologically delivered tests on a broad perspective of comprehensibility

- *Considering that comprehensibility is achieved across a range of L1 and L2 interactants, how is this diversity reflected in the scoring model? Is there reporting of the sample profile that has been used to train and validate the automated scoring system? E.g. range of L1s, age range. Or are there recommendations for which populations the automated scoring system should not be applied to? Is the test provider clear about which target population(s) this test is most appropriate for? Is there clarity about how language variety (i.e. which form or accent of the language) influences the ASR and scoring systems?*
- *Given that comprehensibility is co-constructed, does the automated rating system reflect the TLU listener population, in particular with tests of lingua francas? What is the profile of the rater population whose scores were used to train the system, for example, is this limited to a small group of L1speakers or is it representative of the listeners in the TLU domain?*
- *What linguistic features are used by the machine to generate scores and how do these align with the complex and dynamic interaction of components of comprehensibility? Where algorithym complexity precludes a clear explanation, are the results validated, explained or supported in some other way?*
- *The broader approach to comprehensibility proposes that the communicative context in which the spoken language occurs determines the relative weight of the linguistic and non-linguistic featurs and factors that contribute to compehensibilit. How does the autorating model account for this? Is the scoring model prompt specific (i.e. trained on speech samples elicited in response to a particular task or prompt) which may better reflect the instance of interplay of components in achieving comprehensibility? Or is it trained on generic samples of spoken language, dislocating the linguistic from context?*
- *What is the potential washback of the automated scoring system? Is there the potential for learners to exploit proxy linguistic features (such as the expedient use of low frequency lexis, or of speech speed) at the expense of actual communicative ability?*

***Table 6.2:* Questions about the potential impact of technologically delivered tests on a broad perspective of comprehensibility**

Conclusion

As has been discussed throughout this chapter and, indeed this book, comprehensibility is complex and, while technology can facilitate the assessment of certain comprehensibility-associated features, it could also adversely affect the measurement of other components of the construct and it is essential that there is sufficient consideration of the consequences. The impact on the construct of the use of computers and other devices to deliver tests needs to be factored into validity arguments, for example. Furthermore, the potential validity threats associated with the use of automated rating for spontaneous speech need to be mitigated. Data sets used for machine learning need to be transparent, continuously validated and linked to the test population and TLU-domain. Test developers have an ethical responsibility to inform users of the suitability of their test and the potential consequences for particular test users. Finally, language test stakeholders need to be properly aware of the potential for auto-rating systems to have bias encoded into their data-DNA and this needs to be factored into the interpretation of the test score.

There is reason to be cautiously optimistic, however. As McNamara (2012) suggested, the merging of technological advances with real-life application presents us with a unique opportunity to shape the future, not only of testing but also of the skills that learners develop, of our education systems, and of the societies we live in. Far from suggesting that technology should not be leveraged to make tests of spoken communication faster, better and more accessible, our cautionary note advocates taking an ethical position with regards to technology-enabled language testing so that the variation and essence of human communication is not lost in the interests of mass testing, expediency or commercial gain. Non-specialist understanding of the potential consequences of technology on the assessment of spoken communication ability is key to mitigating ill-considered application or misuse of these tools.

CHAPTER 7

TEACHING TOWARDS A COMPREHENSIBILITY GOAL

In previous chapters, we focused on the concept of comprehensibility from a testing and assessment perspective, highlighting its complex and multidimensional nature and discussing the major linguistic components of speech that contribute to ease or difficulty of understanding a speaker (see Figure 8.1 for a visual representation of the factors contributing to comprehensibility). As discussed earlier, comprehensibility is increasingly considered as an important construct in the assessment of L2 ability in a number of international language tests (e.g. IELTS and TOEFL). Therefore, it is reasonable to argue that comprehensibility should also be of great interest to L2 teaching and learning where learners are planning to take such tests. This refers to the concept of washback effect where a test or assessment process affects the teaching and learning processes. Including comprehensibility as a criterion in language test descriptors and rating scales is inevitably expected to have an impact on what teachers and learners do while preparing for such tests. Previous research has shown that a distinctive characteristic of good language tests is promoting 'beneficial outcomes' of the test including having a positive impact on teaching and learning processes. Such impact includes *positive washback effect*, referring to a situation in which "a testing procedure encourages 'good' teaching practice" (Taylor, 2005: 154). Therefore, including comprehensibility as a criterion/scale in language tests would promote some kind of positive washback effect on what teachers and learners do in L2 classrooms.

Comprehensibility, as defined in this volume (i.e., listener's ease of understanding a speaker), is also believed to have been one of the main goals of language learning. Many L2 learners are aware that their aim is not to become native-like speakers of an L2, but their efforts should focus on being understood by a range of users of the target language (Derwing & Munro, 2015; Levis, 2005). Suzuki and Kormos (2020, p. 144) have argued that most learners in instructional language learning contexts aim to achieve one or all of the three aims of "nativelikeness, comprehensibility, and fluency". They maintain that comprehensibility is far more important than nativelikeness for a large majority of learners. They also argue that comprehensibility is a more realistic learning goal than aiming for nativelikeness for most learners. Suzuki and Kormos's (2020) argument in favour of comprehensibility as a realistic learning goal ties in with our motivation in writing this volume to argue that accurate and appropriate assessment of comprehensibility would support this learning goal.

Despite the importance and dominance of comprehensibility as a learning goal, the concept of teaching comprehensibility as a distinct construct is a new development in the field of L2 teaching. Historically, teachers, teaching materials and curricula paid little attention to the concepts of intelligibility and/or comprehensibility, while the focus of their attention, if any, was just on pronunciation. The teaching of pronunciation was recognised as "a study in extreme" (Levis, 2005, p. 369), with some teaching approaches (e.g. audiolingualism) considering it the "pinnacle of importance", while others (e.g. the communicative language teaching) mostly ignoring it (Levis, 2005). As a result of the move away from the former to the latter approach, a gap in attention to the teaching of pronunciation was observed in the 1980s. Around the mid-1990s, influential work by Munro and Derwing (1994, 1995a, 1995b) attracted attention to the importance of teaching pronunciation and its impact on intelligibility. In the following years, the teaching of pronunciation became popular with a focus on suprasegmental features, but by the 2000s researchers' attention was drawn to the ELF nature of communication and the emergence of new perspectives on teaching pronunciation (e.g. Jenkin's, 2000, lingua franca core) gained currency. Also, as discussed in Chapter 2, for a long time in the history of language teaching and assessment, achieving an idealised L1 speaker's pronunciation was recognised as the goal for most learners and an expected outcome for the corresponding teaching practices. In such perspectives, having a foreign accent was "a marker of poor phonological control" (CEFR companion, 2018, p. 134), and achieving a nativelike pronunciation was considered a prime goal of teaching pronunciation.

Even the more familiar concept of intelligibility with a focus on pronunciation, as discussed in Chapter 1, has not received much attention in language teaching over the past decades. Derwing and Munro (2005) drew researchers and language professionals' attention to this problem by arguing that "the study of pronunciation has been marginalized within the field of applied linguistics" which resulted in teachers being left "to rely on their own intuitions with little direction" (p. 379). Derwing and Munro (2005, p. 382) also argued that L2 teacher materials and training programmes are not informed by the findings of research in L2 phonology, and the "extensive, growing literature on L2 speech" is rarely cited in journals that teachers refer to for their professional practice. A systematic review of the literature conducted by the CEFR (Companion Volume, 2018) found that the vast majority of research in L2 phonology did not focus on teaching and/or learning aspects of second languages; rather, these studies were predominantly interested in identifying patterns in phonology. The review concluded that "much less numerous were the articles focusing specifically on the teaching/learning/assessing of pronunciation" (CEFR, Phonological Scale Revision Process Report, 2016, p. 11). Since this report, there has been some emerging interest in investigating issues related to phonology and intelligibility in pedagogic contexts (e.g. Isaacs & collaborators; Saito & collaborators). While much of this work still focuses on issues related to intelligibility, some researchers have taken an analytic approach to disentangling pronunciation and intelligibility from the concept of comprehensibility (Isaacs & Trofimovich, 2012; Isaacs, Trofimovich & Foote, 2018; Saito, Trofimovich & Isaacs, 2017). This latter group have made invaluable contributions to our understanding of comprehensibility at a research level and have offered significant findings that can lead the teaching of comprehensibility in instructional contexts. What is not known is whether any of this rich body of research has been integrated in teaching and learning documents and practices. This is what this chapter aims to investigate.

The current chapter sets out to examine the extent to which comprehensibility is integrated in teaching and learning contexts. Highlighting the importance of the concept for L2 teachers and learners, the chapter will raise key questions about the extent to which L2 teaching curricula focus on comprehensibility, and whether comprehensibility is taught and practiced in L2 classrooms. Analysing some national curricula for English language teaching, we examine the focus on comprehensibility in these documents and support our arguments by research findings in this area. The chapter will also examine teaching-related research to identify areas of comprehensibility that should be introduced in teaching and teacher training programmes. We will finally provide some examples of what L2 teachers can do to highlight the role of comprehensibility and to prepare their learners to be comprehensible in speaking. Most crucially, the chapter will argue that comprehensibility is important as both a teaching objective and a learning outcome, and as such it is necessary to incorporate it in teaching materials and practices.

Comprehensibility in Curricula and Language Benchmarks

In this section, we provide an analysis of two national and one international L2 curricula/benchmarks to examine the extent to which the concept of comprehensibility is presented in these language teaching policy documents: the Hong Kong English Language Curriculum (2017); the China's Standard English (CSE, 2018); and the Companion Volume document of the CEFR (2020). The prime aim of this analysis is to examine the extent to which comprehensibility is integrated in the teaching and learning documents that recommend good teaching practice in each context. These three policy documents were selected because of the substantial and recent work invested in developing each of of them for national or international purposes. These three rather different documents will provide us with a rich opportunity to evaluate comprehensibility and gain insight into the attention paid to comprehensibility across these different contexts.

Hong Kong English Language Curriculum

The first document to evaluate is the Hong Kong English Language Education Key Learning Area Curriculum Guide (2017) for primary and secondary level education in Hong Kong. Developed by the Hong Kong National Curriculum Council, the document is an ambitious plan for offering the stakeholders a new curriculum that can keep up with the latest developments in the field not only at a local level but in "regional and global landscapes" (Hong Kong Engish Language Education Key Learning Area Curriculum Guide, 2017, p. 2). The curriculum aims to enhance students' English language proficiency for education and beyond-education purposes including employment and leisure. The document evaluates English language in terms of different language skills (listening, speaking, reading and writing) and language strategies (being motivated, independent and responsible).

Our first step in the analysis is a search for the words "comprehensibility" and "intelligibility" in the document, which does not result in any outcome. This, however, does not suggest the concept is not advocated or recommended in the curriculum. A more careful analysis indicates that, as part of speaking skills, the document refers to skills that can be considered relevant to 'intelligibility' or 'comprehensibility'. For example, presenting "information, ideas and feelings clearly and coherently" (Hong Kong Engish Language Education Key Learning Area Curriculum Guide, 2017, p. 157) is stated as a sub-construct of speaking at different stages of learning; this is often defined in terms of correctness of pronunciation and connectedness of speech. It also refers to the role of pronunciation as part of the speaking skills, and uses "appropriate" as an adjective to describe the expected quality "appropriate stress, rhythm and intonation" (Hong Kong Engish Language Education Key Learning Area Curriculum Guide, 2017, p. A35). The document, however, does not highlight these abilities as issues related to comprehensibility. There is plenty of emphasis in this policy document on aspects of pronunciation and cohesiveness including *stress*, *rhythm* and *intonation* and *appropriate use of cohesive devices* that help make speech understandable. It is worth noting that we consider these as aspects of comprehensibility at phonological and discourse level (see Chapters 2 and 3 for further discussions). However, the Hong Kong Curriculum Guide (2017) only mentions these as characteristics of speaking skills, and fails to highlight the importance of how these factors contribute to "ease of understanding". Interestingly, this document has not taken a prescriptive approach to recommending an L1 speaker pronunciation norm; rather, when modelling performance is intended, the document uses adjectives such as "appropriate" and "correct" to describe the quality of learners' expected pronunciation.

Overall, our analysis suggests that the Hong Kong Curriculum Guide (2017) provides a detailed discussion of language skills and strategies needed for successful communication. It also pays attention to fluency and effectiveness of communication by stipulating "Due acknowledgement is given to fluency and effective expression of ideas in students' performance in addition to accuracy" (Hong Kong English Language Education Key Learning Area Curriculum Guide, 2017, p. 91). What it fails to discuss is how these different aspects of speaking contribute to ease/difficulty of the listener understanding the speaker. Based on this analysis, we conclude there is not adequate evidence that the curriculum emphasises the important concept of comprehensibility and the impact it has on the listeners. This also implies that teachers may not benefit from this document when it comes to introducing the concept to their teaching or preparing their learners to be comprehensible.

China's Standards of English (CSE)

In 2018, China's Ministry of Education and the State Language Commission developed China's first evaluation scale for English language ability (CSE) outlining a set of standards for Chinese learners of English. The document focuses on English language use and provides a practical guide for evaluating English language ability. CSE provides a detailed description of proficiency, at nine levels from basic to advanced, for language skills (listening, speaking, reading and writing) and practical skills (translation and interpreting). By providing specific but user-friendly descriptions and can-do statements, CSE aims to provide a document that serves as "one of the fundamental strategies to promote English learning, teaching and assessment in China" (CSE, 2018). For our purpose, we have focused on the speaking ability which is described in the CSE in terms of six aspects of (oral) description, narration, exposition, instruction, argumentation and interaction.

Our search for the words 'comprehensibility' and 'intelligibility' in the CSE document resulted in one example for intelligibility and one for 'comprehensible'. The reference to 'comprehensible', "can give a detailed explanation of topics in his/her own field in a logical and comprehensible manner." (CSE, 2018, p. 59), is made to explain oral exposition at CSE 7, referring to the quality of performance being comprehensible. The word "intelligible' is used to describe the quality of translation strategies for CSE 6: "Can add words or phrases implied in the original, making the translation coherent and intelligible" (CSE, 2018, p. 116).

In describing overall language ability, several references are made to the importance of 'explaining things clearly and speaking with clarity'. For example, at CSE 6, learners are expected to be able to "effectively describe, clarify, … and express him/herself clearly, appropriately, smoothly, and in a conventional manner" (CSE, 2018, p. 6). And learners at CSE 7 are required to "make formal academic presentations and provide further explanations based on questions, using accurate, clear and coherent language" (CSE, 2018, p. 10). These references to 'clear' and 'clearly', however, are not discussed in any depth, and therefore, it is difficult for us to decide whether they refer to the concept of comprehensibility we have proposed in this book. The reference to accuracy further invites attention and analysis. The concept of 'accuracy' (e.g. 'correct pronunciation') is often based on the perception that a dominant variety of the language is the only accurate and/or acceptable norm (also known as 'standard pronunciation'); this concept, in principle, undermines the comprehensibility-oriented approach proposed in this volume.

When discussing oral exposition, the CSE document makes several implicit references to the concept of 'ease of understanding' by referring to clarity of pronunciation as a criterion for being understood. For example, at CSE 3 level, the learner is expected to "grasp the main idea, provided speech is articulated clearly and delivered with standard pronunciation at a slow but natural speed" (CSE, 2018, p. 37). There are also several references to terms such as "appropriate intonation" and "correct pronunciation", or "speech is articulated clearly". Interestingly, clear articulation is often used as a criterion for lower levels of proficiency such as CSE 2, 3 and 4, which implies that incomprehensibility is perhaps a quality associated with lower levels of proficiency. This is an assumption that we have challenged in this book as we have proposed that comprehensibility may affect speaking quality at different levels of proficiency and in a speaker's L1 (see Chapter 1 for a full discussion).

In summary, although comprehensibility is not directly discussed in the CSE document, several references are made to speaking clearly and coherently, and the importance of clarity of articulation is highlighted repeatedly in terms of correctness of pronunciation and speed of delivery. What seems inadequately addressed in this document is the importance of taking the listeners' needs into account and defining speech in terms of how easy it is to understand. Another crucial tenet of the L2 comprehensibility perspective proposed in this volume is prioritising ease of understanding over nativelikeness. As we have seen, while the CSE guidelines in principle refer to the significance of comprehensibility, we have not seen any indication that comprehensibility is distinguished from nativelikeness. These points would inevitably have implications for teachers and learners since a national policy like the CSE is expected to not only set the standards for assessment purposes but to indicate to teachers which areas of language teaching they need to focus on.

CEFR Companion Volume

The third policy-level document we review here is the CEFR Companion Volume (2020). As readers are aware, the CEFR (2001) document was one of the most comprehensive language benchmark policy documents that outlined, in a very detailed manner, L2 communicative ability including language skills and components. One of the strengths of the CEFR document (2001) was that it discussed communicative language ability from teaching, learning and assessment perspectives and provided research-led discussions of L2 ability, its constructs, processes and components. The CEFR Companion Volumes (2018, 2020) aim to update and extend the CEFR initial framework to provide "a transparent, coherent and comprehensive basis for the elaboration of language syllabuses and curriculum guidelines, the design of teaching and learning materials, and the assessment of foreign language proficiency" (CEFR website, 2020).

In the Companion Volume (2020) the 2001 scales are presented as insufficient for assessing phonological control especially in the light of the new research findings and new language use frameworks, for example, English as a Lingua Franca (for a full discussion, see Chapters 1 and 2). Emphasising the inappropriacy of considering 'an idealised native speaker model' when assessing phonological aspects of a second language, the Companion Volume proposes a new framework for conceptualising and evaluating phonological control. The core areas identified in this framework are:

> Articulation, including pronunciation of sounds/phonemes; prosody, including intonation, rhythm and stress – both word stress and sentence stress – and speech rate/chunking; accentedness, accent and deviation from a "norm"; intelligibility, accessibility of meaning for interlocutors, covering also the interlocutors' perceived difficulty in understanding (normally referred to as "comprehensibility"). (p. 133)

The document then explains that due to technical issues related to operationalising the scales, only three categories of the above-mentioned criteria are considered: *Overall phonological control*, *sound articulation*, and *prosodic features* (intonation, stress and rhythm). The more important concept of 'ease of understanding', referred to as *intelligibility* in the Companion Volume, has accordingly been incorporated in global statements of the language ability.

Our analysis of the document highlights a few important findings. First of all, it is evident that the CEFR Companion Volumes are making a valuable effort in attracting attention to issues related to comprehensibility. While the relevant concepts are not always discussed in relation to comprehensibility as defined and perceived in this book, the Companion Volume makes repeated references to different aspects of the spoken performance that affect ease of understanding. It is also very useful to see that the Companion Volumes provide a more careful analysis of issues related to phonological control, highlighting the need to consider 'ease of understanding' or taking the listeners' needs into account. Second, it is surprising to see that the concepts of intelligibility and comprehensibility are sometimes interchangeably used and discussed. The 2018 volume defines intelligibility as "accessibility of meaning for listeners, covering also the listeners' perceived difficulty in understanding (normally referred to as comprehensibility)" (CEFR Companion Volume, 2018, p. 134). The 2020 volume also refers to intelligibility as "how much effort is required from the interlocutor to decode the speaker's message" (CEFR Companion Volume 2020, p. 133). The distinction between concepts of intelligibility and comprehensibility is neither discussed nor explained in these documents. We believe this could lead to ambiguity and/or confusion about the concepts for the end-users of the documents (e.g. teachers and material developers) with a potentially negative impact on how they interact with this document, or how they translate these concept into their teaching and assessment practices. Finally, we note that comprehensibility as a term is frequently used to discuss proficiency not only in speaking but in expressing the intended meaning in writing and translation. This use of the word 'comprehensibility' predictably invites more research to examine the similarities and differences between comprehensibility in speaking and writing and translation.

To summarise, the CEFR companion volumes (2018, 2020), compared to the other two policy documents reviewed earlier, have paid more attention to the concept of comprehensibility and have highlighted the need to consider the listeners' perspective. Although the companion volumes can potentially attract teachers' attention to the concept of comprehensibility, they fail to provide a clear analysis and/or discussion of the construct of comprehensibility.

Comprehensibility and L2 Teachers

Drawing on the evidence provided in this book so far, we argue that comprehensibility is an important aspect of L2 teaching and an area that teachers and teacher training programmes need to pay more attention to. In this section, we examine the existing evidence about the extent to which language teachers are prepared or have been trained to teach the concept of comprehensibility. It is necessary to note that comprehensibility in the sense of 'ease of understanding' is not new to language teaching as it has always been an integral part of what teachers do within the communicative language teaching framework to prepare learners for successful communication.

A good example of a teaching approach active in promoting "ease of understanding" can be seen in the interactionist view of SLA (e.g. Gass, 1997; Long, 1996), a view that informs the theoretical underpinning of currently popular approaches to L2 teaching, such as Task-Based Language Teaching (TBLT) and Content and Language Integrated Learning (CLIL). This view of SLA stipulates that L2 acquisition is facilitated when L2 learners are engaged in conversational interactions with L1 speakers and/or proficient L2 users. The development of L2 learning is therefore expected to be facilitated when interactional encounters provide learners with rich opportunities to work collaboratively to solve communication problems (e.g. clarification requests and comprehension checks). This focus on 'solving communication problems in interaction' is in fact a key principle that underscores the significance of the ability to communicate successfully without the need to sound like a L1 speaker of the target language. This principle, which is at the heart of comprehensibility, has been a familiar concept to teachers adopting teaching approaches such as TBLT and CLIL. Notwithstanding teachers' awareness of and familiarity with the concept, we hypothesise that 'comprehensibility' as a complex and multidimensional construct, presented in this book, is rather recent in the field and as such may not be understood unequivocally by teachers and other professional practitioners.

Several researchers (Isaacs & Trofimovich, 2012; Isaacs, Trofimovich & Foote, 2018; Saito, Trofimovich & Isaacs, 2017, to name a few) investigating the new comprehensibility framework (i.e., a complex and multidimensional construct) have argued that comprehensibility is not a construct explicitly aimed for in teaching and learning practices. Therefore, it is too simplistic to assume that teachers are familiar with the details of the new comprehensibility framework or to expect they should confidently use the framework in their teaching. Isaacs, Trofimovich and Foote (2018, p.193), in particular, argued that teachers and learners "have little practical means of benefiting from research pinpointing the properties of learners' oral performance that optimise or hinder their ability to be understood'. Others (Crowther et al., 2015) expressed concerns about the wide spectrum of domains of linguistic features that contribute to comprehensibility (e.g. phonology, fluency and grammar), and acknowledged that this range may be too broad for language teaching to focus on. While comprehensibility in language teaching remains an under-researched area, our analysis of the literature suggests several lines of enquiry are emerging as important dimensions of comprehensibility for pedagogic purposes. In what follows, we have summarised the most important findings of this body of research under three categories: *the shift (in pronunciation teaching perspective)*, *comprehensibility as a broader concept*, and *comprehensibility in context*. These categories can inform teacher training programmes about important areas that should be included in their agenda to help introduce the new comprehensibility framework to teachers.

The Shift in Pronunciation Teaching Perspective

As discussed before, in more traditional perspectives on language teaching, L2 teachers and teaching materials focused on pronunciation to help promote communication between the speaker and listener. This often involved primarily helping learners develop a pronunciation system that was understandable by L1 speakers of the target language with a set of native norms of pronunciation indicated as the standard. The past two decades, however, has witnessed a shift in understanding pronunciation from a focus on helping learners become L1 speakers to helping them develop speaking ability that is easy to understand and follow. This shift also included a move away from the acquisition of an accent-free and idealised native-speaker norm of pronunciation. In the new perspective, accent reduction or attempts to reduce first language influence is not aimed at; rather, attempts are made to introduce teaching activities that encourage 'easy to understand' speech. The shift has also been associated with the development of new language norms and standards including ELF and English as an international language.

Researchers (Isaacs, 2018; Levis, 2005) have argued that the pedagogical values alluded to teaching aspects of L2 pronunciation have accordingly changed in the minds of teachers, researchers and language testers. With this shift of perspective, the field of language teaching research has started to consider comprehensibility as linguistic features of a speaker's language that make a substantial contribution to making second language (L2) speech easy or difficult to understand. The shift has also invited questions about whether L2 teachers are well-equipped to translate the theoretical shift into everyday practices in their teaching. Evidently, training teachers to integrate comprehensibility as part of teaching speaking is a substantial undertaking that cannot be expected to happen overnight. Such training, as argued by researchers (Derwing & Munro, 2009), is a longitudinal process and needs time and energy investment.

Comprehensibility as a Broader Concept

A second important point with significant implications for teachers and teacher training programmes is the current broader understanding of the construct of 'comprehensibility' in which a wider range of linguistic elements are to be considered. As discussed in previous chapters, research in this area has provided ample evidence that comprehensibility includes a wider spectrum of linguistic elements that contribute to comprehensibility. We have indicated that comprehensibility, although crucial at phonological level, can affect ease/difficulty of understanding at syntactic, discourse and pragmatics levels (see Figure 8.1). This new conceptualisation of comprehensibility will require teachers a revived pedagogic approach to helping learners develop their comprehensibility. To start with, this requires teachers to move beyond focusing on pronunciation of individual sounds to include other aspects of comprehensibility at phonological (e.g. intonation, rhythm and fluency), syntactic (e.g. cohesion), discourse (e.g. coherence) and pragmatic levels (e.g. references to cultural understanding). Clearly, these are all linguistic features that are also important for improved general L2 oral proficiency. However, the emphasis on these features in the comprehensibility perspective is to argue that certain linguistic features (e.g. intercultural awareness) should be prioritised owing to their relative impacts on listener understanding of the message. Teachers' awareness of the influential role of these features in attaining comprehensibility will potentially enable them to help learners promote comprehensibility in an efficient and effective manner. In what follows, we provide examples of studies that have helped promote teachers' awareness of the broader concept of comprehensibility.

Isaacs et al. (2018) worked with a group of EAP teachers to develop rating scales for comprehensibility. This provided the teachers with a unique opportunity to develop their understanding of comprehensibility as they were involved in the research project. The teacher-raters' views in this study suggested that a greater proportion of the variance in comprehensibility ratings was explained by pronunciation and fluency than by the lexical and grammatical aspects of speaking. The finding suggested that for these teachers pronunciation and fluency were more important factors in affecting comprehensibility than vocabulary and grammar. Isaacs et al. (2018) concluded that there is still "the need for a tool to guide teachers on what to focus on in instruction" if teaching the linguistic factors that matter most is expected and to raise teachers and students' awareness about their abilities as well as the expectations they face.

Comprehensibility in Classroom Practice

The discussion presented in the previous sections suggested that a focus on comprehensibility should be included in teaching and learning and the findings of research in this area should be translated to action if learners are expected to benefit from it. We have focused on three aspects of teaching that can help learners develop a reliable understanding of comprehensibility and provide them with rich opportunities to develop their comprehensibility.

Raising Learners' Awareness

The first and perhaps most important aspect of comprehensibility training is to raise learners' awareness about the concept of comprehensibility. Raising awareness about speakers' expectations and judgements and how these relate to different aspects of speech is perhaps the most important message the learners can take away from the awareness raising activities. In order to reach that awareness, it seems necessary to unpack the concept of comprehensibility by discussing the linguistic elements (phonological, syntactic, discourse and pragmatic features) that make someone's speech easy or difficult to understand. Many learners may be aware of the importance of pronunciation both at segmental and suprasegmental levels, but they may not be familiar with features of fluency including repetition, hesitation and pauses that affect comprehensibility. Previous research has provided evidence that awareness raising can have a positive impact on different aspects of L2 performance. Kennedy and Trofimovich (2010), for example, examined the relationship between raising learners' awareness and quality of their pronunciation over a period of 11 weeks. Collecting both qualitative and quantitative data through dialogue journal entries and evaluating learners' pronunciation at the beginning and end of the period, they reported a positive relationship between learner pronunciation ratings and the number of qualitative language awareness comments. The results suggested that higher pronunciation ratings were associated with a larger number of qualitative awareness comments. In a more recent study, Trofimovich and colleagues (Tsunemoto, et al. 2022), used self and peer-assessment to raise learners' awareness about comprehensibility, accentedness and fluency. Collecting data from 25 L2 French learners at a university over a 15-week course, the researchers asked the learners to record two presentations at the beginning and end of the course before assessing their own and peers' speech. The learners' speech samples were also assessed externally by 10 French L1 speakers. The results suggested that the learners in the experimental group "showed greater alignment in self-assessment of comprehensibility than the comparison group" (Tsunemoto et al., 2022, p. 149) in relation to the native-speaking raters' assessment. The study provides support to the claim that awareness raising is an effective approach to helping learners not only develop an understanding of the concept of comprehensibility but to view it from a listener/rater perspective.

Strategy Training

Teaching strategies that can help L2 learners become more comprehensible is another way of helping them promote comprehensibility. There are a range of strategies, such as cognitive, metacognitive and social strategies that can help learners become more comprehensible. Sato (2020) trained a group of Chilean high school learners to use a set of metacognitive strategies to improve their comprehensibility. The strategies were *appeal for help*, *clarification request* and *comprehension check*. A second group that did not receive this training acted as a control group. The learners' comprehensibility was checked before and after the seven-week period of the treatment. Four raters rated the speech samples from the pre and post-tests on a 7-point Likert scale (1 = extremely difficult to understand; 7 = very easy to understand). The results showed that those in the strategy training group improved their comprehensibility significantly compared to the other group. It is worth noting that the strategies were not intended to directly improve the students' comprehensibility; rather, the comprehensibility improvement was observed as a byproduct of more effective interaction.

Working with university level L2 learners, Tavakoli, Campbell and McCormack (2016) taught a group of L2 earners a range of cognitive strategies to avoid pointless repetitions and hesitations that affected their fluency. Drawing the L2 learners' attention on the impact of repetitions on the listener, the authors taught them strategies that helped avoid such repetitions (e.g. using lexical fillers that help buy time when needed). While comprehensibility was not measured as an independent construct in Tavakoli et al. (2016), the results suggested that the group receiving the strategy training performed much better in reducing hesitations and repairs.

The final study we report in this section is Saito and Akiyama (2017). In this study, the authors examined the extent to which Japanese learners of English improved their L2 oral ability, including comprehensibility, over a period of a semester, when engaged in video-based conversational interactions with L1 speakers of English. The L1 speakers were trained to provide recasts, an important type of interactional feedback, when their understanding was affected by the learners' utterances. In other words, the interlocutors used recasts as a strategy to underscore the impact of the speakers' utterances on listeners' understanding. The results suggested two important findings. First, compared to those in the control group, the students in the experimental group, worked on all linguistic features of their language as a response to the interlocutors' feedback. Second, the learners made significant improvements in comprehensibility, fluency and lexicogrammar, while no gains were observed with regard to their accentedness or pronunciation. The study extends support to the hypothesis that strategy training, in this case, negotiating meaning with a proficient interlocutor, has an impact on improving comprehensibility.

The first aim of the strategy training studies reported here seems to be drawing the learners' attention to the co-constructed nature of comprehensibility by making L2 learners aware of the significance of accounting for the listener when presenting their message. Second, they provide learners with strategies that can potentially help them become comprehensible in the co-construction of meaning in the act of communication. The strategy training research reported above ties in well with one of the main claims of this volume: Comprehensibility is shaped in the context of purpose-driven communication between a speaker and a listener (see Chapter 1 for a full discussion).

Instruction to Promote Comprehensibility

Instruction has been shown to have a positive impact on the development of comprehensibility. One of the earliest studies providing evidence for the role of instruction in improving comprehensibility is Derwing, Munro and Wiebe (1998). In two interrelated experiments, the researchers examined whether L2 learners improve their comprehensibility, accent and fluency as a result of instruction over a 10-week period. Two experimental groups receiving different instructions, focusing on segmental features in one group and working with global features of pronunciation in another, were compared with a control group. The results indicated that improvements were observed in the learners reading of sentences and narrative retellings in both experimental groups. The results also suggested that both types of instruction had a positive impact on the learners' comprehensibility as rated by L1 speakers and ESL experienced teachers. More recently, Zhang and Yuan (2020), examining the effects of explicit pronunciation instruction (segmental versus suprasegmental) on Chinese

L2 learners of English over an 18-week period, partially confirmed the findings of Derwing et al. (1998). Their results suggested that while both groups demonstrated improvement in their general pronunciation, the suprasegmental instructional group made statistically significant progress in their comprehensibility at the post test and they maintained it till the delayed posttest. Similarly, Gordon and Darcy (2022) examined gains in comprehensibility as a result of pronunciation instruction in three groups (segmental, suprasegmental and a combination of both) of L2 learners in a university in Costa Rica. The improvement, however, was only observed in the suprasegmental group for comprehensibility and fluency. No improvement was observed in accentedness across the three groups. The results of these studies provide evidence that explicit instruction can help learners improve (aspects of) their comprehensibility.

As discussed in previous chapters, comprehensibility is shown to be a dynamic construct that evolves through the course of interaction (see Figure 8.1). Research in this area (Kennedy & Trofimovich, 2019) has suggested that raters' ratings of comprehensibility improve when they listen to a long sample of the speaker's speech during the course of interaction, implying that longer interactions are often rated as more comprehensible. The pedagogic implication of this dynamicity is that teachers should encourage L2 speakers to engage in spoken interactions that are not brief by nature (Kennedy & Trofimovich, 2019). Longer interactions can provide learners with an opportunity to learn more about their listener's needs and about how they can improve their speaking to cater for those needs. The classroom context offers a range of such opportunities including group discussions, brainstorming and dialogic tasks, and interviews.

Investigating the effects of instructional techniques adapted from drama on fluency, comprehensibility and accentedness of Brazilian L2 learners of English, Galante and Thompson (2017) found that drama-based activities can help learners develop their fluency and comprehensibility, but the instruction did not have much impact on accentedness. In a study investigating the effects of instruction on comprehensibility, Saito (2011) provided a group of 20 Japanese learners of English with some explicit phonetic instruction to examine the effects of such instruction (segmental features of æ,f,v,θ,ð,w,l) on the ratings of comprehensibility. The results of the study suggested that explicit instruction positively improved comprehensibility, but it did not have an impact on accent reduction. The examples provided in this section, taken together, indicate that tailor-made instruction can have a positive impact on helping learners become comprehensible.

Conclusion

In this chapter, we have reviewed research on the pedagogic aspects of comprehensibility. By examining language teaching curricula/benchmarks, research in teacher training and classroom practice, we have provided some evidence that the new perspective to comprehensibility is not carefully, rigorously or methodically considered in language teaching. Our analysis of the three documents reviewed above (Hong Kong English Language Curriculum, CEFR Companion Volume, and CSE) suggests that the concept of comprehensibility is neither systematically nor sufficiently discussed in these language policy documents. The only exception was the CEFR companion volumes in which a fresh attempt has been made to disentangle the concept of phonological control, and as a result a discussion has opened up about ease/difficulty of understanding the speaker and taking into account the listener's need and perspective.

Language curricula and policy documents are powerful pedagogic resources to which a range of stakeholders and practitioners refer to for professional use. Teachers writing lesson plans, material developers designing textbooks and language test writers developing tests are only some of the professional users referring to these documents. If these documents do not provide a clear and detailed discussion of comprehensibility and its different aspects and criteria, it would be unrealistic to expect comprehensibility to be exercised in language teaching practice, teacher training programmes or syllabus design. Accordingly, it would be unrealistic to expect teachers to be familiar with the new conceptualisation of comprehensibility or to be able to promote it effectively in their classrooms. Eventually, it would be unjust to assess a learner on a criterion for which she has neither received a clear explanation of the construct nor some proper training. We have highlighted some areas of comprehensibility that teacher training programmes can focus on, and have provided examples of classroom activities that can help learners become more comprehensible. Overall, our discussion in this chapter calls for more research in this area and is an indication of what can be done to help stakeholders develop an in-depth and reliable understanding of the concept of comprehensibility.

CHAPTER 8

CONCLUSION

This volume has been motivated by the need we have felt, in our professional careers, to understand and highlight the crucial role of comprehensibility in communication, and the inconsistency we have observed in the conceptualisation and assessment of comprehensibility in different language tests. The volume has provided a strong position on the importance of developing an in-depth and multifaceted understanding of comprehensibility in the context of real-world language use (particularly lingua francas), and the impact such understanding would have on improving practice in language testing, language teaching and use of automated procedures in assessment of second language ability. This volume has also addressed the limitations we have observed in existing approaches to defining, operationalising and assessing comprehensibility. These approaches, tending to be reductionist in nature (i.e., often focusing on intelligibility rather than comprehensibility), have usually focused on identifying a narrow range of linguistic indicators of comprehensibility (e.g. phonological or lexical aspects), and have disregarded higher-level linguistic, paralinguistic and contextual factors that contribute to comprehensibility. As we have seen, two approaches have been adopted for the evaluation of comprehensibility: either a reductionist/narrow approach to understanding and operationalising comprehensibility, where discrete linguistic indicators are the main focus; or a holistic, subjective, listener-privileged approach to evaluating comprehensibility. Both these approaches – whether used in tandem or alone – have led to limitations and issues in the assessment of spoken language ability, including test reliability, construct under-representation and construct coverage. These are some of the issues we have discussed throughout the volume (see Chapters 2, 3, 4 and 7 for example). Before presenting a summary, however, it is necessary to review the key underlying principles informing our proposed approach in the current manuscript.

First, our analysis of the construct of comprehensibility in this book is informed by some major shifts in perspectives in our discipline over the past decades. The first shift is the move away from understanding comprehensibility as "the phonological control of an idealised native speaker" (Council of Europe, 2018, p143) in which accent was seen as an indication of the speaker's poor phonological skills. Although this shift was in principle introduced to the field some time ago (e.g. Gass & Varinos, 1984; Smith & Nelson, 1985), it had been disregarded in language testing and teaching for a long time. The proposed approach here, therefore, highlights this shift and considers one's accent irrelevant to comprehensibility if the message is easy to understand. The second important shift informing our proposed approach is the move away from considering an *idealised native speaker* as a baseline for successful communication. As discussed in Chapters 1 and 2, this is a perspective that has been widely challenged by researchers in our field, and as such many language testing organisations now acknowledge that considering a *L1 speaker* model in language assessment is inappropriate and/or irrelevant to most L2 users, learners and test-takers. Our current approach to understanding comprehensibility underlies the importance of communication in a world in which a language like English is spoken by a range of L1 speakers and serves as a lingua franca in a variety of social, academic and professional contexts. These shifts have inevitably influenced our current understanding of the construct of comprehensibility and informed our suggestions (e.g. to broaden the construct to include a range of variations in these lingua francas) on its assessment.

In addition to these shifts, development of other phenomena will influence the assessment of comprehensibility in future. The development of digital technology and an increase in human mobility, for example, have already affected not only how we communicate but also how we learn (Werner & Todeva, 2022); such changes inevitably require new perspectives to testing language skills. In the backdrop of this change, there are two important developments to consider when assessing comprehensibility. First, human communication today is multimodal in nature and therefore accounting for its multimodality when assessing comprehensibility seems indispensable. What appears to be incomprehensible in an aural mode might well be comprehensible in a multimodal context. Second, plurilingualism, or the ability to communicate with "proficiency of varying degrees, in several languages, and experience of several cultures" (Council of Europe, 2001, p. 5), and the advantages of plurilingual communication are increasingly acknowledged and appreciated (Vallejo & Dooly, 2020). While current approaches to assessing comprehensibility predominantly focus on assessment in a single language, it would be difficult to assess plurilingual speakers' linguistic ability, including comprehensibility, with reference to only one of their languages (Shohamy, 2022).

In our discussions in this volume, we have recognised the complexity of the construct of comprehensibility and the cumulative effect of a myriad of linguistic and non-linguistic components that contribute to it. We have also appreciated the dynamic interplay of both linguistic and non-linguistic variables that contribute to comprehensibility, and of speaker and listener communicative goals and strategies in achieving mutual comprehensibility. Our proposed approach highlights the importance of the co-constructed nature of comprehensibility which is continuously shaped, reshaped and constructed by both the speaker and listener during the act of communication. Comprehensibility, in this volume, is understood as a dynamic and malleable construct influenced by the context and purpose of communication and the communicative goals speakers and listeners bring to the act of communication. The significant impact that context-of-use and purpose-of-communication has on comprehensibility has been specifically underlined in Chapters 3 and 4 where a range of different discoursal, contextual, sociolinguistic and sociocultural factors are suggested to affect comprehensibility (e.g. L1, familiarity, gender).

The primary aim of this volume has been to analyse the complex construct of comprehensibility and propose a new approach to understanding and operationalising comprehensibility for assessment purposes. Our analysis has demonstrated the contrast between intelligibility and comprehensibility where the former refers to a listener's actual understanding of phonological features of speech, while the latter focuses on the ease (or difficulty) a listener experiences when listening to a given speaker. We have also argued that a key difference between the two constructs is that intelligibility focuses on phonological characteristics of speech, whereas comprehensibility encapsulates a broader sense of overall understanding, covering a range of phonological, temporal, discoursal and pragmatic features of speech. Most importantly, comprehensibility is different from intelligibility as it is not a characteristic specifically displayed by a speaker or a listener; rather, comprehensibility is a joint endeavour co-constructed between the listener and the speaker when they engage in an act of communication and in relation to the purpose and context of communication.

The proposed approach considers comprehensibility from a broader, contemporary, language-in-use perspective and explores how different linguistic characteristics of speech and the context in which the speech takes place affect comprehensibility. Understanding and defining comprehensibility in this way complements previous research in this area which focused on the significance of comprehensibility at word and utterance level. We have argued that comprehensibility is affected at word, utterance, temporal, discourse and pragmatic levels of communication, and that understanding the message is usually affected by factors at more than one level. The pinnacle of our primary discussions of comprehensibility in this volume underscored the complex and multidimensional construct of comprehensibility; our discussion also suggested that the variety in the conceptualisation and measurement of comprehensibility across different language testing organisations can be explained in the light of the complex nature of comprehensibility (see Chapter 1 for a full discussion) and by the fast developing research into linguistic correlates of the construct. In the absence of an analytical framework in which comprehensibility can be carefully defined and analysed, this volume has called for a research-oriented and evidence-based model that provides an analytic framework for understanding, defining and assessing comprehensibility, one that is informed by the context of use and the purpose of the test. Comprehensibility is context- and communicative purpose dependent, and the relative importance of the different components discussed throughout this book and how they combine varies accordingly. In this volume, we have invited researchers, teachers, and language test designers to consider comprehensibility as a broader construct than what previous research had contended. That is to say, in order to understand the construct of comprehensibility and to measure it accurately, it is not enough to examine only the phonological characteristics of speech; comprehensibility should also be assessed in the light of temporal features of speech and discoursal and pragmatic characteristics of the content that is being communicated.

Figure 8.1 is a visual representation of the broader model of comprehensibility that we have proposed in this book. In the diagram, the speech event or instance of spoken communication is located at a specific confluence of contributing factors that work together to render the communicative act comprehensible. In the centre of Figure 8.1, the ovals represent the more easily measurable or quantifiable (at least to some extent) features at work in making meaning in spoken language. These are features that could be included explicitly in rating scales, manipulated in autorating systems, or extracted through complex statistical modelling of human scores. The different shades are intended to represent the relative weight or burden the particular set of features carries in getting the speaker's meaning across; the darker the shading of the oval, the greater the relative contribution to, or importance of, that category of features to comprehensibility. In this case, the particular (hypothetical) speech event relies more on purely linguistic features (darkest shade), then discourse features, then pragmatic factors (lightest shade) to achieve communicative success. In this figure, l*inguistic feature*s include phonological, temporal, morphological and lexical features of speech, *discourse features* refer to characteristics of speech at text level including cohesion and coherence, and *pragmatic factors* refer to a range of elements that help make the intended meaning comprehensible particularly with regard to sociolinguistic and sociocultural factors (see Chapters 2, 3 and 4 for a detailed discussion of each).

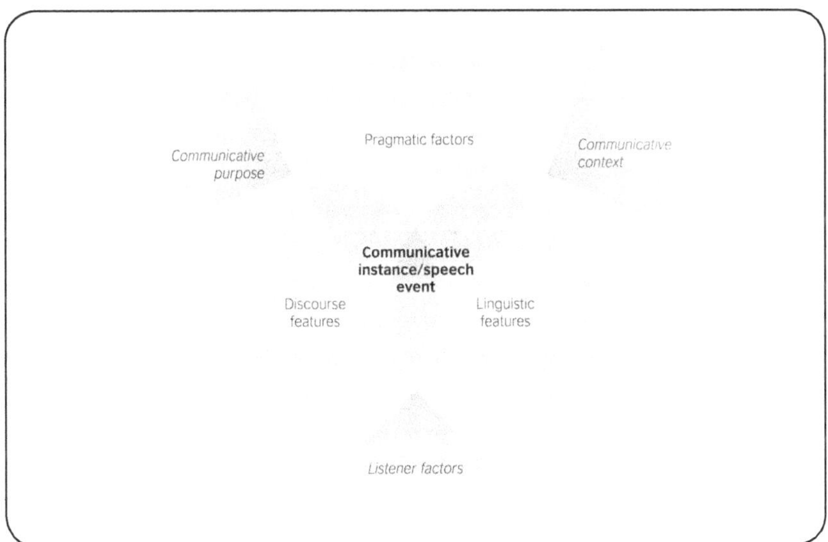

Figure 8.1 A broader perspective on comprehensibility

As can be seen in Figure 8.1, which features are tasked with the greater communicative burden is shaped by the immediate ecosystem of the speech event: the context in which the communication occurs (e.g. whether there are visual cues that reduce the need for precision in lexis), the purpose of the communicative act (e.g. simple transfer of information in a culturally neutral situation), and the support the listener brings to the instance of spoken communication (e.g. willingness to tolerate pauses and repetition). Our premise is that the wider context (including listener factors and communicative purpose) will shape the profile of more measurable features that are necessary to achieve comprehensibility, and that this will change not only between different communicative contexts, but also within the same conversation. The figure also demonstrates that comprehensibility is a dynamic construct as the set of components contributing to it is shifting and dynamic.

One primary objective of the volume has been to examine the extent to which the proposed approach to understanding comprehensibility can be incorporated in language testing in order to reflect the realities of L2 communication. In doing so, we have identified a major challenge: comprehensibility is a multifaceted, dynamic phenomenon determined by a range of characteristics from both the speakers' speech (i.e., speaker factors) and listeners' backgrounds (i.e., listener factors). Certain listeners, for example, may assign more lenient ratings to the same speech sample when they have greater familiarity with the particular foreign accent of the speech (e.g. Kennedy & Trofimovich, 2019), relevant training experience (e.g. Isaacs & Thomson, 2013), and bilingual and multilingual experiences (Shintani, Saito, & Koizumi, 2019). This listener-based approach to comprehensibility has strong ecological validity, as it reflects how speech communication develops in real-life. However, this view challenges the current approach adopted in high-stakes proficiency tests, where professional raters are typically trained to assign and agree on a single rating following criteria outlined by professional testing boards. What these tests do, in principle, is to minimise the effect of listener factors and to consider the speaker primarily responsible for the degree of comprehensibility assigned to the speaker. Putting the speaker at the centre of comprehensibility assessment will be a complex issue, particularly as language testing is moving towards using more technological advancements (e.g. AI enabled) in the assessment of L2 speaking ability (see Chapter 6 for a full discussion). Based on our proposed approach, we argue that language testing should stop adopting a speaker-only perspective to comprehensibility and take steps towards recognising the dynamic nature of comprehensibility. Rating descriptors and rater training materials, for example, should reflect the dynamic relationship between the speaker and listener by emphasising the role of the listener and listener factors.

In what follows, we will provide a summary of our conclusions and discuss the key points that researchers and practitioners can take away from these discussions. In addition, we highlight areas in which further research is needed to improve professional practice in relevant fields such as language testing and teaching.

Comprehensibility at a Phonological Level

In Chapter 2, we examined the essential contribution of phonological features of speech to the construct of comprehensibility and highlighted a number of issues related to linguistic characteristics of pronunciation that affect the assessment of communicative ability. Examining the link between phonological features of speech and comprehensibility, we have argued that this relationship and its realisation in language tests throw up some major challenges in the assessment of pronunciation, particularly when assessing a language which acts as a lingua franca. In what follows, we summarise some such challenges.

The existing research evidence has shown that while top-down processing of the message (i.e., starting from higher-level features such as overall meaning and context and moving down to phonological features and individual phonemes) is essential in achieving comprehensibility, other linguistic contributors such as articulation of individual sounds may play a more crucial role in determining the clarity of meaning where macro-level features are absent or sparse. Because accent is primarily associated with pronunciation, a crucial point to underline is that phonological features of speech are important only when they affect the meaning of the message to be communicated. As discussed throughout the book, adhering to a *L1 speaker norm* in the assessment of communicative ability is inappropriate and irrelevant to most stakeholders in most L2 testing contexts. Assessing phonologic features of speech where meaning is not impacted would lead to judgments of language beyond its linguistic and communicative value (see Chapter 2 for a full discussion).

Research in this area draws on different approaches to examining the relationship between phonological features of speech and comprehensibility. The four approaches discussed in this volume are *the empirical*, *the core-inventory*, *the Functional Load Principle*, and *the dynamic* approaches. While each approach has its own characteristics, merits and drawbacks, we have drawn on the findings of research in these different approaches to determine which phonological features of speech are related to comprehensibility. The summary of research presented in Chapter 2 suggests that a considerably large amount (49%) of linguistic features affecting comprehensibility are related to segmental (consonants and vowels) and suprasegmental features (e.g. stress and rhythm) of speech. With regard to segmental features, we have reported a range of consonants, vowels and consonant clusters and their different characteristics (e.g. quality, duration and position) shown to be central to comprehensibility. One would inevitably expect that the specific phonemes affecting comprehensibility and how salient they are in achieving comprehensibility to depend on other factors such as L1 background, and the listener's experience and expertise. For suprasegmental features, we have also reported stress, intonation, pitch, rhythm and tone to be factors that directly impact comprehensibility.

The important and complex contribution that phonological features of speech make to overall comprehensibility raises several challenges to language testers and scale developers. Firstly, our discussion has shown that the relative importance of phonological features is varied and dynamic, depending on speakers, communicative context, and the purpose of the test. Furthermore, given the influence of context on the impact of particular features, the scales used to assess comprehensibility should have a different focus to those used to rate phonological control in spontaneous speech. In this way the relative contribution of different features in different contexts will be reflected in the rating scales. This is an enormous challenge that the language testing discipline will need to address. Human-rated pronunciation scales are also reported to be difficult to design and operationalise as identifying specific differences in phonological features of speech needs sufficient linguistic expertise that not all raters might have. Finally, machine-rating of pronunciation also brings new challenges for the assessment of phonological features of speech. This topic is further discussed below.

Comprehensibility at Discourse and Pragmatic Levels

Our key argument in discussing comprehensibility at discourse level is based on the fact that ease or difficulty of understanding a speaker goes beyond understanding her/him at phoneme, word or utterance level. To promote ease of understanding of a given speaker, meaning needs to be transparent at discourse and pragmatic levels. We have argued that at discourse level the way utterances and idea units are connected to each other and how the spoken text is organised are important factors that can potentially affect comprehensibility. The study of discourse includes a broad range of linguistic factors such as ellipses, conjunctions and lexical organisation. However, not all these factors may affect comprehensibility at a similar level. For reasons of scope, we have focused on how cohesion and coherence of speech affect comprehensibility. Chapter 3 argues that speech that is poorly organised due to lack of cohesion or coherence is difficult to understand. This difficulty is not because of the listener not understanding the individual words or utterances, but because the listener cannot connect the individual elements of speech into a coherent whole at the extended discourse level.

Chapter 3 also highlighted the dearth of research in this area. The few studies examining the relationship between discourse features and comprehensibility provide emerging evidence that a speaker's use of cohesive devices and phonological features can indirectly affect comprehensibility of the message. This small body of research also suggests that the use of discourse features seems to have a substantial impact on understanding the intended meaning. In the absence of adequate research examining the relationship between comprehensibility and different aspects of discourse, it is difficult to make any final conclusions about the extent to which discourse features affect comprehensibility. Future research is certainly needed to provide us with a more in-depth knowledge of the relationship between comprehensibility and understanding the intended meaning.

We have argued that comprehensibility should also be considered at a pragmatic level because the ability to comprehend others takes place in the context of communication, and therefore it is inevitably shaped by social and cultural factors. Based on this rationale and drawing on the literature in this area, we have proposed that two groups of variables potentially influence comprehensibility: *contextual factors* (those related to the context of language use) and *sociolinguistic and socio-cultural factors* (those related to social and cultural aspects of language use).

Implied meaning, topic familiarity, and interpreting implicatures are some contextual factors that affect comprehensibility. Understanding the speaker's intended and implied meaning, affected by a range of contextual and socio-cultural factors, for example, plays an important role in the degree of comprehensibility of a listener. Given that comprehensibility is a joint endeavour, listeners' interpretation of the intended meaning is as crucial as the speakers' output; this, therefore, determines at least to some extent the degree of the listener's understanding of the message.

For sociolinguistic and sociocultural features, we discussed several factors that affect comprehensibility including richness of social experience, familiarity with L2 varieties, and differences in cultural and communication norms. The most widely researched aspects of the sociocultural factors affecting comprehensibility seems to be raters' background and attitudes. Studies investigating this topic have predominantly examined the concept of comprehensibility in terms of familiarity with, and attitudes to, L2 varieties. This has been an increasingly important area of research as new varieties are emerging and familiarity with all these varieties is essentially impossible. Notwithstanding the importance of familiarity, there are other sociolinguistic and/or sociocultural features of speech that should be examined as potential features affecting comprehensibility. Examining cultural norms, L1 and professional backgrounds are only some of the sociolinguistic factors affecting comprehensibility that need focused research.

Our discussions in Chapter 4 also focused on the assessment of comprehensibility in some international tests of English as to whether the pragmatic aspects were reflected in these tests. Focusing on the scales of speaking in TOEFL iBT and IELTS, our analysis indicated that comprehensibility is not assessed on a distinct set of scales. Rather, it is combined with a range of other sub-constructs including fluency, coherence and delivery with varying length of the scales (from 4 to 9 points), and use of polar adjectives (*easy/hard to understand* or *totally comprehensible/incomprehensible)* to rate the varying degrees of comprehensibility. Our analysis offered two main outcomes: it highlighted the importance of issues related to rater variability in ratings of comprehensibility; and it reiterated the need for more research in examining comprehensibility in rating scales and descriptors.

Fluency and Comprehensibility

A significant contribution of this volume has been to shed light on the important and intricate relationship between fluency and comprehensibility. Fluency, a multidimensional construct itself, represents fluidity, smoothness and uninterrupted production of the intended meaning in real time. Fluency can be defined in terms of cognitive, perceived, and utterance fluency (see Chapter 5 for a full discussion). We have shown that the smooth and effortless production of speech may be challenged by a number of cognitive factors including incomplete linguistic knowledge, difficulty in processing information, and cognitive complexity of the speaking task. A disruption in the production of fluent speech, regardless of its cognitively oriented source, would have an impact on comprehensibility. Speaking with long and disruptive pauses in the middle of an utterance when searching for lexical and grammatical units, for example, would inevitably affect a listener's perception of the ease with which they understand the intended meaning. In addition to the cognitive aspect of fluency, and following Tavakoli and Wright (2020), we have considered fluency from an interactionist perspective in which the listener is an active component of the meaning making process and an effective partner in understanding the meaning in interaction.

Our analysis in Chapter 5 suggests that the relationship between fluency and comprehensibility is interrelated and of a symbiotic nature. We discussed the existing research evidence that demonstrates speakers' fluency to affect listeners' comprehensibility. Suzuki and Kormos (2020), for example, provide empirical evidence that articulation rate, a measure of speed fluency, is to a great extent related to the ease of understanding. Other research also provides similar evidence highlighting the relationship between different aspects of fluency (speed, breakdown and repair) and listeners' ease or difficulty with which they understand a speech sample (Saito et al., 2017). More importantly, we highlighted research (e.g. Derwing et al, 2004; O'Brien, 2014) that claims the effects of fluency on comprehensibility are greater than the contribution of accentedness (see Chapter 5 for further details). Finally, we reviewed research that has shown raters' comprehensibility and fluency judgements to be strongly associated, and therefore highly comprehensible speech is likely to be perceived as highly fluent speech as well (Suzuki & Kormos, 2020).

Given the strong research evidence from a second language acquisition perspective about the interrelationship between the two constructs, it is necessary for language testing research to examine this relationship in more depth. We have noted a paucity of research examining the interaction between fluency and comprehensibility across levels of proficiency, in different language tests, with different test tasks and with different rating scales. The evidence provided in Chapter 5 has established that the contribution of fluency to comprehensibility is an important research topic that warrants further research. Such research would have significant implications for developing and validating rating scales and for designing rater training materials.

Technology and Comprehensibility

As technology is increasingly leveraged for different purposes in the field of language assessment, our volume would have been incomplete if we did not explore the effects of technology use in the assessment of comprehensibility. In Chapter 6, we argued that while the development of technology is overall beneficial to the assessment of language, the potential detrimental effects on the evaluation of spoken communication need to be carefully considered and mitigated against, particularly in the context of high-stakes tests. Chapter 6 considered the potential impact of technology on the assessment of comprehensibility from two broad perspectives: first, when tests are delivered using technological devices and second, the use of automated rating to assess spoken performance.

In terms of technology-enabled delivery of speaking tests, we pointed out that this brings several potential threats to assessing comprehensibility: narrowing the construct (i.e. measuring only a small part of the ability due to a change in delivery mode); introducing construct irrelevance (i.e. where abilities outside of the intended ability are being measured as a result of the use of technology); and impacting the reliability of test scores. In the first instance, we argued that a narrowing of the construct could arise as a result of various factors, including a restriction of the range of task types that can be delivered on technological devices, with implications for the skills that can be evaluated, for instance in cases where the use of extended monologues is more prevalent in technology-enabled delivery and interactive skills may be less adequately represented, or highly reduced opportunities to draw on context-level factors that contribute to comprehensibility. Technology-mediated test-tasks also risk introducing construct-irrelevant factors, such as computer literacy and ability to interact in an online environment, skills that are extraneous to being able to communicate effectively in the spoken language. In terms of reliability, we argued that technical aspects of the test (e.g. whether audio or video samples are collected, whether the quality of acoustic signals are of an acceptable standard, etc.) have an impact on the assessment of comprehensibility with predictable consequences for reliability as well as construct validity. On the other hand, one of the benefits of moving towards computer-mediated language testing is that it reflects the increasing move towards digital communication, and, arguably, the ability to interact in a digital world is a central part of the communicative construct in the contemporary world.

In terms of issues related to automated assessment, we argued that the auto-rating of the speaking ability has a potentially significant impact on the assessment of comprehensibility. We discussed a number of factors that might result in the automated assessing machine to evaluate the speaker as not comprehensible or less comprehensible and identified a few potential sources of threat to validity and reliability of the test score: construct coverage; reliability; representative sampling; potential encoding of bias; and construct obfuscation. First, automated rating carries with it the risk of narrowing the construct coverage if priority is given to the linguistic indicators a machine can most easily and accurately measure over less quantifiable communicative devices which are no less important for assessment of comprehensibility. Secondly, automated rating is most reliable when assessing highly predictable, non-spontaneous speech (Zechner et al., 2020). This means one may expect a less reliable outcome when assessing performance that is unpredictable and non-spontaneous. This would have significant implications for language varieties and language samples that are not recognised by the machine. As a result of this, it is possible that a creative and strong student could receive a lower score than one who employs test-wise strategies. This may lead to a negative washback effect as it encourages test-takers to focus on form and rely on rote-learning. Another important issue we discussed in this regard is data sampling and underrepresentation. Auto-rating systems 'learn' from data and therefore they are most reliable when the learning is used for a test-taker population that is exactly the same or very similar to the data set from which the learning has emerged. Therefore, using the same auto-rating system with a different group of test-takers would affect the reliability of the scoring, thus establishing a clear link between the data used to train the machine and the target population of test-takers is crucial. Representative sampling is also important from the rater perspective: if the judges of what is comprehensible speech are drawn from a narrow group, this bias is likely to be encoded. Finally, the lack of transparency in terms of how the auto-rating systems are arriving at the scores – particularly in the case of deep learning systems – risks construct obfuscation.

On the positive side, despite the use of scale descriptors and robust human-marker training and monitoring systems, the operationalisation of the comprehensibility construct in the minds of examiners is also far from clear, and auto-rating presents a solution – at least in part – to the rating of the extremely complex and multifaceted ability of making oneself understood. Following the discussion of technology-enabled language assessment, Chapter 6 concluded that technology in testing is not to be blamed in and of itself, calling, rather, for careful consideration of how technology is adopted, what the potential consequences of introducing it could be, and the steps that that need to be taken to mitigate negative effects, such as hybrid models that draw on both human and auto-rating systems.

Comprehensibility in Pedagogic Contexts

In Chapter 7, we examined the concept of comprehensibility from a teaching and learning perspective. We argued that achieving comprehensibility is now recognised as a realistic and auspicious learning goal by most L2 learners. We also argued that appropriate and accurate assessment of comprehensibility would have a positive washback effect on encouraging teachers and learners to aim for the development of comprehensibility rather than a L1 speaker norm of speech. Reviewing the literature on comprehensibility in pedagogic contexts, we identified two crucial limitations. First, we have argued that little attention has been paid to encouraging learners to develop comprehensibility; this is perhaps because language pedagogy, like other sub-disciplines of applied linguistics, in the past was preoccupied with the concepts of L1 speaker norms and therefore achieving a native-like pronunciation was imposed on teachers and learners as a teaching objective or learning outcome. This imposition has made pedagogic practices less successful, leading to some teachers' and learners' frustration and demotivation. The second limitation reported here is that even the narrow concept of intelligibility with its focus on pronunciation was not sufficiently practiced in teacher textbooks, teacher education programmes and or L2 classrooms. We have shown that over the past decade there has been a significant shift of perspective in understanding, researching and analysing the construct of comprehensibility. One would expect this shift to have found its way into pedagogic practices. Our primary analysis of some teaching benchmarks and curricula has unfortunately suggested that comprehensibility is hardly discussed or represented in L2 teaching textbooks and materials.

The chapter endeavoured to answer two key questions. In response to the question of the extent to which L2 teaching curricula focus on comprehensibility, we reviewed three national and international L2 teaching curricula/benchmarks. Our analysis suggested that the CEFR Companion Volumes (2018, 2020), compared to the other two documents, have paid more attention to comprehensibility and focused on the listeners' perspective. This document, however, does not provide a clear analysis of what constitutes comprehensibility or how it can be achieved. The second question the chapter focused on was whether comprehensibility is taught and practiced in L2 classrooms. The existing evidence suggests that L2 teachers are not familiar with the new perspective on the complex and multidimensional construct of fluency. Some researchers, including Crowther et al. (2015), have also argued that the wide spectrum of domains of linguistic features that contribute to comprehensibility (e.g. phonology, fluency and grammar) might be too broad to focus on in L2 teaching. Given the crucial role of comprehensibility in both language communication and language assessment, it is striking to see very little research has been conducted to explore comprehensibility in L2 education. This should be considered as an important item on the L2 research agenda to which researchers and teachers will need to attend. Despite all these limitations, the most important finding we report here is that instruction works well with the development of comprehensibility. The emerging research evidence is adequately robust to imply explicit instruction positively improves comprehensibility.

Implications for Language Testing

Our discussions throughout the volume have offered some significant implications for the language testing discipline. These stem out of two main areas that this book, overall, has highlighted: the inconclusive evidence currently available to support a purely feature-driven model of comprehensibility, and the dynamic nature of comprehensibility on a number of different levels. Indeed, the inconclusive evidence is also a result of the dynamic nature of the construct.

Our analysis of the existing approaches to assessing comprehensibility has underlined the need for data-driven evidence to support the inclusion of specific linguistic features and the exclusion of others in rating scales (human or machine) in the assessment of comprehensibility. The lack of adequate evidence for a definitive range of linguistic indicators of comprehensibility has implications, especially for a generalised, atomic-based approach to assessing the construct, particularly where the population of test-takers is drawn from a wide range of language backgrounds. This raises questions around the extent to which linguistic features should be explicitly realised in scale descriptors or auto-rating systems unless the test-taker population is narrowed-down and clearly defined, as informed by research-generated evidence. For high-stakes, globalised tests with a diverse test-taker population, a holistic approach might be preferred, both in terms of human and auto-rating systems, provided the raters are representative of the real-life listeners and users of the language, particularly in the case of lingua francas where a standard benchmark is, as we have argued, difficult to justify.

As we have discussed, the construct of comprehensibility is dynamic not only in terms of speaker language background, but also from the communicative purpose and context of use perspectives. Again, marking systems (whether realised in examiner-applied scale descriptors or auto-rating systems) designed to assess general proficiency across a range of tasks and contexts, face the greatest challenges. For example, linguistic features that are crucial to successfully communicating a message in one context – such as exhibiting a sophisticated range of lexical devices in a monologic, academic presentation – may have less relevance in another, such as a spontaneous, interactive and informal speech event. This suggests that scales – and auto-rater models – need to, at least to some degree, account for task-level contributors to comprehensibility.

Mitigation of the challenges associated with assessing an under-researched, complex, and dynamic construct is necessary. Claims about the evaluation of a test-taker's ability to make themselves understood should be made responsibly, with transparency about which test-taker population the scores are valid for, and the communicative purpose and context to which the scores apply made explicit.

Final Remarks

To conclude this volume, there are a few final remarks to which we would like to draw the readers' attention. First of all, this book is built on our professional experiences in language teaching, testing and research in these areas over the past decades; it is also informed by the findings of research in comprehensibility and intelligibility in language assessment. While these two rich sources have been fundamental in the formation and development of the ideas presented, they are inevitably limited in a number of ways. Firstly, our analysis has predominantly focused on tests of English as a second language with only minor parts of analysis examining tests of other languages. The main reason for our focus has been due to issues of access to and availability of such tests. Many tests of English have robust and detailed performance descriptors available publicly, most probably due to the high-stakes involved for a very large and diverse test-taker population. Also, many tests of other languages have their detailed documentations published in their native languages which makes access to these rich sources of information difficult for researchers not familiar with these languages. This is a limitation that future research can more progressively attend to.

Second, as indicated throughout the manuscript, there is a paucity of research on issues related to comprehensibility in language testing. Our analysis has demonstrated that not much research has been conducted to examine comprehensibility in general and with regard to linguistic features of speech beyond the utterance level in particular. For instance, very little research has so far examined the effects of discourse and pragmatic aspects of speech on comprehensibility, the interaction between fluency and comprehensibility, and the use of machine rating in the assessment of comprehensibility. This volume should therefore be considered as a call for more research in these areas.

As moving towards automated assessment of language seems both inevitable and imminent, it is necessary to investigate the impact of machine-rating on the assessment of comprehensibility. The language testing discipline needs to define what is necessary to ensure the validity and reliability of automated assessment of this complex construct can be promoted. Finally, we consider this book as a small but emerging and significant contribution to the field of language testing. We envisage that forthcoming research will offer an opportunity to question, complement and/or validate our proposed approach.

REFERENCES

Abercrombie, D. (1949). Teaching pronunciation. *English Language Teaching, 3*, 113–122. https://doi.org/10.1093/elt/III.5.113

Ahn, S.-Y., & Kang, H.-S. (2017). South Korean university students' perceptions of different English varieties and their contribution to the learning of English as a foreign language. *Journal of Multilingual and Multicultural Development, 38*(8), 712–725. https://doi.org/10.1080/01434632.2016.1242595

American Council for the Teaching of Foreign Languages (ACTFL). (2012). *Proficiency Guidelines*. https://www.actfl.org/resources/actfl-proficiency-guidelines-2012/english/speaking

American Council for the Teaching of Foreign Languages (ACTFL). *Oral Proficiency Interview (OPI)*. Retrieved 14 January, 2023, from https://www.actfl.org/assessment-research-and-development/actfl-assessments/actfl-postsecondary-assessments/oral-proficiency-interview-opi

Anderson-Hsieh, J.R., & Koehler, K. (1988). The effect of foreign accent and speaking rate on native speaker comprehension. *Language Learning, 38*(4), 561–593. https://doi.org/10.1111/j.1467-1770.1988.tb00167.x

Anderson-Hsieh, J., Johnson, R., & Koehler, K. (1992). The relationship between native speaker judgments of nonnative pronunciation and deviance in segmentals, prosody, and syllable structure. *Language Learning, 42*(4), 529–555. https://doi.org/10.1111/j.1467-1770.1992.tb01043.x

Australian Associated Press. (2017, August 8). *Computer says no: Irish vet fails oral English test needed to stay in Australia*. https://www.theguardian.com/australia-news/2017/aug/08/computer-says-no-irish-vet-fails-oral-english-test-needed-to-stay-in-australia

Bachman, L.F. (1990). *Fundamental considerations in language testing*. Oxford University Press.

Bachman, L.F., & Palmer, A.S. (1996). *Language testing in practice*. Oxford University Press.

Bernaisch, T., & Koch, C. (2015). Attitudes towards Englishes in India. *World Englishes*, *35*(1), 118–132. https://doi.org/10.1111/weng.12174

Berns, M. (2006). World Englishes & communicative competence. In B.B. Kachru, Y. Kachru, & C.L. Nelson (Eds.), *The handbook of world Englishes* (pp. 718–730). Blackwell. https://doi.org/10.1002/9780470757598.ch40

Bernstein, J. (1999). PhonePass testing: Structure and construct. Ordinate. https://www.ordinate.com/pdf/StructureAndConstruct990826.pdf

Bernstein, J., Van Moere, A., & Cheng, J. (2010). Validating automated speaking tests. *Language Testing*, *27*(3), 355–377. https://doi.org/10.1177/0265532210364404

Berry, A. (1994). Spanish and American turn-taking styles: A comparative study. *Pragmatics and Language Learning*, *5*, 180–90.

Best, C., & Tyler, M. (2007). Nonnative and second-language speech perception: Commonalities and complementarities. In M.J. Munro, O. Bohn (Eds.), *Language experience in second language speech learning: In honor of James Emil Flege* (pp.13–34). John Benjamins. https://doi.org/10.1075/lllt.17.07bes

Blevins, J. (1996). The syllable in phonological theory. In J.A. Goldsmith (Ed.), *The Handbook of phonological theory* (pp. 206–244). Blackwell Publishing. https://doi.org/10.1111/b.9780631201267.1996.00008.x

Bolton, K., & Kwok, H. (1990). The dynamics of the Hong Kong accent: Social identity and sociolinguistic description. *Journal of Asian Pacific Communication*, *1*(1), 147–172.

Bosker, H., Pinget, A., Quené, H., Sanders, T., & de Jong, N.H. (2012). What makes speech sound fluent? The contributions of pauses, speed and repairs. *Language Testing*, *30*(2), 159–175. https://doi.org/10.1177/0265532212455394

Brown, A. (1988). Functional load and the teaching of pronunciation. *TESOL Quarterly*, *22*(4), 593–606. https://doi.org/10.2307/3587258

Camarata, S. (2019). Comprehensibility. In S. Damico & M.J. Ball (Eds.), *The SAGE encyclopedia of human communication sciences and disorders* (pp. 448–449). SAGE Publications. https://doi.org/10.4135/9781483380810

Cambridge English. (2015). *Cambridge English: First for Schools sample paper 1 Speaking*. Cambridge: Cambridge English Language Assessment.

Canale, M. (1983). From communicative competence to communicative language pedagogy. In J. Richards & R. Schmidt (Eds.), *Language and communication* (pp. 2–27). Longman.

Canale, M., & Swain, M. (1980). Theoretical bases of communicative approaches to second language teaching and testing. *Applied Linguistics*, *1*(1), 1–47. https://doi.org/10.1093/applin/1.1.1

Carey M.D., Mannell, R.H., & Dunn, P.K. (2011). Does a rater's familiarity with a candidate's pronunciation affect the rating in oral proficiency interviews? *Language Testing*, *28*(2), 201–219. https://doi.org/10.1177/0265532210393704

Carrell, P.L. (1982). Cohesion is not coherence. *Tesol Quarterly*, *16*(4), 479–488. https://doi.org/10.2307/3586466

Catford, J.C. (1987). Phonetics and the teaching of pronunciation: a systemic description of English phonology. In J. Morley (Ed.), *Current perspectives on pronunciation: Practices anchored in theory* (pp. 87–100). TESOL.

Celcé-Murcia, M. (2008). Rethinking the role of communicative competence in language teaching. In E. Alcon Soler & M.P. Safont Jorda (Eds.), *Intercultural language use and language learning* (pp. 41–57). Springer. https://doi.org/10.1007/978-1-4020-5639-0_3

Chapelle, C.A., & Voss, E. (2016). 20 years of technology and language assessment in Language learning & technology. *Language Learning & Technology*, *20*(2), 116–128. http://llt.msu.edu/issues/june2016/chapellevoss.pdf

Chen, L., Zechner, K., Yoon, S., Evanini, K., Wang, X., Loukina, A., Tao, J., Davis, L., Lee, C.M., Ma, M. Mundkowsky, R. Lu, C., Leong, C.W., & Gyawali, B. (2018). Automated scoring of nonnative speech using the SpeechRaterSM v.5.0 engine *ETS Research Report Series*, 2018(1), 1–31. https://doi.org/10.1002/ets2.12198

China's Standards of English Language Ability (2018). Ministry of Education of the People's Republic of China. https://cse.neea.edu.cn/html1/report/18112/9627-1.htm

Chukharev-Hudilainen, E., & Ockey, G.J. (2021). The Development and Evaluation of Interactional Competence Elicitor for Oral Language Assessments. ETS Research Report Series, 2021: 1–20. https://doi.org/10.1002/ets2.12319

Chun, D. (2002). Discourse intonation: From theory and research to practice. John Benjamins. https://doi.org/10.1075/lllt.1

Clark, H., & Fox Tree, J. (2002). Using *uh* and *um* in spontaneous speaking. *Cognition*, *84*(1), 73–111. https://doi.org/10.1016/S0010-0277(02)00017-3

Clark, J.L.D. (1979). Direct versus semi-direct tests of speaking proficiency. In E.J. Briere, and F.B. Hinofotis (Eds), *Concepts in language testing: Some recent studies* (pp. 35–49). TESOL.

Council of Europe. (2018). *Common European framework of reference, companion volume with new descriptors*. Council of Europe Publishing. https://rm.coe.int/cefr-companion-volume-with-new-descriptors-2018/1680787989

Council of Europe. (2020). *Common European Framework of Reference for Languages: Learning, teaching, assessment – Companion volume*. Council of Europe Publishing. www.coe.int/lang-cefr

Council of Europe. (2016). Common European Framework of Reference for Languages: Learning, teaching, assessment, Phonological scale revision process report. Council of Europe Publishing. https://rm.coe.int/phonological-scale-revision-process-report-cefr/168073fff9

Cook, G. (1989). Discourse, language teaching: A scheme for teacher education. Oxford University Press.

Cooke, S. (2020). Assessing real-world use of English as a Lingua Franca (ELF): A validity argument. *VNU Journal of Foreign Studies*, *36*(4). https://doi.org/10.25073/2525-2445/vnufs.4574

Council of Europe. (2001). Common European framework of reference for languages: Learning, teaching, assessment. Cambridge University Press.

Council of Europe. (2011). *Common European framework of reference for languages: learning, teaching, assessment*. Council of Europe. https://rm.coe.int/16802fc1bf

Council of Europe. (2018). *Common European Framework of Reference for Languages: Learning, Teaching, Assessment. Companion Volume*. https://rm.coe.int/cefr-companion-volume-with-new-descriptors-2018/1680787989

Council of Europe. (2018). *Common European framework of reference for languages: Learning, teaching and assessment – Companion volume* with new descriptors. Language Policy Division, Council of Europe. http://www.coe.int/lang-cefr

Council of Europe. (2011). *Manual for language test development and examining*. http://www.coe.int/t/dg4/linguistic/ManualLanguageTest-Alte2011_EN.pdf

Cribb, M. (2012). Semantic and pragmatic miscues in non-native spoken extended discourse. *Journal of Pragmatics*, *44*(1), 71–82. https://doi.org/10.1016/j.pragma.2011.10.005

Crowther, D., Trofimovich, P., & Isaacs, T. (2016). Linguistic dimensions of second language accent and comprehensibility. *Journal of Second Language Pronunciation*, *2*(2), 160–182. https://doi.org/10.1075/jslp.2.2.02cro

Crowther, D., Trofimovich, P., Isaacs, T., & Saito, K. (2015). Does a speaking task affect second language comprehensibility? *Modern Language Journal*, *99*(1), 80–95. https://doi.org/10.1111/modl.12185

Crowther, D., Trofimovich, P., Saito, K., & Isaacs, T. (2015). Second language comprehensibility revisited: Investigating the effects of learner background. *TESOL Quarterly*, *49*(4), 814–837. https://doi.org/10.1002/tesq.203

Crowther, D., Trofimovich, P., Saito, K., & Isaacs, T. (2018). Linguistic dimensions of L2 accentedness and comprehensibility vary across speaking tasks. *Studies in Second Language Acquisition*, *40*(2), 443–457. https://doi.org/10.1017/S027226311700016X

Crystal, D. (1992). An encyclopedic dictionary of language and languages. Blackwell.

Cutler, A. (1984). Stress and accent in language production and understanding. In D. Gibbon & H. Richter (Eds.), *Intonation, accent and rhythm: Studies in discourse phonology* (pp. 77–90). Berlin: Library of Congress Cataloging. https://doi.org/10.1515/9783110863239.77

Cutler, A. (2015). Lexical stress in English pronunciation. In: M. Reed & J.M. Levis (Eds.), *The Handbook of English Pronunciation* (pp. 106–124.). Wiley Blackwell. https://doi.org/10.1002/9781118346952.ch6

De Jong, N.H., & Bosker, H. (2013). Choosing a threshold for silent pauses to measure second language fluency. In R. Eklund (Ed.), *Proceedings of the 6th workshop on Disfluency in Spontaneous sSpeech (DiSS)* (pp. 17–20). Royal Institute of Technology (KTH).

De Jong, N., & Perfetti, C. (2011). Fluency training in the ESL classroom: An experimental study of fluency development and proceduralisation. *Language Learning*, *61*(2), 533–568. https://doi.org/10.1111/j.1467-9922.2010.00620.x

Demuth, K. (2009). The prosody of syllables, words and morphemes. In E. Bavin (Ed.), *Cambridge Handbook on Child Language* (pp. 183–198). Cambridge University Press. https://doi.org/10.1017/CBO9780511576164.011

Derwing, T.M., & Munro, M.J. (1997). Accent, intelligibility and comprehensibility: Evidence from four L1s. *Studies in Second Language Acquisition*, *19*(1), 1–16. https://doi.org/10.1017/S0272263197001010

Derwing, T.M., & Munro, M.J. (2005). Second language accent and pronunciation teaching: A research-based approach. *TESOL Quarterly*, *39*(3), 379–397. https://doi.org/10.2307/3588486

Derwing, T.M., & Munro, M.J. (2013). The development of L2 oral language skills in two L1 groups: A 7-year study. *Language Learning*, *63*(2), 163–185. https://doi.org/10.1111/lang.12000

Derwing, T.M., & Munro, M.J. (2015). Pronunciation fundamentals: Evidence-based perspectives for L2 teaching and research. John Benjamins North America. https://doi.org/10.1075/lllt.42

Derwing, T.M., Munro, M.J., Foote, J.A., Waugh, E., & Fleming, J. (2014). Opening the window on comprehensible pronunciation after 19 years: A workplace training study. *Language Learning*, *64*(3), 526–548. https://doi.org/10.1111/lang.12053

Derwing, T.M., Rossiter, M.J., Munro, M.J., & Thomson, R.I. (2004). Second language fluency: Judgments on different tasks. *Language Learning*, *54*(4), 655–679. https://doi.org/10.1111/j.1467-9922.2004.00282.x

Derwing, T.M., & Rossiter, M.J. (2003). The effects of pronunciation instruction on the accuracy, fluency, and complexity of L2 accented speech. *Applied Language Learning*, *13*(1), 1–17.

Derwing, T.M., Thomson, R.I., & Munro, M.J. (2006). English pronunciation and fluency development in Mandarin and Slavic speakers. *System*, *34*(2), 183–193. https://doi.org/10.1016/j.system.2006.01.005

Derwing, T., & Munro, M. (2009). Putting accent in its place: Rethinking obstacles to communication. *Language Teaching*, *42*(4), 476–490. https://doi.org/10.1017/S026144480800551X

Derwing, T., Munro, M.J., & Wiebe, G. (1998). Evidence in favor of a broad framework for pronunciation instruction. *Language Learning*, *48*(3), 393–410. https://doi.org/10.1111/0023-8333.00047

Deterding, D. (2013). Misunderstandings in English as a lingua franca: An analysis of ELF interactions in South-East Asia. Walter de Gruyter. https://doi.org/10.1515/9783110288599

Deterding, D., & Kirkpatrick, A. (2006). Emerging South-East Asian Englishes and intelligibility. *World Englishes*, *25*(3–4), 391–409. https://doi.org/10.1111/j.1467-971X.2006.00478.x

Dewaele, J.-M. (1996). How to measure formality of speech? A model of synchronic variation. In K. Sajavaara and C. Fairweather (Eds.), *Approaches to second language acquisition, Jyväskylä Cross-Language Studies 17* (pp. 119–133). University of Jyväskylä.

Dimova, S. (2018). Pronunciation assessment in the context of World Englishes. In O. Kang & A. Ginther (Eds.), *The Routledge handbook of contemporary English pronunciation* (pp. 49–66). Routledge. https://doi.org/10.4324/9781315170756-4

Duolingo. *Duolingo English Test.* (n.d.). https://englishtest.duolingo.com/readiness

Duolingo. (2023). Duolingo English Test: Official Guide for Test Takers. https://englishtest.duolingo.com/prepare/guide

Duran-Karaoz, Z., & Tavakoli, P. (2020). Predicting L2 fluency from L1 fluency behaviour: The case of L1 Turkish and L2 English speakers. *Studies in Second Language Acquisition*, *42*(4), 671–695. https://doi.org/10.1017/S0272263119000755

Early, M., Kendrick, M., & Potts, D. (2015). Multimodality: Out from the margins of English language teaching. *TESOL Quarterly*, *49*(3), 447–460. https://doi.org/10.1002/tesq.246

Educational Testing Service (ETS). (n.d.). *TOEFL iBT speaking section*. https://www.ets.org/toefl/test-takers/ibt/about/content/speaking/

Educational Testing Service (ETS). (2023). *TOEFL iBT Independent Speaking Rubric*. https://www.ets.org/content/dam/ets-org/pdfs/toefl/toefl-ibt-speaking-rubrics.pdf

Elder, C., & Davis, A. (2006). Assessing English as a lingua franca. *Annual Review of Applied Linguistics*, *26*, 282–301. https://doi.org/10.1017/S0267190506000146

Field, J. (2005). Intelligibility and the listener: The role of lexical stress. *TESOL Quarterly*, *39*(3), 399–423. https://doi.org/10.2307/3588487

Flege, J.E., Munro, M.J., & MacKay, I.R.A. (1995). Effects of age of second-language learning on the production of English consonants. *Speech Communication*, *16*(1), 1–26. https://doi.org/10.1016/0167-6393(94)00044-B

Flege, J.E., & Bohn, O.S. (2021). The revised speech learning model (SLM-r). *Second language speech learning: Theoretical and empirical progress*, 3–83. https://doi.org/10.1017/9781108886901.002

Foote, J.A., & Trofimovich, P. (2018). Is it because of my language background? A study of language background influence on comprehensibility judgements. *The Canadian Modern Language Review*, *74*(2), 253–278. https://doi.org/10.3138/cmlr.2017-0011

Foster, P., & Skehan, P. (1996). The influence of planning and task type on second language performance. *Studies in Second Language Acquisition*, *18*(3), 299–323. https://doi.org/10.1017/S0272263100015047

Foster, P. (2020). Oral fluency in a second language: A research agenda for the next ten years. *Language Teaching*, *53*(4), 44–461. https://doi.org/10.1017/S026144482000018X

Foster, P., & Skehan, P. (1996). The influence of planning and task type on second language performance. *Studies in Second Language Acquisition*, *18*(3), 299–323. https://doi.org/10.1017/S0272263100015047

Foster, P., Tonkyn, A., & Wigglesworth, G. (2000). Measuring spoken language: A unit for all reasons. *Applied Linguistics*, *21*(3), 354–375. https://doi.org/10.1093/applin/21.3.354

Freed, B. (2000). Is fluency, like beauty, in the eyes (and ears) of the beholder? In H. Riggenbach (Ed.), *Perspectives on fluency* (pp. 243–265). University of Michigan Press. https://doi.org/10.3998/mpub.16109

Fulcher, G. (1996). Does thick description lead to smart tests? A data-based approach to rating scale construction. *Language Testing*, *13*(2), 208–238. https://doi.org/10.1177/026553229601300205

Fulcher, G. (2003). *Testing second language speaking*. Pearson Education. doi.org/10.4324/9781315837376

Fulcher, G. (2010). *Practical language testing*. Hodder Education. doi.org/10.4324/980203767399

Fung, L., & Carter, R. (2007). Discourse markers and spoken English: Native and learner use in pedagogic settings. *Applied Linguistics*, *28*(3), 410–439. https://doi.org/10.1093/applin/amm030

Galaczi, E.D., French, A., Hubbard, C., & Green, A. (2011). Developing assessment scales for large-scale speaking tests: A multiple-method approach. *Assessment in Education: Principles, Policy & Practice*, *18*(3), 217–237. https://doi.org/10.1080/0969594X.2011.574605

Galante, A., & Thomson, R.I. (2017). The effectiveness of drama as an instructional approach for the development of second language oral uency, comprehensibility, and accentedness. *TESOL Quarterly*, *51*(1), 115–142. https://doi.org/10.1002/tesq.290

Gass, S., & Varonis, E.M. (1984). The effect of familiarity on the comprehensibility of non-native speech. *Language Learning*, *34*(1), 65–87. https://doi.org/10.1111/j.1467-1770.1984.tb00996.x

Gernsbacher, M.A., & Givón, T. (1995). Introduction: coherence as a mental entity. In M.A. Gernsbacher & T. Givón (Eds.), *Coherence in spontaneous text* (pp. vi–x). John Benjamins. https://doi.org/10.1075/tsl.31.01ger

Gesellschaft für Akademische Studienvorbereitung und Testentwicklung e. V. (2012). *TestDaF-Institut, Bochum – TestDaF-Levels Subtest level descriptions*. https://www.testdaf.de/de/teilnehmende/warum-testdaf/testdaf-levels-englisch/

Ghanem, R., & Kang, O. (2018). Pronunciation features in rating criteria. In O. Kang & A. Ginther (Eds.), *The Routledge handbook of contemporary English pronunciation* (pp. 115–136). Routledge. https://doi.org/10.4324/9781315170756-7

Goldsmith, J.A. (2011). The syllable. In J.A. Goldsmith, J. Riggle, & A.C.L. Yu (Eds.), *The Handbook of phonological theory (2nd ed.)* (pp. 165–196). Blackwell Publishing Ltd. https://doi.org/10.1002/9781444343069.ch6

Gordon, J., & Darcy, I. (2022). Teaching segmentals and suprasegmentals: Effects of explicit pronunciation instruction on comprehensibility, fluency, and accentedness. *Journal of Second Language Pronunciation, 8*(2), 168–195. https://doi.org/10.1075/jslp.21042.gor

Graddol, D. (1999). The decline of the native speaker. In D. Graddol & Meinhof, U.H. (Eds.). *English in a Changing World. AILA Review*, 13, 57–68.

Green, C.F. (1998). Competing criteria in the comprehensibility of interlanguage texts: order of information versus discourse miscues. *RELC Journal*, *29*(2), 72–89. https://doi.org/10.1177/003368829802900204

Hahn, L.D. (2004). Primary stress and intelligibility: research to motivate the teaching of suprasegmentals. *TESOL Quarterly*, *38*(2), 201–223. https://doi.org/10.2307/3588378

Halliday, M.A.K., & Hasan, R. (1976). *Cohesion in English.* Longman. https://doi.org/10.4324/9781315836010

Halliday, M.A.K., & Matthiessen, C. (2013). *Halliday's introduction to functional grammar* (4th ed.). Routledge. https://doi.org/10.4324/9780203431269

Hansen Edwards, J., Zampini, M., & Cunningham, C. (2018). The Accentedness, Comprehensibility, and Intelligibility of Different Varieties of Asian English. *World Englishes*, *37*(4), 538–557. https://doi.org/10.1111/weng.12344

Hansen Edwards, J., Zampini, M., & Cunningham, C. (2019). Listener judgments of speaker and speech traits of varieties of Asian English. *Journal of Multilingual and Multicultural Development*, *40*(8), 691–706. https://doi.org/10.1080/01434632.2018.1549057

Harding, L. (2017). Validity in pronunciation assessment. In O. Kang, & A. Ginther (Eds.), *Assessment in second language pronunciation.* Routledge. https://doi.org/10.4324/9781315170756-3

Harding, L., & Mcnamara, T. (2017). Language assessment: The challenge of ELF. In J. Jenkins, W. Baker & M. Dewey (Eds.), *The Routledge handbook of English as a lingua franca* (pp. 570–582). Routledge. https://doi.org/10.4324/9781315717173-46

Harris, Z.S. (1952). Discourse analysis. *Language*, *28*(1), 1–30. https://doi.org/10.2307/409987

Hasan, R. (1984). Coherence and cohesive harmony. In J. Flood (Ed.), *Understanding reading comprehension: Cognition, language, and the structure of prose* (pp. 181–219). International Reading Association. https://doi.org/10.1558/equinox.25229

Heaney, S. (1975). *North.* London: Faber and Faber.

Hong Kong English Language Education Key Learning Area Curriculum Guide (2017). https://www.edb.gov.hk/attachment/en/curriculum-development/kla/eng-edu/Curriculum%20Document/ELE%20KLACG_2017.pdf

Hymes, D. (1971). On communicative competence. In Pride, J. & J. Holmes (Eds.), *Sociolinguistics* (pp. 269–293). Penguin.

Ingram, D. (1985). Assessing proficiency: An overview of some aspects of testing. In K. Hyltenstam & M. Pienemann (Eds.), *Modelling and assessing second language development* (pp. 215–276). Multilingual Matters.

International English Language Testing System (IELTS). (n.d.). Ensuring quality and fairness. https://www.ielts.org/about-ielts/ensuring-quality-and-fairness

International English Language Testing System (IELTS). (n.d.). *IELTS Speaking: Band Descriptors (public version).* British Council, IDP: IELTS Australia and Cambridge English Language Assessment. https://assets.cambridgeenglish.org/webinars/ielts-speaking-band-descriptors.pdf

Isaacs, T. (2018). Fully automated speaking assessment: Changes to proficiency testing and the role of pronunciation. In O. Kang, R. I. Thomson, & J. M. Murphy (Eds.), *The Routledge handbook of contemporary English pronunciation* (pp. 570–584). Routledge. https://doi.org/10.4324/9781315145006-36

Isaacs, T. (2018). Shifting Sands in Second Language Pronunciation Teaching and Assessment Research and Practice. *Language Assessment Quarterly*, *15*(3), 273–293. https://doi.org/10.1080/15434303.2018.1472264

Isaacs, T., & Harding, L. (2017). Pronunciation assessment. *Language Teaching*, *50*(3), 347–366. https://doi.org/10.1017/S0261444817000118

Isaacs, T., & Thomson, R. (2013). Rater experience, rating scale length, and judgments of L2 pronunciation: Revisiting research conventions. *Language Assessment Quarterly*, *10*(1), 135–159. https://doi.org/10.1080/15434303.2013.769545

Isaacs, T., & Trofimovich, P. (2016). *Second language pronunciation assessment: interdisciplinary perspectives.* Multilingual Matters. https://doi.org/10.21832/9781783096855-003

Isaacs, T., & Trofimovich, P. (2012). Deconstructing comprehensibility: Identifying the linguistic influences on listeners' L2 comprehensibility ratings. *Studies in Second Language Acquisition*, *34*(4), 475–505. https://doi.org/10.1017/S0272263112000150

Isaacs, T., Trofimovich, P., & Foote, J.A. (2018). Developing a user-oriented second language comprehensibility scale for English-medium universities. *Language Testing*, *35*(2), 193–216. https://doi.org/10.1177/0265532217703433

Isaacs, T., Trofimovich, P., Yu, G., & Muñoz Chereau, B. (2015). Examining the linguistic aspects of speech that most efficiently discriminate between upper levels of the revised IELTS Pronunciation scale. *IELTS Research Reports Online Series*, *4*, 48. https://ielts.org/researchers/our-research/research-reports/examining-the-linguistic-aspects-of-speech-that-most-efficiently-discriminate-between-upper-levels-of-the-revised-ielts-pronunciation-scale

Ishiguro, K. (2021). *Klara and the sun*. Faber & Faber. https://doi.org/10.1007/978-3-476-05728-0_23324-1

Iwashita, N., & Vasquez, C. (2015). *An examination of discourse competence at different proficiency levels in IELTS speaking part 2*. British Council, Cambridge English Language Assessment, and IDP: IELTS Australia. https://ielts.org/researchers/our-research/research-reports/an-examination-of-discourse-competence-at-different-proficiency-levels-in-ielts-speaking-part-2

Iwashita, N., May, L., & Moore, P. (2017). Features of discourse and lexical richness at different performance levels in the Aptis speaking test. British Council https://www.britishcouncil.org/sites/default/files/iwashita_et_al_layout_1_revised.pdf

Jenkins, J. (2000). *The phonology of English as an international language*. Oxford University Press. http://eprints.soton.ac.uk/id/eprint/65985

Jenkins, J., Cogo, A., & Dewey, M. (2011). Review of developments in research into English as a lingua franca. *Language Teaching*, *44*(3), 281–315. Cambridge University Press. https://doi.org/10.1017/S0261444811000115

Jin, T., & Mak, B. (2013). Distinguishing features in scoring L2 Chinese speaking performance: How do they work? *Language Testing*, *30*(1), 23–47. https://doi.org/10.1177/0265532212442637

Jurado-Bravo, M. (2018). Vowel quality and vowel length in English as a lingua franca in spain. *Miscelánea*, *57*, 13–34. https://doi.org/10.26754/ojs_misc/mj.20186310

Kachru, B., Kachru, Y., & Nelson, C. (2006). *The handbook of world Englishes*. Blackwell. https://doi.org/10.1111/b.9781405111850.2006.00003.x

Kachru, B.B. (1985). Standards, codification and sociolinguistic realism: the English language in the outer circle. In R. Quirkand H. Widdowson

(Eds). *English in the World: Teaching and Learning the Language and Literatures* (11–30). Cambridge University Press. https://www.teachingenglish.org.uk/sites/teacheng/files/F044%20ELT-60%20English%20in%20the%20World%20-%20Teaching%20and%20Learning%20the%20Language%20and%20Literatures_v3_1.pdf

Kachru, Y. (2008). Cultures, contexts, and interpretability. *World Englishes*, *27*(3), 309–318. https://doi.org/10.1111/j.1467-971X.2008.00569.x

Kager, R. (1996). The Metrical theory of word stress. In J.A. Goldsmith (Ed.), *The Handbook of Phonological Theory* (pp. 367–402). Blackwell. https://doi.org/10.1111/b.9780631201267.1996.00012.x

Kahng, J. (2014). Exploring utterance and cognitive fluency of L1 and L2 English speakers: temporal measures and stimulated recall. *Language Learning*, *64*(4), 809–854. https://doi.org/10.1111/lang.12084

Kang, O. (2010). Relative salience of suprasegmental features on judgments of L2 comprehensibility and accentedness. *System*, *38*(2), 301–315. https://doi.org/10.1016/j.system.2010.01.005

Kang, O. (2012). Impact of rater characteristics and prosodic features of speaker accentedness on ratings of international teaching assistants' oral performance. *Language Assessment Quarterly*, *9*(3), 249–269. https://doi.org/10.1080/15434303.2011.642631

Kang, O., & Moran, M. (2014). Functional loads of pronunciation features in nonnative speakers' oral assessment. *TESOL Quarterly*, *48*(1), 176–187. https://doi.org/10.1002/tesq.152

Kang, O., Rubin, D., & Kermad, A. (2019). The effect of training and rater differences on oral proficiency assessment. *Language testing*, *36*(4), 481–504. https://doi.org/10.1177/0265532219849522

Kang, O., Rubin, D., & Pickering, L. (2010). Suprasegmental measures of accentedness and judgments of English language learner proficiency in oral English. *The Modern Language Journal*, *94*(4), 554–566. https://doi.org/10.1111/j.1540-4781.2010.01091.x

Kennedy, S., & Trofimovic, P. (2019). Comprehensibility: A Useful Tool to Explore Listener Understanding. *The Canadian Modern Language Review*, *75*(4), 275–284. https://doi.org/10.3138/cmlr.2019-0280

Kennedy, S., & Trofimovich, P. (2010). Language awareness and second language pronunciation: A classroom study. *Language Awareness*, *19*(3), 171–185. https://doi.org/10.1080/09658416.2010.486439

Kennedy, S., Blanchet, J., & Trofimovich, P. (2014). Learner pronunciation, awareness and instruction in French as a second language. *Foreign Language Annals*, *47*(1), 79–96. https://doi.org/10.1111/flan.12066

Kerswill, P. (2014). The objectification of 'Jafaican': the discoursal embedding of Multicultural London English in the British media. In J. Androutsopoulos (Ed.) *The Media and sociolinguistic change* (428–455). Walter De Gruyter. https://doi.org/10.1515/9783110346831.427

King, R.D. (1967). A measure for functional load. *Studia Linguistica, 21*, 1–14. https://doi.org/10.1111/j.1467-9582.1967.tb00545.x

King, R.D. (1967). Functional load and sound change. *Language*, *43*(4), 831–852. https://doi.org/10.2307/411969

Kirkpatrick, A. (2007). *World Englishes: Implications for international communication and English language teaching*. Cambridge University Press. https://doi.org/10.1017/S0047404509990376

Knoch, U. (2016). What can pronunciation researchers learn from research into second language writing? In T. Isaacs and Trofimovich, P. (Eds.), Second language pronunciation assessment: Interdisciplinary perspectives, 54–71. Multilingual Matters. https://doi.org/10.21832/9781783096855-006

Knoch, U., Fairbairn, J., & Huisman, A. (2015). *An evaluation of the effectiveness of training Aptis raters online*. British Council. http://www.britishcouncil.org/sites/britishcouncil.uk2/files/evaluation-of-effectiveness-aptis-online-training.pdf

Kress, G. (2000). Multimodality: Challenges to Thinking About Language. *TESOL Quarterly*, *34*(2), 337–340. https://doi.org/10.2307/3587959

Kormos, J., & Denés, M. (2004). Exploring measures and perceptions of fluency in the speech of second language learners. *System*, *32*(2), 145–164. https://doi.org/10.1016/j.system.2004.01.001

Ladefoged, P., & Johnson, K. (2014). *A course in phonetics (7th ed.)*. Cengage Learning.

Lado, R. (1961). *Language testing: The construction and use of foreign language tests*. Longman. https://api.semanticscholar.org/CorpusID:59853602

Lazaraton, A. (2002). A qualitative approach to the validation of oral language tests. Cambridge University Press. https://www.cambridge.org/gb/cambridgeenglish/catalog/teacher-training-development-and-research/qualitative-approach-validation-oral-language-tests/qualitative-approach-validation-oral-language-tests-paperback?isbn=9780521002677&format=PB

Leech, G. (1983). *Principles of pragmatics*. Longman. https://doi.org/10.4324/9781315835976

Lennon, P. (1990). Investigating fluency in EFL: A quantitative approach. *Language Learning*, *40*(3), 387–417. https://doi.org/10.1111/j.1467-1770.1990.tb00669.x

Lennon, P. (2000). The lexical element in spoken second language fluency. In H. Riggenbach (Ed.), *Perspectives on Fluency* (pp: 25–42). University of Michigan Press. https://doi.org/10.3998/mpub.16109

Leung, C., & Lewkowicz, J. (2006). Expanding horizons and unresolved conundrums: Language testing and assessment. *TESOL Quarterly*, *40*(1), 211. https://doi.org/10.2307/40264517

Levis, J.M., & Wichmann, A. (2015). English Intonation – Form and Meaning. In M. Reed & J.M. Levis (Eds.), *The handbook of English pronunciation* (pp. 139–156). Wiley Blackwell. https://doi.org/10.1002/9781118346952.ch8

Levis, J.M. (2005). Changing contexts and shifting paradigms in pronuniciation Teaching. *TESOL Quarterly*, *39*(3), 369–377. https://doi.org/10.2307/3588485

Levis, J.M. (2006). Pronunciation and the assessment of spoken language. In R. Hughes (Ed.), *Spoken English, TESOL and applied linguistics: Challenges for theory and practice* (pp. 245–70). Palgrave Macmillan. https://doi.org/10.1057/9780230584587_11

Liao, S. (2009). Variation in the use of discourse markers by Chinese teaching assistants in the US. *Journal of Pragmatics*, *41*(7), 1313–1328. https://doi.org/10.1016/j.pragma.2008.09.026

Linell, P. (1998). *Approaching dialogue: Talk interaction and contexts in dialogical perspectives*. John Benjamins. https://doi.org/10.1075/impact.3

Litman, D., Strik, H., & Lim, G.S. (2018). Speech technologies and the assessment of second language speaking: Approaches, challenges, and opportunities. language *Assessment Quarterly*, *15*(3), 294–309. https://doi.org/10.1080/15434303.2018.1472265

Lotherington, H., & Jenson, J. (2011). Teaching Multimodal and Digital Literacy in L2 Settings: New Literacies, New Basics, New Pedagogies. *Annual Review of Applied Linguistics*, *31*(Mar), 226–246. https://doi.org/10.1017/S0267190511000110

Low, E.L. (2006). Cross-Varietal comparison of deaccenting and given information: Implications for international intelligibility and pronunciation teaching. *TESOL Quarterly*, *40*(4), 739–761. https://doi.org/10.2307/40264306

Low, E.L. (2015). The Rhythmic patterning of English(es): Implications for pronunciation teaching. In M. Reed & J.M. Levis (Eds.), *The handbook of English pronunciation* (pp. 125–138). Wiley Blackwell. https://doi.org/10.1002/9781118346952.ch7

Luchini, P.L., & Kennedy, S. (2013). Exploring sources of phonological unintelligibility in spontaneous speech. *International Journal of English and Literature*, *4*(3), 79–88. https://academicjournals.org/journal/IJEL/article-full-text-pdf/B8E3F993858

MacIntyre, P.D. (2012). The idiodynamic method: A closer look at the dynamics of communication traits. *Communication Research Reports*, *29*(4), 361–367. https://doi.org/10.1080/08824096.2012.723274

Major, R.C. (2007). Identifying a foreign accent in an unfamiliar language. *Studies in Second Language Acquisition*, *29*(4), 539–556. https://doi.org/10.1017/S0272263107070428

Major, R., Fitzmaurice, S., Bunta, F., & Balasubramanian, C. (2002). The Effects of nonnative accents on listening comprehension: Implications for ESL assessment. *TESOL Quarterly*, *36*(2), 173–190. https://doi.org/10.2307/3588329

McCarthy, M. (1991). *Discourse analysis for language teachers*. Cambridge University Press. https://sacunslc.files.wordpress.com/2015/03/michael-mccarthy-discourse-analysis-for-language-teachers-cambridge-language-teaching-library-1991.pdf

McNamara, T. (2006). Validity in language testing: The challenge of Sam Messick's legacy. *Language Assessment Quarterly*, *3*(1), 31–51. https://doi.org/10.1207/s15434311laq0301_3

McNamara, T. (2012). English as a lingua franca: The challenge for language testing. *Journal of English as a Lingua Franca*, *1*(1), 199–202. https://doi.org/10.1515/jelf-2012-0013

Meyer, F.K. (2012). Language proficiency testing for Chinese as a foreign language: An argument-based approach for validating the Hanyu Shuiping Kaoshi (HSK). Peter Lang. http://doi.org/10.3726/978-3-653-03934-4

Meyerstein, R.S. (1970). Functional load: Descriptive limitations, alternatives of assessment and extensions of application. Mouton. https://doi.org/10.1515/9783111354163

Müller, S. (2005). Discourse markers in native and non-native English discourse. John Benjamins. https://doi.org/10.1075/pbns.138

Munro, M.J., & Derwing, T.M. (1994). Evaluations of foreign accent in extemporaneous and read materials. Language Testing, *11*(3), 254–266. https://doi.org/10.1177/026553229401100302

Munro, M.J., & Derwing, T.M. (1995). Foreign accent, comprehensibility, and intelligibility in the speech of second language learners. Language Learning, *45*(1), 73–97. https://doi.org/10.1111/j.1467-1770.1995.tb00963.x

Munro, M.J., & Derwing, T.M. (1998). The effects of speaking rate on listener evaluations of native and foreign-accented speech. *Language Learning*, *48*(2), 159–182. https://doi.org/10.1111/1467-9922.00038

Munro, M.J., & Derwing, T.M. (2006). The functional load principle in ESL pronunciation instruction: An exploratory study. *System*, *34*(4), 520–531. https://doi.org/10.1016/j.system.2006.09.004

Munro, M.J., & Derwing, T.M. (1995). Processing time, accent, and comprehensibility in the perception of native and foreign-accented speech. *Language and Speech*, *38*, 289–306. https://doi.org/10.1177/002383099503800305

Nagle, C., Trofimovich, P., & Bergeron, A. (2019). Toward a dynamic view of second language comprehensibility. *Studies in Second Language Acquisition*, *41*(4), 647–672. https://doi.org/10.1017/S0272263119000044

Nakamura, S. (2011). Characteristics of contrast between the stressed and the unstressed in rhythm units observed in duration structure in English speech by Japanese learners. *Pan-Pacific Association of Applied Linguistics*, *15*(1), 177–189. https://files.eric.ed.gov/fulltext/EJ939946.pdf

Nakatsuhara, F., Inoue, C., Berry, V., & Galaczi, E. (2017). Exploring performance across two delivery modes for the IELTS Speaking Test: face-to-face and video-conferencing delivery (Phase 2). IELTS Partnership Research Papers, 3. IELTS Partners: British Council, Cambridge English Language Assessment and IDP: IELTS Australia. https://www.ielts.org/teaching-and-research/research-reports

Neri, A., Cucchiarini, C., & Strik, H. (2006). Selecting segmental errors in non-native dutch for optimal pronunciation training. *IRAL, International Review of Applied Linguistics in Language Teaching*, *44*(4), 357–404. https://doi.org/10.1515/IRAL.2006.016

Nespor, M., & Vogel, I. (1986). *Prosodic Phonology*. Foris Publications. https://doi.org/10.1515/9783110977790

Newman, P. (1996). Hausa tonology: Complexities in an "easy" tone language. In J.A. Goldsmith (Ed.), *The handbook of phonological theory* (pp. 762–781). Blackwell Publishing. https://doi.org/10.1111/b.9780631201267.1996.00028.x

Nguyen, C.L., Ingram, J., & Pensalfini, R. (2008). Prosodic transfer in Vietnamese acquisition of English contrastive stress patterns. *Journal of Phonetics*, *36*(1), 158–190. https://doi.org/10.1016/j.wocn.2007.09.001

O'Brien, M.G. (2014). L2 learners' assessments of accentedness, fluency, and comprehensibility of native and nonnative German speech. *Language Learning*, *64*(4), 715–748. https://doi.org/10.1111/lang.12082

O'Brien, M.G., Jackson, C.N., & Gardner, C.E. (2014). Cross-linguistic differences in prosodic cues to syntactic disambiguation in German and English. *Applied Psycholinguistics*, *35*(1), 27–70. https://doi.org/10.1017/S0142716412000252

O'Sullivan, B. (2020). Taxonomy for Terms Related to Human & Automated Rating Systems. British Council Internal Report.

O'Loughlin, K.J. (2001). *The equivalence of direct and semi-direct speaking tests*. Cambridge University Press.

Pearson. (2018). *Versant Spanish Test: Test description and validation summary*. Version 1118M. Palo Alto: Pearson. https://www.pearson.com/content/dam/one-dot-com/one-dot-com/english/SupportingDocs/Versant/ValidationSummary/Versant-Spanish-Test-Description-Validation-Summary.pdf

Pearson Education Ltd. (2023). *PTE Academic Score Guide for Test Takers: Version 19*. Palo Alto: Pearson. https://assets.ctfassets.net/yqwtwibiobs4/3Bm0RMkKoNVOoOxUe38mg4/f565a92a97e8f3cf60c5506d347dedb8/PTE_Academic_Score_Guide_for_Test_Takers_June_2023.pdf

Pearson Education, Inc. (2022). *Versant English Test: Test Description and Validation Summary*. https://www.pearson.com/content/dam/one-dot-com/one-dot-com/pearson-languages/en-gb/pdfs/versant-resources/versant-english-test-description-validation-summary.pdf

Pearson Education, Inc. (n.d.). *Other spoken language tests*. https://www.pearson.com/english/versant/tests/other-spoken-language-tests.html

Peltonen, P. (2018). Exploring connections between first and second language fluency: A mixed methods approach. *The Modern Language Journal*, *102*(4), 676–692. https://doi.org/10.1111/modl.12516

Pickering, L. (2001). The role of tone choice in improving ITA communication in the classroom. *TESOL Quarterly*, *35*(2), 233–255. https://doi.org/10.2307/3587647

Pickering, L. (2009). Intonation as a pragmatic resource in ELF interaction. *Intercultural Pragmatics*, *6*(2), 235–255. https://doi.org/10.1515/IPRG.2009.013

Préfontaine, Y., & Kormos, J. (2016). A qualitative analysis of perceptions of fluency in second language French. *International Review of Applied Linguistics in Language Teaching*, *54*(2), 151–169. https://doi.org/10.1515/iral-2016-9995

Préfontaine, Y. (2013). Perceptions of French fluency in second language speech production. *Canadian Modern Language Review*, *69*(3), 324–348. https://doi.org/10.3138/cmlr.1748

Préfontaine, Y., Kormos, J., & Johnson, D. (2016). How do utterance measures predict raters' perceptions of fluency in French as a second language? *Language Testing*, *33*(1), 53–73. https://doi.org/10.1177/0265532215579530

Purpura, J. (2004). *Assessing Grammar.* Cambridge University Press. https://doi.org/10.1017/CBO9780511733086

Read, J., & Nation, P. (2006). An investigation of lexical dimension of the IELTS speaking tests. *IELTS Research Reports*, *6*, 1–25. https://ielts.org/researchers/our-research/research-reports/an-investigation-of-the-lexical-dimension-of-the-ielts-speaking-test

Reid, K.T., Trofimovich, P., & O'Brien, M. (2019). Social attitudes and speech ratings: Effects of positive and negative bias on multilingual listeners' judgement of second language speech. *Studies in Second Language Acquisition*, *41*(2), 419–442. https://doi.org/10.1017/S0272263118000244

Rover, C. (2011). Testing of second language pragmatics: Past and future. *Language Testing*, *28*(4), 463–481. https://doi.org/10.1177/0265532210394633

Saito, K. (2020). Multi- or single-word units? The role of collocation use in comprehensible and contextually appropriate second language speech. *Language Learning*, *70*(2), 548–588. https://doi.org/10.1111/lang.12387

Saito, K. (2011). Examining the role of explicit phonetic instruction in native-like and comprehensible pronunciation development: an instructed SLA approach to L2 phonology. *Language Awareness*, *20*(1), 45–59. https://doi.org/10.1080/09658416.2010.540326

Saito, K., & Akiyama, Y. (2017). Linguistic correlates of comprehensibility in second language Japanese speech. *Journal of Second Language Pronunciation*, *3*(2), 199–217. https://doi.org/10.1075/jslp.3.2.02sai

Saito, K., Trofimovich, P., & Isaacs, T. (2015). Second language speech production: Investigating linguistic correlates of comprehensibility and accentedness for learners at different ability levels. *Applied Psycholinguistics*, *37*(2), 217–240. https://doi.org/10.1017/S0142716414000502

Saito, K., Trofimovich, P., & Isaacs, T. (2015). Using listener judgements to investigate linguistic influences on L2 comprehensibility and accentedness: A validation and generalization study. *Applied linguistics*, *38*(4), 439–462. https://doi.org/10.1093/applin/amv047

Saito, K., Trofimovich, P., & Isaacs, T. (2016). Second language speech production: Investigating linguistic correlates of comprehensibility and accentedness for learners at different ability levels. *Applied Psycholinguistics*, *37*(2), 217–240. https://doi.org/10.1017/S0142716414000502

Saito, K., Trofimovich, P., & Isaacs, T. (2017). Using listener judgements to investigate linguistic influences on L2 comprehensibility and accentedness: A validation and generalization study. *Applied Linguistics*, *38*, 439–462. https://doi.org/10.1093/applin/amv047

Saito, K., Trofimovich, P., Isaacs, T., & Webb, S. (2016). Re-examining phonological and lexical correlates of second language comprehensibility: The role of rater experience. In T. Isaacs, & P. Trofimovich (Eds.), *Second Language Pronunciation Assessment: Interdisciplinary Perspectives* (pp. 141–156). https://doi.org/10.21832/ISAACS6848

Saito, K., Webb, S., Trofimovich, P., & Isaacs, T. (2016). Lexical profiles of comprehensible second language speech. *Studies in Second Language Acquisition*, *38*(4), 677–701. https://doi.org/10.1017/S0272263115000297

Saito, K., Tran, M., Suzukida, Y., Sun, H., Magne, V., & Ilkan, M. (2019). How do second language listeners perceive comprehensibility of foreign accented speech?: Roles of first language profiles, second language proficiency, age, experience, familiarity and metacognition. *Studies in Second Language Acquisition*, *41*(5), 1133–1149. https://doi.org/10.1017/S0272263119000226

Sato, M. (2020). Metacognitive instruction for collaborative interaction: The process and product of self-regulated learning in the Chilean EFL context. In C. Lambert and R. Oliver (Eds.) *Using tasks in second language teaching: Practice in diverse contexts* (pp. 215–236). Multilingual Matters. https://doi.org/10.21832/9781788929455

Schmidt, M., & Fägersten, K. (2010). Disfluency markers in L1 attrition. *Language Learning*, *60*(4), 753–791. https://doi.org/10.1111/j.1467-9922.2010.00575.x

Schmidt, R. (1992). Psychological mechanisms underlying second language fluency. *Studies in Second Language Acquisition*, *14*(4), 357–385. https://doi.org/10.1017/S0272263100011189

Sealey, A. (2020). Introduction to discourse: Definitions, debates, and decisions. In C. Hart (Ed.), *Researching Discourse: A Student Guide* (pp. 6–19). Routledge. https://doi.org/10.4324/9780367815042-2

Seedhouse, P., & Harris, A. (2011). Topic development in the IELTS Speaking Test. *IELTS Research Reports*, *12*, 1–56. https://www.ielts.org/-/media/research-reports/ielts_rr_volume12_report2.ashx

Segalowitz, N. (2010). The Cognitive Bases of Second Language Fluency. Routledge. https://doi.org/10.4324/9780203851357

Segalowitz, N. (2016). Second language fluency and its underlying cognitive and social determinants. *International Review of Applied Linguistics in Language Teaching*, *54*(2), 79–95. https://doi.org/10.1515/iral-2016-9991

Seidlhofer, B. (2009). Common ground and different realities: World Englishes and English as a lingua franca. *World Englishes*, *28*(2), 236–245. https://doi.org/10.1111/j.1467-971X.2009.01592.x

Seidlhofer, B. (2011). *Understanding English as a Lingua Franca*. Oxford University Press. https://doi.org/10.1002/9781405198431.wbeal0243

Sewell, A. (2017). Functional load revisited: Reinterpreting the findings of 'lingua franca' intelligibility studies. *Journal of Second Language Pronunciation*, *1*(3), 57–79. https://doi.org/10.1075/jslp.3.1.03sew

Sheppard, B., Elliott, N., & Baese-Berk, M. (2017). Comprehensibility and intelligibility of international student speech: Comparing perceptions of university EAP instructors and content faculty. *Journal of English for Academic Purposes*, *26*, 42–51. https://doi.org/10.1016/j.jeap.2017.01.006

Shintani, N., Saito, K., & Koizumi, R. (2019). The relationship between multilingual raters' language background and their perceptions of accentedness and comprehensibility of second language speech. *International Journal of Bilingual Education and Bilingualism*, *22*(7), 849–869. https://doi.org/10.1080/13670050.2017.1320967

Shohamy, E. (2022). Critical Language Testing, Multilingualism and Social Justice. *TESOL Quarterly*, *56*(4), 1445–1457. https://doi.org/10.1002/tesq.3185

Sicola, L., & Darcy, I. (2015). Integrating pronunciation into the language classroom. In M. Reed & J. Levis (Eds.), *Handbook of English pronunciation* (pp. 467–483). Wiley-Blackwell. https://doi.org/10.1002/9781118346952.ch26

Skehan, P. (2003). Task based instruction. *Language Teaching*, *36*(1), 1–14. https://doi.org/10.1017/S026144480200188X

Skehan, P. (2009). Modelling second language performance: Integrating complexity, accuracy, fluency, and lexis. *Applied Linguistics*, *30*(4), 510–532. https://doi.org/10.1093/applin/amp047

Skehan, P. (2014). Limited attentional capacity, second language performance, and task-based pedagogy. In P. Skehan (Ed.), *Processing perspectives on task performance* (pp. 211–260). John Benjamins. https://doi.org/10.1075/tblt.5.08ske

Smith, L.E., & Nelson, C.L. (1985), International intelligibility of English: Directions and resources. *World Englishes*, *4*(3), 333–342. https://doi.org/10.1111/j.1467-971X.1985.tb00423.x

Spezzini, S. (2004). English immersion in Paraguay: Individual and sociocultural dimensions of language learning and use. *International Journal of Bilingual Education and Bilingualism*, *7*(5), 412–431. https://doi.org/10.1080/13670050408667823

Surendran, D., & Levow, G. (2004). The Functional load of tone in Mandarin is as high as that of vowels. In. *Speech prosody, international conference* (pp. 99–102). https://sprosig.org/sp2004/PDF/Surendran-Levow.pdf

Suzuki, S., & Kormos, J. (2020). Linguistic dimensions of comprehensibility and perceived fluency: An investigation of complexity, accuracy and fluency in second language argumentative speech. *Studies in Second Language Acquisition*, *42*(1), 251. https://doi.org/10.1017/S0272263119000627

Suzuki, S., & Kormos, J. (2022). The multidimensionality of second language oral fluency: Interfacing cognitive fluency and utterance fluency. *Studies in Second Language Acquisition*, 1–27. https://doi.org/10.1017/S0272263121000899

Suzuki, S., Kormos, J., & Uchihara, T. (2021). The Relationship Between Utterance and Perceived Fluency: A Meta-Analysis of Correlational Studies. *The Modern Language Journal (Boulder, Colo.)*, *105*(2), 435–463. https://doi.org/10.1111/modl.12706

Suzukida, Y., & Saito, K. (2021). Which segmental features matter for successful L2 comprehensibility? Revisiting and generalizing the pedagogical value of the functional load principle. *Language Teaching Research*, *25*(3), 435–450. https://doi.org/10.1177/1362168819858246

Suzukida, Y., & Saito, K. (2022). What is second language pronunciation proficiency? An empirical study. *System (Linköping)*, *106*, 102754. https://doi.org/10.1016/j.system.2022.102754

Szczepek Reed, B.B. (2012). A conversation analytic perspective on teaching English pronunciation: The case of speech rhythm. *International Journal of Applied Linguistics*, *22*(1), 67–87. https://doi.org/10.1111/j.1473-4192.2011.00293.x

Taguchi, N. (2005). Comprehending implied meaning in English as a foreign language. *The Modern Language Journal*, *89*(4), 543–562. https://doi.org/10.1111/j.1540-4781.2005.00329.x

Taguchi, N. (2007). Development of speed and accuracy in pragmatic comprehension in English as a foreign language. *TESOL Quarterly*, *41*(2), 313–338. https://doi.org/10.1002/j.1545-7249.2007.tb00061.x

Taguchi, N. (2011). Rater variation in assessment of speech acts. *Pragmatics*, *21*(3): 453–474. https://doi.org/10.1075/prag.21.3.08tag

Taguchi, N. (2012). Context, individual differences, and pragmatic competence. Multilingual Matters. https://doi.org/10.21832/9781847696106

Tajima, K., Port, R., & Dalby, J. (1997). Effects of temporal correction on intelligibility of foreign accented English. *Journal of Phonetics*, *25*, 1–24. https://doi.org/10.1006/jpho.1996.0031

Tan, R.S.K., & Low, E.L. (2014). Rhythmic patterning in Malaysian and Singapore English. *Language and Speech*, *57*(2), 196–214. https://doi.org/10.1177/0023830913496058

Tannen, D. (1980). Spoken/Written Language and the Oral/Literate Continuum. In E. B. Caron et al. (Eds.), *Proceedings of the Sixth Annual Meeting of the Berkeley Linguistics Society* (pp. 207–218). Berkeley Linguistic Society. https://doi.org/10.3765/bls.v6i0.2133

Tanskanen, S.K. (2006). Collaborating towards coherence: Lexical cohesion in English discourse. John Benjamins. https://doi.org/10.1075/pbns.146

Tauroza, S., & Luk, J. (1997). Accent and second language listening comprehension. *RELC Journal*, *28*(1), 54–71. https://doi.org/10.1177/003368829702800104

Tavakoli, P., & Skehan, P. (2005). Strategic planning, task structure, and performance testing. In R. Ellis (Ed.), *Planning and task performance* (pp. 239–273). John Benjamins. https://doi.org/10.1075/lllt.11.15tav

Tavakoli, P., & Foster, P. (2008). Task design and second language performance: The effect of narrative type on learner output. *Language Learning*, *58*(2), 439–73. https://doi.org/10.1111/j.1467-9922.2008.00446.x

Tavakoli, P. (2011). Pausing patterns: differences between L2 learners and native speakers. *ELT Journal*, *65*(1), 71–79. https://doi.org/10.1093/elt/ccq020

Tavakoli, P., Campbell, C., & McCormack, J. (2016). Development of Speech Fluency Over a Short Period of Time: Effects of Pedagogic Intervention. *TESOL Quarterly*, *50*(4), 447–471. https://doi.org/10.1002/tesq.244

Tavakoli, P., & Hunter, A.-M. (2018). Is fluency being 'neglected 'in the classroom'? Teacher understanding of fluency and related classroom practices. *Language Teaching Research*, *22*(3), 330–349. https://doi.org/10.1177/1362168817708462

Tavakoli, P., & Uchihara, T. (2020). To what extent are multiword sequences associated with oral fluency? *Language Learning*, *70*(2), 506–547. https://doi.org/10.1111/lang.12384

Tavakoli, P., & Wright, C. (2020). *Second language speech fluency: From research to practice*. Cambridge University Press. https://doi.org/10.1017/9781108589109

Tavakoli, P., Nakatsuhara, F., & Hunter, A-M. (2020). Aspects of oral fluency across assessed levels of proficiency: Do "fluency profiles" for different proficiency levels exist? *Modern Language Journal*, *104*(1). https://doi.org/10.1111/modl.12620

Taylor, L. (2005). Washback and impact. *ELT Journal, Key concepts*, *59*(2), 154–5. https://doi.org/10.1093/eltj/cci030

Thompson, S.E. (1994). Aspects of cohesion in monologue. *Applied Linguistics*, *15*(1), 58–75. https://doi.org/10.1093/applin/15.1.58

Thomson, R. (2017). Measurement of accentedness, intelligibility, and comprehensibility. In *Assessment in second language pronunciation* (pp. 11–29). Routledge. https://doi.org/10.4324/9781315170756-2

Trinity College. (n.d.). ISE Rating Scales. https://www.trinitycollege.com/qualifications/english-language/ISE/ISE-results-and-certificates/ISE-rating-scales

Tian, Y. Maruyama, T., & Ginzburg, J. (2017). Self-addressed questions and filled pauses: A cross-linguistic investigation. *Journal of Psycholinguistic Research*, *46*(4), 905–922. https://doi.org/10.1007/s10936-016-9468-5

Trofimovich, P., & Isaacs, T. (2012). Disentangling accent from comprehensibility. *Bilingualism: Language and Cognition*, *15*(4), 905–916. https://doi.org/10.1017/S1366728912000168

Trofimovich, P., Kennedy, S., & Blanchet, J. (2017). Development of second language French oral skills in an instructed setting: A focus on speech rating. *The Canadian Journal of Applied Linguistics, Special Issue*, *20*(2), 32–50. https://doi.org/10.7202/1042675ar

Tsunemoto, A., Trofimovich, P., Blanchet, J., Bertrand, J., & Kennedy, S. (2022). Effects of benchmarking and peer-assessment on French learners' self-assessments of accentedness, comprehensibility, and fluency. *Foreign Language Annals*, *55*(1), 135–154. https://doi.org/10.1111/flan.12571

Universities UK International. (2018). *International facts and figures: Higher Education 2018*. University Press. https://www.universitiesuk.ac.uk/sites/default/files/field/downloads/2022-07/InternationalFactsandFigures-2018_web.pdf

Vallejo, C., & Dooly, M. (2020). Plurilingualism and translanguaging: Emergent approaches and shared concerns. *International Journal of Bilingual Education and Bilingualism*, *23*(1), 1–16. https://doi.org/10.1080/13670050.2019.1600469

Van Moere, A. (2012). A psycholinguistic approach to oral language assessment. *Language Testing*, *29*(3), 325–344. https://doi.org/10.1177/0265532211424478

Van Moere, A., & Downey, R. (2016). 21. Technology and artificial intelligence in language assessment. In *Handbook of second language assessment* (pp. 341–358). De Gruyter Mouton. https://doi.org/10.1515/9781614513827-023

Varonis, E.M., & Gass, S. (1982). The comprehensibility of non-native speech. *Studies in Second Language Acquisition*, *4*(2), 114–136. https://doi.org/10.1017/S027226310000437X

Webb, S., & Rodgers, M.P.H. (2009). Vocabulary demands of television programs. *Language Learning*, *59*(2), 335–366. https://doi.org/10.1111/j.1467-9922.2009.00509.x

Webb, S., & Rodgers, M.P.H. (2009). The lexical coverage of movies. *Applied Linguistics*, *30*(3), 407–427. https://doi.org/10.1093/applin/amp010

Weismer, G. (2008). Speech intelligibility. In M.J. Ball, M.R. Perkins, N. Mueller, & S. Howard (Eds.), *Handbook of clinical linguistics* (pp. 568–580). https://doi.org/10.1002/9781444301007.ch35

Wennerstrom, A. (1994). Intonational meaning in English discourse: A study of non-native speakers. *Applied Linguistics*, *15*(4), 399–420. https://doi.org/10.1093/applin/15.4.399

Wennerstrom, A. (2001). Intonation and evaluation in oral narratives. *Journal of Pragmatics*, *33*(8), 1183–1206. https://doi.org/10.1016/S0378-2166(00)00061-8

Wennerstrom, A. (2001). The music of everyday speech: Prosody and di scourse analysis. Oxford University Press.

Werner, R., & Todeva, E. (2022). Plurilingualism and multimodality: The metanoia within reach. *TESL Canada Journal*, *38*(1), 214–227. https://doi.org/10.18806/tesl.v38i2.1362

White, S. (1989). Backchannels across cultures: A study of Americans and Japanese. *Language in Society*, *18*(1), 59–76. https://doi.org/10.1017/S0047404500013270

Wichmann, A. (2000). *Intonation in text and discourse: Beginnings, middles and ends*. Routledge. https://doi.org/10.4324/9781315843599

Widdowson, H.G. (2004). Text, context, pretext: Critical issues in discourse analysis. Blackwell. https://doi.org/10.1002/9780470758427

Wigglesworth, G., & Elder, C. (2010). An investigation of the effectiveness and validity of planning time in speaking test tasks. *Language Assessment Quarterly*, *7*(1), 37–41. https://doi.org/10.1080/15434300903031779

Winke, P., Gass, S., & Myford, C. (2013). Raters' L2 background as a potential source of bias in rating oral performance. *Language Testing*, *30*(2), 231–252. https://doi.org/10.1177/0265532212456968

Winters, S., & O'Brien, M.G. (2013). Perceived accentedness and intelligibility: The relative contributions of F0 and duration. *Speech Communication*, *55*(3), 486–507. https://doi.org/10.1016/j.specom.2012.12.006

Wood, D. (2010). *Formulaic language and second language speech fluency: Background, evidence and classroom applications*. Bloomsbury. https://doi.org/10.5040/9781474212069

Wray, A. (2000). Formulaic sequences in second language teaching: Principle and practice. *Applied Linguistics*, *21*(4), 463–489. https://doi.org/10.1093/applin/21.4.463

Wray, A. (2002). *Formulaic Language and the Lexicon*. Cambridge University Press. https://doi.org/10.1093/applin/21.4.463

Xi, X. (2010). Automated scoring and feedback systems: Where are we and where are we heading? *Language Testing*, *27*(3), 291–300. https://doi.org/10.1177/0265532210364643

Xi, X. (2012). Validity and the automated scoring of performance tests. In G. Fulcher & F. Davidson (Eds.), *The Routledge handbook of language testing* (pp. 438–451). Routledge. https://doi.org/10.4324/9780203181287

Xi, X., Higgins, D., Zechner, K., & Williamson, D. (2012). A comparison of two scoring methods for an automated speech scoring system. *Language Testing*, *29*(3), 371–394. https://doi.org/10.1177/0265532211425673

Yates, L., Zielinski, B., & Pryor, E. (2011). The Assessment of pronunciation and the new IELTS Pronunciation scale. IELTS Research Reports 12. https://ielts.org/researchers/our-research/research-reports/the-assessment-of-pronunciation-and-the-new-ielts-pronunciation-scale

Yip, M. (1996). Tone in East Asia languages. In J.A. Goldsmith (Ed.), *The handbook of phonological theory* (pp. 476–494). Blackwell Publishing. https://doi.org/10.1111/b.9780631201267.1996.00015.x

Zechner, K., Higgins, D., Xi, X., & Williamson, D. (2009). Automatic scoring of non-native spontaneous speech in tests of spoken English. *Speech Communication*, *51*(10), 883–895. https://doi.org/10.1016/j.specom.2009.04.009

Zechner, K., & Evanini, K. (Eds.). (2020). Automated speaking assessment: Using language technologies to score spontaneous speech. Routledge. https://doi.org/10.4324/9781315165103

Zhang, R., & Yuan, Z.M. (2020). Examining the effects of explicit pronunciation instruction on the development of L2 pronunciation. *Studies in Second Language Acquisition*, *42*(4), 905–918. https://doi.org/10.1017/S0272263120000121

Zielinski, B.W. (2008). The listener: No longer the silent partner in reduced intelligibility. *System*, *36*(1), 69–84. https://doi.org/10.1016/j.system.2007.11.004

Zielinski, B. (2015). The segmental/suprasegmental debate. In M. Reed & J.M. Levis (Eds.), *The handbook of English pronunciation* (pp. 397–412). Wiley-Blackwell. https://doi.org/10.1002/9781118346952.ch22

APPENDIX 1

CAMBRIDGE B2 FIRST SPEAKING TASK

What might be difficult for the people about trying to win in these situations?	1

Reproduced with kind permission of Cambridge University Press and Assessment.

APPENDIX 2

IELTS DESCRIPTORS

SPEAKING: Band Descriptors (public version)

Band	Fluency and coherence	Lexical resource	Grammatical range and accuracy	Pronunciation
9	• speaks fluently with only rare repetition or self-correction; any hesitation is content-related rather than to find words or grammar • speaks coherently with fully appropriate cohesive features • develops topics fully and appropriately	• uses vocabulary with full flexibility and precision in all topics • uses idiomatic language naturally and accurately	• uses a full range of structures naturally and appropriately • produces consistently accurate structures apart from 'slips' characteristic of native speaker speech	• uses a full range of pronunciation features with precision and subtlety • sustains flexible use of features throughout • is effortless to understand
8	• speaks fluently with only occasional repetition or self-correction; hesitation is usually content-related and only rarely to search for language • develops topics coherently and appropriately	• uses a wide vocabulary resource readily and flexibly to convey precise meaning • uses less common and idiomatic vocabulary skilfully, with occasional inaccuracies • uses paraphrase effectively as required	• uses a wide range of structures flexibly • produces a majority of error-free sentences with only very occasional inappropriacies or basic/non-systematic errors	• uses a wide range of pronunciation features • sustains flexible use of features, with only occasional lapses • is easy to understand throughout; L1 accent has minimal effect on intelligibility
7	• speaks at length without noticeable effort or loss of coherence • may demonstrate language-related hesitation at times, or some repetition and/or self-correction • uses a range of connectives and discourse markers with some flexibility	• uses vocabulary resource flexibly to discuss a variety of topics • uses some less common and idiomatic vocabulary and shows some awareness of style and collocation, with some inappropriate choices • uses paraphrase effectively	• uses a range of complex structures with some flexibility • frequently produces error-free sentences, though some grammatical mistakes persist	• shows all the positive features of Band 6 and some, but not all, of the positive features of Band 8
6	• is willing to speak at length, though may lose coherence at times due to occasional repetition, self-correction or hesitation • uses a range of connectives and discourse markers but not always appropriately	• has a wide enough vocabulary to discuss topics at length and make meaning clear in spite of inappropriacies • generally paraphrases successfully	• uses a mix of simple and complex structures, but with limited flexibility • may make frequent mistakes with complex structures, though these rarely cause comprehension problems	• uses a range of pronunciation features with mixed control • shows some effective use of features but this is not sustained • can generally be understood throughout, though mispronunciation of individual words or sounds reduces clarity at times

Band				
5	• usually maintains flow of speech but uses repetition, self correction and/or slow speech to keep going • may over-use certain connectives and discourse markers • produces simple speech fluently, but more complex communication causes fluency problems	• manages to talk about familiar and unfamiliar topics but uses vocabulary with limited flexibility • attempts to use paraphrase but with mixed success	• produces basic sentence forms with reasonable accuracy • uses a limited range of more complex structures, but these usually contain errors and may cause some comprehension problems	• shows all the positive features of Band 4 and some, but not all, of the positive features of Band 6
4	• cannot respond without noticeable pauses and may speak slowly, with frequent repetition and self-correction • links basic sentences but with repetitious use of simple connectives and some breakdowns in coherence	• is able to talk about familiar topics but can only convey basic meaning on unfamiliar topics and makes frequent errors in word choice • rarely attempts paraphrase	• produces basic sentence forms and some correct simple sentences but subordinate structures are rare • errors are frequent and may lead to misunderstanding	• uses a limited range of pronunciation features • attempts to control features but lapses are frequent • mispronunciations are frequent and cause some difficulty for the listener

APPENDIX 3

FLUENCY INDICATORS

Adopted from Tavakoli, Nakatsuhara & Hunter (2020)

Speed measure

Articulation rate: Total number of syllables divided by total amount of phonation time (excluding pauses) multiplied by 60

Composite measures

Speech rate: Total number of syllables divided by total performance time (including pauses) multiplied by 60

Mean length of run: The mean number of syllables between two pauses

Breakdown measures

Phonation time ratio: percentage of performance time spent speaking

Mean length of silent pauses at mid-clause and end-clause positions

Mean length of filled pauses at mid-clause and end-clause positions

Frequency of silent pauses silent pauses at mid-clause and end-clause position

Frequency of filled pauses silent pauses at mid-clause and end-clause position

Repair measures

Frequency of all repairs per 60 seconds

Frequency of false starts and/or reformulations per 60 seconds

Frequency of partial or complete repetitions per 60 seconds

Frequency of self-corrections per 60 seconds

A pause threshold is necessary for measuring silence. While most current studies use a threshold of 250 ms, longer thresholds of up to 1 second have also been observed.

APPENDIX 4

EXAMPLE OF A TEST TASK

Check out each question type

- Listen carefully. Some fake words may have small differences from real ones.
- Click on the speaker icon to replay each word as many times as you want.

About this Challenge

Question Type: Listen and Select

Time Limit: 1.5 minutes

Subscores: Comprehension, Conversation

Select the real English words in this list

WORD 1	WORD 2	WORD 3
WORD 4	WORD 5	WORD 6
WORD 7	WORD 8	WORD 9

Figure 1: Duolingo English Test sample task type. Retrieved on 4 July, 2021, from https://englishtest.duolingo.com/readiness Reproduced with kind permission from Duolingo.

INDEX

www.ingramcontent.com/pod-product-compliance
Lightning Source LLC
LaVergne TN
LVHW010444080826
844660LV00026B/1214

* 9 7 8 1 8 0 0 5 0 4 3 3 2 *